CRADDOCK ON THE CRAFT OF PREACHING

by

FRED B. CRADDOCK

edited by Lee Sparks & Kathryn Hayes Sparks
foreword by Thomas G. Long

CHALICE ®
PRESS
ST. LOUIS, MISSOURI

"These chapters are 'classic Craddock' in the sense that they are a unique mixture of deep scholarship, a humble spirit, a keen sense of literature, and a decades-long dedication to the craft of preaching."
■ EDITORS LEE AND KATHRYN SPARKS

"New and 'old' preachers alike will be inspired again to observe, read, study, listen. We remember that preaching is more important than we may feel about it on any given day, and that while the rigors of it and its relentless and unremitting nature will test us, it is a wondrous calling."
■ MARY DONOVAN TURNER, PACIFIC SCHOOL OF RELIGION

"Preachers have flocked to Fred Craddock's lectures and workshops on preaching for years...We attend, seeking homiletical wisdom that works, stories that entertain and inspire, but mostly encouragement. Then we return to our ministries with a full heart, but not necessarily full of notes. Here is the ultimate Craddock workshop, and in print that we might turn to it again and again."
■ MIKE GRAVES, SAINT PAUL SCHOOL OF THEOLOGY

For everyone who has been and will be encouraged by the wisdom of Dr. Fred B. Craddock.

www.chalicepress.com

Paperback: 9780827205376   EPUB: 9780827205543
Hardcover: 9780827205536   EPDF: 9780827205550

Cataloging-in-Publication Data available from
the Library of Congress

Printed in the United States of America

Contents

Foreword by Thomas G. Long   vii

Message from Fred B. Craddock   ix

Introduction by Lee Sparks and Kathryn Hayes Sparks   1

1. Between the Ear and the Mouth   5

2. New Testament Theology as a Pastoral Task   9

3. Preaching as Storytelling: For Instance   19

4. Preaching as Storytelling: Sustaining the Power   31

5. Preaching as Storytelling: The Form   41

6. Preaching as Storytelling: Additional Practical Suggestions   53

7. The Sermon as a Twice-Told Tale: What Is a "Twice-Told Tale"?   65

8. The Sermon as a Twice-Told Tale: Funds in the Memory Bank   75

9. The Sermon as a Twice-Told Tale: Resonance with Human Experience   85

10. The Sermon as a Twice-Told Tale: The Form of the Sermon   97

11. The Sermon as a Twice-Told Tale: New Words to Old Tunes   105

12. Preaching and the Nod of Recognition   117

13. Preaching and the Shock of Recognition   127

14. Preaching the Same Sermon Every Week   137

15. Wanting Out   147

16. Thirteen Ways to End a Sermon   157

17. The Habit of the Sermon   169

18. Once More with Feeling   179

Notes   195

Foreword

Mention the name of Fred Craddock to a group of pastors and the results are inevitable. Someone will surely recount a favorite "Craddock story," not a story *about* Craddock, mind you, but a story told *by* Craddock, one of the homespun slice-of-life narratives that populate his sermons and burst forth as luminous epiphanies of the gospel in everyday life. Someone else will recite one of Craddock's wry aphorisms, his delightful and angular observations about human experience that generate cloudbursts of laughter and leave listeners cleansed and refreshed. Yet another will testify how it was hearing Fred Craddock preach that forever changed her own way of creating and delivering sermons, prompting others to confess, sometimes sheepishly, to attempts of preaching Craddock-inspired sermons to their own congregations.

Fred Craddock is so well known and so well loved as a preacher, a storyteller, a fascinating and witty speaker, a master of the oral performance that sometimes it is easy to forget that Craddock is also a consummate teacher of homiletical theory and practice. We know of the deep impression he has made on so many by standing in the pulpit and preaching, but what should not be forgotten are the equally rich contributions Craddock has made at the writing desk and in the classroom.

One of Craddock's early books, *As One without Authority*, originally published in 1971, stands at the top of a very short list of pivotal books in homiletics to appear in the last century. Craddock's attention to the needs and capacities of the listeners—his advocacy of inductively shaped sermons inviting the hearers on a journey of discovery—and his notion that sermons are most effective not when the preacher begins by announcing the "point" at the beginning but when the listeners gasp with insight at the end were novel and even counterintuitive ideas when Craddock introduced them almost half a century ago, tilting the homiletical world on its axis. The fact that such notions are now the prevailing wisdom for countless preachers, and in many classrooms, is a tribute to the power and value of Craddock's homiletical creativity.

The chapters of this book lie in that fertile but perilous middle ground between theory and performance. They are concerned with the workaday task of putting together sermons with language and story, with biblical interpretation and the habits of a pastor's week, and with sermon beginnings and endings—that is, with the *craft* of preaching. This is a rich place (this territory between theory and performance) because it is here that the proclamation of the gospel takes on concrete and embodied form. But it is also a perilous place because so many homileticians who have ventured here have skidded off the highway and ended up in the ditch of banalities and trivia (e.g., "start your sermon with a heart-warming story; tell a joke halfway through"). Craddock, a brilliant craftsman himself, exposes the richness of the homiletical craft while never condescending to the preacher or treating the task of sermon development as if it were merely a set of techniques. For Craddock, the art of preaching involves the practicalities of mixing pigments and applying brush strokes, but it is never reduced to a simplistic "paint by the numbers."

Consider, for example, what Craddock says about telling stories. Those readers hoping for a formula, a narrative template, will be disappointed. Instead, Craddock remains firmly at the level of the homiletical artisan:

> So I want to make sure that my stories are life-like. That the stories have depth and height and breadth. And not little, old, flat, one dimensional simple, clever, tricky, cute, little things. If there is a disease in the preaching that I hear most often it's not that what the minister says is wrong. It's that it is just too small.[1]

Fred Craddock's ideas have changed the world of homiletics. His preaching has challenged and inspired a generation of congregations and preachers. In this book, though, Craddock pulls up a chair beside the preacher at work in the study. He points to our sermon drafts and inquires whether these are the very best words we can find to tell the gospel. He reminds us who will be out there in the pews and helps us find ways to weave the truth of scripture into the fabric of their lives. He pulls an old book of poetry off the shelf and shows how the stanzas dance with meaning and delight. Here in the study we are not on the windy mountaintop of theoretical break-throughs nor are we in the brightly lit pulpit with the eyes of the people focused on us. We are in the quiet and solitude of the study; and it is here that the words come together, that the sermon takes faithful shape–or not. Whenever we yearn to be relieved of the demanding task of crafting the sermon, whenever we wish, on the one hand, for some urgent pastoral need to call us away from the desk, or if we are tempted, on the other, to set aside the sermon in favor of playing solitaire on the computer, there is Fred Craddock, whispering in our ear, "Do not be seduced by the fact that much of your seminary education is designed to prepare you to handle crises. Most likely it will not be the crises so much as the routine demands of ministry that will really test your mettle."[2]

Thomas G. Long
Bandy Professor of Preaching
Candler School of Theology

Message from Fred B. Craddock

I hope you are encouraging each other as preachers and pastors. We need to encourage each other because other ministers are the ones most in a position to do it and most able to do it, and, I hope, willing to do it. Those of us who have preached for a time realize that there are no real clear clues as to our effectiveness. If a number of persons respond to our preaching, we know that the seed was planted and watered by our predecessors. The preaching we do today may be just planting seeds that will be harvested after we are long gone. Neither popularity nor unpopularity are reliable keys to effective preaching.

During the 1960s, if you were unpopular that was a measure of your "prophetic" effectiveness. Two "prophets" talked about how things were going at their respective churches.

"How's your church doing?"

"Well, when I went there, there were about three hundred in attendance, but we've gotten it down to eighty-three."

"Oh, you're doing really well. Great job!"

It was called being *prophetic* but as I look back on it, maybe it was really just being *obnoxious.* There is a difference.

As I said, we need to encourage each other because we don't really know how to measure our effectiveness. People develop ears for our preaching as we grow into a relationship with them as pastor, which is no measure really of the sermon but of a relationship.

Not even our own *feelings* give us an adequate clue. You can preach a sermon and feel that it went over the pulpit like a wingless dove. You heard it hit the floor–thud. And you are embarrassed but you're glad it's over and thus want to go home. And then somebody will say to you, "You spoke to me today in a way that you haven't in some time and I want to thank you."

You can't expect to have the effectiveness of your preaching confirmed by your pulse. How we "feel" about it is not usually an accurate indicator. Some things are true and some things are significant apart from the way I feel. This is why my morning prayer has been the same for decades– "Gracious God, I'm grateful for the work that is more important than how I happen to feel about it on any given day"–because some things are true and some things are important even while I'm asleep.

We need, therefore, to encourage each other because what we want to do and what we have to do–while they coincide sometimes, a lot of times–stand at some distance from each other, and the call to faithfulness is more painful than usual. But none of this, however high and lofty one holds the pulpit, requires our being heavy spirited. Søren Kierkegaard said, "Seriousness of purpose does not require heaviness of manner." We ought to stay light on our feet because I'm not God and you're not God and so we should enjoy this and be somewhat amused by the fact we are in the ministry, of all people.

So we need to encourage each other, pray for each other, and pray for ourselves. Sometimes pastors get so busy going down the list they forget to pray for themselves. It is prayer *to* God that authorizes our speaking *about* God. And I can tell when preachers are busy talking about God or whether they are persons who speak with God. Without the work of the Holy Spirit, we're just making speeches.

I hope this book is an encouragement to you, as you have been to me.

Fred B. Craddock
Cherry Log, Georgia

Introduction

Craddock on the Craft of Preaching grew out of a series of serendipitous events. In 2006, we attended Dr. Craddock's two-day workshop "What I Have Learned in 60 Years of Preaching (So Far)," a regional gathering of preachers at Heart of the Rockies Christian Church (Disciples of Christ) in Fort Collins, Colorado. As usual, Dr. Craddock did not disappoint. We were inspired, encouraged, and challenged in ways that no other speaker-preacher can pull off.

At about the same time, I received publicity information from Chalice Press about Dr. Craddock's *Connecting the Dots*, his (then) forthcoming book, in my role as managing editor of *Rev! Magazine*. I became even more respectful of Dr. Craddock's lifework in the context of his humble beginnings and honest reflections about his calling. We published an excerpt of the book in the magazine.

It occurred to us that even though Dr. Craddock has published extensively, it has been many years since the 1986 release of *Preaching*, his venerable textbook used in many homiletics classes. But what about preachers who have been in the field long enough to know they don't know everything about preaching and who are open to critical reflection of their work by one of the few universally respected teachers of preachers?

We knew that one of Dr. Craddock's postprofessorial missions has been to teach preachers in smaller venues and churches, and we knew that there were many recordings of his preaching workshops, lectures, and sermons. Discussions ensued with Cyrus White, publisher of Chalice Press, who proposed the idea of a collection of lectures from Dr. Craddock that could be "translated" from the oral form to a written one. Mr. White's enthusiasm led to conversations with Dr. Craddock, who expressed his surprise that anyone would want to hear anything more from him in print on the topic of preaching. Nonetheless, he agreed to the project and gave his blessing to it in the hope that it would be encouraging to preachers.

We then gathered over one hundred lectures and workshops led by Dr. Craddock through the years. We listened to well over two hundred hours of his material. Even though it was a major task to discern what to include in this book, it was a wonderful experience to listen to Dr. Craddock for all of those hours.

These chapters are "classic Craddock" in the sense that they are a unique mixture of deep scholarship, a humble spirit, a keen sense of literature, and a decades-long dedication to the craft of preaching. They show how his mind has developed over time. They show how, even though Dr. Craddock has traveled the world to share his views with an international audience, and even though he has numerous books of high-quality scholarship, he remains true to the humble roots of the boy who grew up poor in Depression-era Tennessee.

Chapter 1 is about "P301," Dr. Craddock's introduction to preaching class, and his fourteen basic beliefs about preaching. Chapter 2 looks at the question of whether New Testament theology is practical and looks to Paul as a reflective theologian dealing with practical problems. Chapters 3, 4, 5, and 6 deal with preaching as a form of storytelling, a major theme in Dr. Craddock's work. In the next five chapters, Dr. Craddock explores the idea of the sermon as a "twice-told tale," the premise of which is that effective preaching creates a sense of "rehearing" in the listener.

He further develops that theme in chapters 12 and 13, in which he suggests that sermons do best when they create a "nod of recognition" and a "shock of recognition" in the listeners.

Chapters 14 through 18 deal with some of the more *practical* aspects of Dr. Craddock's views of preaching, such as naming a biblical text as central to one's theology, what to do when a sense of wanting out comes on us, thirteen ways to end sermons, developing a habit of study, and how to approach emotion in preaching.

In recent years, illness has slowed Dr. Craddock down. In the fall of 2009, he gave what he said would be his last lecture on preaching at the Cherry Log Preaching Festival. When the audience of preachers gave him a rousing standing ovation before he said one word of his "Once More with Feeling" lecture (chapter 18), he replied, "Yeah, you love me now that I'm *done*."

The truth is that Dr. Craddock has been loved by generations of preachers. His life's work in the world of preaching has left a permanent and indelible mark. In his own inimitable way, he is regarded as one of the giants of preaching. Contrary to his opening words in his last lecture, his work is not "done"—it continues on in the lives of the thousands of preachers and teachers who have been, and will be, impacted by his legacy.

It's been an honor to work on this project with Dr. Craddock. He has been willing to share his material freely with us, and he has been a joy to work with. He embodies the scripture he claims as the text for his life, from Luke 6:35b: "[God] is kind to the ungrateful and the wicked" (see chapter 14). We hope this project finds its way to preachers who are open to critical reflection on their craft and are encouraged and challenged by it. We also hope more than a few seminary and college students will tap sooner rather than later into the wit and wisdom of Dr. Craddock.

We thank the many people who contributed to this project with their time and talents, including the helpful librarians who supplied audio recordings from their organization's collections: Ms. Ann Knox of Union Theological Seminary, Richmond, Virginia; Marilyn Schertz of Candler School of Theology, Atlanta, Georgia; The Walter Scott Society of Christian Theological Seminary, Indianapolis, Indiana; Duke Divinity School, Durham, North Carolina; and Bell Tower Productions, Marietta, Georgia.

We also thank the following transcriptionists for their diligent efforts in turning Dr. Craddock's oral words into written words: Nancy Depperschmidt, Sue Freeburg, Allison Lococo, and Marian Sparks. Finally, we thank our young son Elijah for his understanding and waiting while Mom and Dad were working on this project.

Lee Sparks and Kathryn Hayes Sparks
Loveland, Colorado

1

Between the Ear and the Mouth

I have had the privilege of hearing the first quivering sermons of many students. Some people who don't understand what that is like will sometimes say to me, "Poor Fred, you had to listen to all of those beginning sermons." In my teaching career first at Phillips Graduate Seminary and then at Candler School of Theology, I listened to thousands of first sermons in "introduction to preaching" class. I want the persons who have been my students to know that I had the best job on the faculty.

In the beginning of my teaching career, I taught mostly New Testament and a little preaching. Over the years, I shifted to teaching mostly preaching and some New Testament. When I moved to teaching mostly preaching, I worried that my ear would be bombarded and I would grow homiletically deaf. I feared that I would get to a point where I was not really listening to the student up there quivering through that first sermon—that my mind would be wandering and I would be groaning (to myself), "Here we go again."

Not through any discipline of mine, nor through any activity or exercise of my own, God saw fit to grace me with a listening ear through all of those sermons. For reasons I don't quite understand, each one of those first sermons was also a "first sermon" to me as the listener. Some of those first sermons were as rough as a corncob. But every once in a while a student would preach that first sermon and it would move me to the point where I found it difficult to start the discussion because I wanted us to just sing the doxology and leave. But I felt I owed it to the students to make comments, just to give them their money's worth in tuition.

As a starting point to this project, I have decided, wisely or unwisely, to go back to the material in the folder that is marked "P301: Introduction to Preaching." Gail O'Day and I taught the course at Candler. We assigned adjuncts and helpers in other classes. But we were very careful about that course—we did not let anybody else teach P301. If there were visiting faculty members who could teach preaching, we would let them teach an advanced elective, but *we* taught P301. That was the important course in the field because that's where the students were introduced to the importance of the ear and the mouth: to learn how to listen.

The Bible takes listening very seriously. The Bible's term for "listening" is translated most often as "obey." But the Bible doesn't know the difference between "listen" and "obey." Listening is a fundamental word, but it is so hard to do. We all have marvelous mechanisms for not listening. The Bible recognizes this. Recall that marvelous passage about the suffering servant in Isaiah 50:4b–5, "Morning by morning he wakens—wakens my ear to listen as those who are taught. The Lord God opened my ear, and I was not rebellious." The wording literally is "God dug out my ear."

You don't just listen—it takes an act of God to *really* listen. And in order to serve, the servant said, "I gave my back to those who struck me, and my cheeks to those who pulled out the beard; I did not hide my face from insult and spitting" (Isa. 50:6).

So we start with the introduction of the ear because it is the person who can hear the gospel who can preach the gospel. Preaching is like singing. If you don't have the ear, then you don't have the voice. We start with listening—it's so extremely important.

P301 also deals, of course, with the mouth. Speaking. Because our culture tends to minimize speaking, "sticks and stones may break my bones but words will never harm me"—all of that is false. It's false. Unless students begin with a profound respect for words and what happens when they say something to somebody, they will not understand that speaking is the fundamental human sacrament. You can mow the yard with the extremities of your body. You can paint the basement of the church with the extremities of your body. But if you witness for Jesus Christ, you get a lump in your throat because that's so hard to do. And anybody who says "words, words, words" or "anybody can talk" has never tried to bring up an important subject with anybody.

Preaching is a matter of drawing the breath in pain to tell the Story. This is why it is so difficult to preach: to stand up in a room and see strangers there and yet share with them matters that are more intimate than those in your family—more important than life—to folk that might have been just passing by or stopping in.

The ear and the mouth are connected. Isaiah 50:4 says, "The Lord God has given me the tongue of a teacher, that I may know how to sustain the weary with a word. Morning by morning he wakens—wakens my ear to listen as those who are taught." You don't just go hear lectures on preaching and then prepare a sermon. It's not that easy—it's not that smooth. One doesn't just hear preaching, or hear a little about preaching, and then go preach. There's a lot of distance between the ear and the mouth: ear, brain, heart, soul, and out the mouth.

What I want to do is review P301. This may not be wise, and if you don't think it's wise or if you feel insulted, don't tell me about it. I'm a fragile human being. It may have been a long time since you took P301, so this will be a "refresher" for you. For others, this will be a preview. In P301 we didn't start immediately on exegesis of the text–to get something to say so that we could design a sermon and fashion a way to say it. We don't start there. We start with comments prior to that.

I opened the third drawer down in my filing cabinet. In that drawer was a folder, and there was one sheet in that folder for each semester I taught in which I condensed years of lectures on preaching and wrote their essence into the following statements. These few statements were what I told students before they ever started working on sermons. These are for preachers who never had me in P301–and for those who did but were not listening at the time. Most of what I said in that opening session was the same every time. I changed it a little bit to make the dean think I was continuing to create and all that, but basically it was the same.

I boiled it down to fourteen statements. If you recognize them, good. I would be *keenly* disappointed if there was nothing in these fourteen statements that you have not already embraced and lived out in your ministry.

1. We have all heard good preachers, but no one preaches well enough to be imitated. Find your own voice and prepare your own sermons. Your favorite preacher may be a violin and you may discover that you're a trumpet.

2. The key to consistently effective preaching is the discipline of daily work. I'm sorry that the daily work is very often *not* exciting. But remember there is more to walking than dancing. You have the right to label the simplest tasks "Mickey Mouse" *only* after you have mastered them.

3. The surest way to stop growing is to stop reading. The surest way to rest, satisfied with your achievements, is to stop reading. So to read thoroughly and to master one good book will enable you to read all other books with greater speed, with greater ease, and with greater profit.

4. Carry through on every impulse to its conclusion before other new and fresh impulses smother the preceding one. A preacher cannot live very long on impulses unattended.

5. Even the most careful professional attention to the sins of others does not release you from struggles with your own. When attending to your own soul, select resource material that makes a demand on you, because many devotional books weaken rather than strengthen character. Be aware that there are sins of the spirit as well as sins of the flesh. Be on guard when an answer to prayer leaves you feeling smug, superior, or exempt.

6. Learn to live with the fact that there are few, if any, clues to your effectiveness as a preacher. Both popularity and unpopularity are absolutely worthless as tests of the value of your preaching.

7. Do not expect everything you preach to be confirmed by your pulse. Not all sermons will have visceral support. How you feel about a matter may not be a true register of its importance or its merit. Some things are true even while we're asleep.

8. You are not obliged to be everywhere and to say everything. Leave some things unsaid and some meetings unattended. Choose your times and your places carefully, so that your words will proceed out of silence and your presence will proceed out of absence.

9. Do not be seduced by the fact that much of your seminary education is designed to prepare you to handle crises. Most likely it will not be the crises so much as the routine demands of ministry that will really test your mettle.

10. Major tasks do not simply consume energy—they generate energy. Put both of your hands to a significant assignment and you will discover miraculously that you have even two more hands to take care of your other duties. The minister who burns little energy has little energy.

11. Seriousness of purpose does not require heaviness of manner. In other words, it doesn't mean you have to look like a sad dork. Remaining light on your feet does not contradict but honors the importance of your work. And being pleasant, cheerful, and full of good humor will serve your listeners as a sure sign of the presence of God's grace.

12. Remember that preaching is not simply talking about Christian subjects but is itself a Christian act. What this means, at its very minimum, is that the preacher respects *all* listeners as centers of value, of meaning, of decision, of thought, of feeling, and of action. Every listener must be given room to say "no" to your sermon. Otherwise, their "yes" will be meaningless.

13. There will be times when what you want to do and what you have to do exactly coincide. Thank God for those occasions because they will be rare. There will be many times—many occasions—when what you want to do stands at some distance from what as minister of the gospel you have to do.

14. You very likely, while in seminary and beyond, will experience lapses of your own personal faith. Do not panic. In the interim between the lapse of faith and the return of faith, I suggest you do two things. First, let the church believe for you until your own faith returns. And second, remember that even when you are experiencing distance from God and feeling all alone, it is still better to be true than false, to be brave than cowardly, to be generous than selfish, and to be kind than cruel.

2

New Testament Theology as a Pastoral Task

The question, "can theology be practical?" is often translated into the more popular question: "will it preach?" Through the years I have grown to hate the idea of "will it preach?" That question assumes the minister is a "consumer," running around with a notebook, attending conferences to steal ideas, combing through books, and hearing, receiving, and sharing only that which is really for "retail." The preacher who operates with a "will it preach?" paradigm has no appreciation for the reservoir but instead stands desperately at the faucet for a cupful for next Sunday. So I don't like that expression, and that is not my task in this chapter.

My task here is to deal with the question, "is it possible that New Testament theology be practical?" Now that is a big task, of course, because it assumes the existence of New Testament theology. And it assumes that we can just go from that and jump into the question of whether or not it is practical. Actually, the subject of New Testament theology is itself a nest full of briars and confusion. If you go to the seminary library and look through titles under New Testament theology, you will notice that most of the titles end in question marks. For example, when I came to Candler School of Theology, my colleague Henry Boers had just published a very important book on New Testament theology, and the title is *What Is New Testament Theology?*

Is there any such thing as New Testament theology? If by theology one means a systematic and coherent focus of thought around the concept of God, then there is no such thing as New Testament theology. The New Testament provides the raw material for theology, but it is not a theology itself.

The problem began, or at least came to full expression, with the Protestant Reformation. Most of us who are Protestants like to relish the thought that the Reformation gave the Bible back to the church. While there is some truth in that, there is the darker side that the Reformation took the Bible *away* from the church. It was believed at that time the church owned, possessed, controlled, and used the Bible as a proof text to authorize doctrines, practices, moral instruction, and ritual. And with the Reformation the Bible was taken away, and some distance was put between the Bible and the church so that the Bible could do its proper work: to stand over and against the church, to call the church into question, and to bring the church under the judgment of God. With that distance, however, unintended consequences began to emerge. One important unintended consequence was that the Bible came to be studied at a distance from the church, outside the church, outside the community of faith.

Methods of scholarship were devised for studying the Bible with the assumption that faith is a disadvantage when you are studying this book. The emerging scholarship assumed faith blurs your vision, makes you sentimental, and makes you protective. You should be clear-eyed, level gazed, and totally objective. We must engage in "values-free" research according to this viewpoint.

A whole body of approaches arose that we generally classify as the "historical critical" study of the Bible. We are much indebted to the historical-critical approach. We know things about the Bible, about its text, its literary structure, and historical sources that we would have never known without it. And we could never go back to the era prior to the historical critical study, even if we wanted to.

We are much in debt to the historical critical study of the Bible. But with that came the growing concern that with this distance between the church and Bible, how can we get the Bible back to the church? How can the distance be bridged? How can the gulf be crossed? How can the Bible be given back to the community from which it came and to which it speaks?

One approach was the development of what is called New Testament theology to get at the meaning of the text, the theological insight, the thrust of the text, what the text says to the human spirit. On March 30, 1787, a professor joined the theological faculty of the University of Altdorf in Switzerland. Professor Johann Philipp Gabler, for his inaugural lecture as a new member of that faculty, took for himself the task of distinguishing between dogmatic theology and biblical theology, drawing their lines of purpose, their definitions of direction, and their methods.

And many New Testament scholars believe that was the beginning of what is called New Testament theology. The issues raised in that marvelous address more than two hundred years ago are still the issues pursued in New Testament study—in New Testament theology in particular. How does one get at the meaning if there is a truth for all time, caught in the historical relativities and circumstances of the New Testament? How does one extricate the message without leaving behind the historical reality in which the church lives, did live, and in which we live? How can this book, caught in time and place, be normative for every time and place? How can I draw up its message and its meaning for the church? Shall I go by the theology of the authors: Paul, John, or Luke? Or shall I affirm the unity of the New Testament and just develop some topics: reign of God, eschatology, God, Christology, salvation, or redemption?

Do I decide what is the heart and soul of the New Testament–the so-called canon within the canon–and let that be the magnet that I pass over all the material? And whatever is attracted to the "magnet" is good and whatever is not is no good?

How does one "do" New Testament theology? Well, while that will continue to be debated and discussed, wherever it has been given a chance, the Bible has continued to make its impact in the lives of people: triggering new insight, new revelation; giving new vision and new life. Wherever it has been heard, it has continued to address a wide range of occasions and a wide range of issues. The content of the Bible has been lifted up and rendered as a valid alternative, as a serious alternative to materialism, to futility, and to other ways of life. The Bible, when given a chance, has continued to intersect the questions and the categories and the lifestyles of people all over the world.

There is, however, one thing that has not happened. With the separation of the church and the Bible beginning with the Reformation, the study of the Bible has in many ways been a study of one-half of a conversation. I am convinced that the relationship between the community of believers and the Bible is such that the community sits under the Bible, but the Bible is the community's book. That relationship is so important that to take them apart is to lose something that cannot be recovered by a disinterested researcher or by a casual passerby.

It is the task of the pastor to put the book and the church together. It's *that* task that's not being done. Theological faculty members, including myself, have been accused of taking the Bible away from the church. And it may be true that faculty members of theological schools are under an "indictment" of distancing the Bible from the church, but I would like to make an indictment of my own: pastors have kept the Bible from the church. Now I'll try to build my case. Instead of devising or constructing a new schema or a new grid for putting the Bible and the church together, I would like to move inside the Bible and see how one pastor functioned theologically within the tradition, with a body of material, and was brilliant in his craft.

The pastor I have in mind is the apostle Paul; the church I have in mind is the church at Corinth. How did this pastor deal effectively with a church with a body of material that for us is scripture and for him was the tradition?

Paul was a pastor, by any definition. If to love and long for the people and to love them with the compassion of Christ is to be a pastor, then Paul was a pastor. If to feel the burden of all the lost and confused people is to be a pastor, then Paul was a pastor. "As God is my witness, my heart's desire is for them that they be saved" (Rom. 10:1). "I could almost wish myself to be damned if it would save my people" (Rom. 9:3). If to be anxious about the condition of the church is to be a pastor, Paul was a pastor. In addition to the many bruises and stripes, shipwrecks, chases, jails and hatreds that he endured, if daily anxiety for the churches is to be a pastor, he was a pastor. If to get angry is to be a pastor, then he was a pastor. If to pray for the people all the time is to be a pastor, he was a pastor. "I make mention of you continually in my prayers" (Rom. 1:9). If knowing when to use the milk of the gospel and when to use the meat of the gospel is to be a pastor, then Paul was a pastor. If to be hurt by the very people to whom you minister is to be a pastor, then Paul was a pastor.

> What happened for the affection you felt, when I came to you sick, you received me as an angel of the Lord, as Christ Jesus himself, you would have plucked out your eyes for me, what happened? I long for you, I wish I could see you, I feel like a woman in travail trying to have a child. (Gal. 4)

Paul was a pastor.

And the church at Corinth, as you know, had a lot of problems. Some of the problems stemmed from their background. They were converted from a background that had many differing values from Christianity. Their views of women, their views of sex, and their views of the human body were very different from the gospel. This created a problem, because no matter how radical and clean and good your conversion is, you can't get rid of the past like you shake dust from your coat. It's still there in the vocabulary and the images. It was still there and they were struggling with that.

Part of the problem was that some of their pre-Christian practices were very similar to Christianity. Apparently, many of them had belonged to pagan cults that had some sort of ritual meal, something like communion. The one they worshiped they called "lord." They have other experiences, for example, such as speaking in tongues. There was chewing the laurel leaf, getting into a sort of state, and then uttering this unutterable stuff, and having an interpreter there. And now they've come into the church with the gifts of the Spirit.

They had problems. Part of the problem was Paul had introduced them to something that they found extremely strange and difficult to understand. And that is what was called a "congregation." Are you aware of how radically different a congregation is from anything in the world? They came from religions that had shrines where they would slip in and slip out alone.

Part of the problem stemmed from the fact that they had a lot of ministers going through town. And some liked Apollos, some liked Peter, some liked Paul. And Paul himself contributed to the problem. In Acts 18:11, Luke said Paul was just there only eighteen months—how more itinerate can you be? With only eighteen months in Corinth, of course they had problems.

Let's observe a pastor at work with a church that has problems. One of them was the menu. Do we eat meat sacrificed to idols? (1 Cor. 8) Now, some said no, of course not. So radical was their conversion, they didn't want anything to do with the past. Others on rational grounds said, "I'm not going to do it because that's financing the idols. I'm not going to do it." Others were of a tender conscience and just could not see themselves doing it. Still others said, "Look, there's only one God, those idols are nothing, so there's nothing wrong with the meat."

They had all the right answers. But in the church, even the right answers are sometimes wrong. And there was a problem. Now, this is a very practical problem, and it seems a petty problem today. Here they are writing to the apostle of the Lord, the apostle Paul, to talk about the *menu*. He could have said,

> I didn't go through all the training and all the years and the discipline, prayer, and struggle to deal with this little thing. Look, handle it yourselves. Let the people whose last names begin with A–G bring salad or vegetables. Let H–K bring the meat, and L–Z bring dessert. Serve it buffet style, eat what you like, and let it go.

Instead, what does the apostle Paul do with this practical problem? He says,

> First of all, let me remind you of our faith. There is one God, creator of us all from whom is everything and for whom we all live. And there is one Lord Jesus Christ through whom is everything and through whom we live. Now, there is the instruction about what you eat and how you eat. And there's the instruction on eating together. Now let's work through the problems involved.

Did you notice what Paul the pastor did? He reminded them of their tradition, he quoted the confession of faith, which served to enlarge the conversation so that they weren't discussing just the menu; they were in dialogue about what it is to be a Christian.

Then there was the Lord's supper. It was in shambles. All kinds of problems arose. It was disturbing, it was noisy. Some apparently came late and didn't get anything to eat. The economic differences within the membership began to divide. Those who had money and could bring food had food. And those who didn't have money didn't have any food, didn't bring any food, and didn't get any food. And so some were full and asleep and others were hungry and bothered. It was a very serious problem. Well, obviously, this is a practical problem that needs to be worked out. What do you do? Paul could have said something like,

> Well, it seems to me like you are having the meal at the wrong time. I think if we moved it up to 7:00 instead of 6:30 everyone can be here at the same time. I know that some of the working people can't get off early, and they have to pick up their kids and then they get home and they get here. Let's move it to 7:00, OK? Or perhaps we have it on the wrong night. Trying to tuck it in with choir practice may be a little too packed in there. Why don't we move it to Tuesday? I think everybody would be freer on Tuesday at 7:00.

Instead, here's what Paul the pastor said:

> I want to remind you of the tradition that I traditioned to you. That the Lord Jesus on the night he was betrayed took bread. And he broke it and when he had given thanks he said, "This is my body." Likewise, after the supper he took the cup and said, "This cup is the new covenant in my blood. Do this in remembrance of me." (1 Cor. 11:23–25)

Do you see what Paul did? He took the tradition and said, essentially, "We will set our meal together in the tradition. Remember the tradition, the continuity. If it is not the Lord's supper we're eating, what are we doing? Just eat at home" (1 Cor. 11:33). Very practical.

If you go a little further to chapter 12 of 1 Corinthians, there is a problem with speaking in tongues. It concerned the *pneumata*, the spiritual things or the spiritual people. They were very much concerned about the manifestations of the Spirit. First thing Paul did was to change the word; he didn't want to use *pneumata* (spiritual things). He changed the word to *charismata* (gifts). There were people who apparently were making speaking in tongues the norm for really having the Spirit. Others who didn't speak in tongues felt kind of put out and left out, not having a very significant gift. Those with the extraordinary gifts rose to the top, came to the front, and got all the attention, disturbing others. What will Paul do about this practical problem?

Paul could have said something like,

> Well, just make sure none of those charismatics gets to be chair of any committees. Don't let any of them in on the pastor-parish relations committee. Don't put any of them on the worship committee. I mean we don't want to scare anybody off. I will also occasionally in my sermons refer to the fact that only six blocks away is a church where everybody speaks in tongues. Don't you

think you'd be more at home down there? I mean this is a practical problem, we've got the unity of the church to think about and we can't put up with all these disturbances.

Instead, Paul said,

It's tough, but we're not going to relinquish the diversity of the people of God in order to get a quick unity. I will not grant emergency powers to the leadership to shut down the tongues. Now here's what I'd like you to think about: Do you remember our creed? It's the trinity, do you remember the trinity? There are the diversities of gifts, but there's one Holy Spirit. There are diversities of services, but there is one Lord Jesus Christ. There are diversities of works, but there is one God who is energizing *ta panta in pasin* (the totality in the totality).

Why did Paul do that? Was he pulling out his old seminary education on them so they'd all be subordinated and say, "Paul really knows his theology, doesn't he?" No, no, no. Paul was saying, in essence,

There is one Lord Jesus Christ. Whenever you talk about the working of the Holy Spirit, is it leading you to serve in the ways that Jesus served—to help, to love, to care, to reach, to give, to suffer? There's the canon by which you measure if you have the working of the Spirit. And Christ himself comes under the one God, who is the energizing force of the totality of all creation. Do you want a canon by which to measure whether you have the spirit and whether you have Jesus in your heart? Does it reach out, touch, and is it set in the context of *all* human relationships and *all* creation? Or is it just something you have "nestled in your heart?"

I'm talking practical theology here.

So here we have a church with problems, we have a pastor, and we have his, shall we say, his scripture, his tradition. And he brings the tradition to bear upon those problems, to enlarge the conversation, to give them context, to give them roots, and to give them direction. And in the process of doing it, we find the tradition itself being rephrased and reworked—that's the way tradition moves forward.

But that's not really the whole story. In my judgment that's not the important thing about it. What I want to call to your attention is that in Paul's use of his theology on practical problems, he says, "Let me remind you. This is what I delivered to you. Do you remember?" What made it effective was that he brought to their attention *what they already knew.*

It was what *they* believed, not just what Paul brought in to take care of a problem. There is a world of difference between saying, "now, I think this is the point where I need to bring some theology in on this" and saying, "do you remember how we hammered it out together, one Spirit, one Christ, one Lord? Do you remember how we said it together when we worshiped together? On the night on which he was betrayed, Jesus took bread. Do you remember that?"

The power of Paul's use of theology is in the fact that when he uses it he is not introducing it for the first time; he is *reminding* them of what they already know. Now, how did they know it?

Part of their knowledge came from Paul's predecessors. There were others who preached before Paul. The difference apparently was that Paul had invested significant time in Corinth. Paul and the Corinthians had gone through life together. It was not Paul's theology that he brought from Jerusalem or Damascus or anywhere else. It was *theirs*, and he says, "Let me remind you now of what we shared at the beginning." It was theirs. They could say their theology didn't just depend on Paul.

I marvel at Paul's ability to draw from the *shared* theology that he developed with the Corinthians. At the same time, I wonder how truly effective I've been as a pastor, preacher, and teacher in the church. How well have I been able to remind people of what they already know—and then help them to work through their theology again? How well have I helped them to name their theology?

In contrast, many people who belong to the rigid and conservative theological circles can articulate what they believe. It may be true that much of their theology is too small and too easily packaged. It's snatched from various places. But when you ask them a question, they will have three things to say about it. If you have another question, they can recite four spiritual precepts. It's a little too simple, but what strikes me is those persons' ability to *say it*.

How are they able to say it? Someone has helped them to be able to say it. Someone has helped their church to find its tongue, to say what they believe. Then when a problem arises the pastor can say, "Now let's say it again together. There is one spirit. Do you remember? On the night he was betrayed . . ."

It is my judgment that a lack of tradition is one reason there is so much resistance in many churches to things that are considered new. Take for instance the ordination of women, the phenomenon of the appearance of women in the pulpits of our churches. There has been, as you may have observed here and there, some resistance to this.

Now it is customary to hear somebody say, "Our church is so firm and established in its conviction that they are going to be awfully hard to move and bend and change and this and that." That's not my judgment. My judgment is this: the reason there is so much resistance in many places is that the people do not have, and cannot express, their tradition; what they believe; what they've worked out about God, and Christ, and the world, and salvation, and life together.

And where there is no substance, no articulated faith, the church is undernourished. An undernourished church, when it is hit with something new, rushes to the bulwark with the only weapons it can gather in a moment: cliché, fear, prejudice, and quickly purchased slogans.

We are not talking about bad people. We are talking about people who have survived on junk food because they have not been fed nourishing food. I think almost any problem faced by a church can be overcome if that church has worked through and can say, "This is who we are and this is what we believe." Now, it might go underground and be forgotten, but you will come along as the pastor and say, "Well first of all, let me help you to say again what it is that we believe. Do you remember? Now let's go from there."

Our churches have intelligent people. They are also hungry, anxious, and willing. They are as capable of careful theological reflection as any of us. All they lack is the vocabulary. I do not believe that the church can go far into the twenty-first century continually carried on the back of the clergy. The clergy are holding too many things away from the church. When it is the church, it is the body of Christ; it's the church where the presence of Christ dwells.

Those of us on theological faculties have been far from successful in bridging the gulf between the Bible and the church. But the same has been true of pastors. So how are we to do it? The only thing I can think of is this: To teach, to teach, to teach, to teach. And then when the dark cloud forms, somebody will probably beat you to it and say, "First of all, let's remember what we believe."

3

Preaching as Storytelling

For Instance

In this chapter, and the three that follow, I will look at preaching as storytelling. My focus will be on the *method* of preaching and not so much on the content of preaching. I do not wish to erode the central importance of content by dwelling on style. We must have *something* to say; we cannot carve beautiful sculptures out of nothing. In preaching, we first have to ask, "What?" Second, we ask, "So what?" And then we say, "For instance." I am going to deal with "for instance" in this section. However, my silence on "What?" and "So What?" in this section is neither a judgment upon it nor a neglect of it in myself.

There are two ways to improve preaching: there is the event itself, but there is before it rehearsal and there is following it reflection. In my usual setting, the seminary, we deal with preaching in terms of rehearsal–the preparation for the event. And that is very important.

But in our case here, we move to the other side and deal with the *reflection* on our craft. Most experiences are never complete until we *reflect* on them. Because at the time something's happening we cannot absorb it all. We cannot learn in a maximum way from the experience unless we reflect on it.

This is true of a trip. I've gone with a group on a tour and taken all those pictures, but suitcases, maps, dysentery, and everything else distract me. I cannot really enjoy the experience until I get home and get the pictures developed. When I look through the photos, I finally enjoy the trip. It is a delightful thing because the trip is not really *made* until I reflect on the trip.

It's true of marriage. On my wedding day, I wasn't thinking of marriage. I was thinking of much more important things at the time, such as "I'm still on my feet. Don't fall down." I wanted to say the right things and stand in the right places to get through the ceremony. After the wedding was over, and now for almost sixty years, I've reflected on the implications of two words: "I will."

It's true of baptism. At the time I was baptized when I was fifteen, I was thinking about how to breathe, how to hold the handkerchief, whether to bend my knees or keep my feet on the bottom, and what the depth and temperature of the water in the baptistery would be. Would it be embarrassing? The minister was reciting Romans 6 and the Great Commission and all of that. That was all well and good, but I was concerned about these other things. But I have reflected for sixty-five years what was meant by my baptism.

It's important to reflect on our craft as preachers. It helps to have distance from our usual place of activity. It's important to hear others tell their stories. When we hear others' stories, we are more able to laugh about things that two months ago we *wept* over. It's also important to take walks along the back roads and rivers of the mind–to crawl away into the monastery of one's own solitude and reflect.

Therefore my task is to bring to the conscious level of reflection what we do all the time and to learn from what we do and to think about and understand what we already know.

A highly prized form of learning is to understand what we know, as Luke said to Theophilus, "So that you may know the truth concerning the things about which you have been instructed" (Lk. 1:4). And by the way, that is also important in preaching. It is very important that people have the experience of understanding what they already know. At least 90 percent of every sermon should be such that they can say, "Amen." They do not wish to be insulted or put down. Every day the world serves them a hot cup of despair along with a generous serving of a big put-down. So I think we ought to engage in the ministry of encouragement to each other. I hope I can do that with you.

I enjoy talking about preaching as storytelling because the biblical material is appropriate to storytelling. Much of it exists in forms of stories. Some of it still carries the residue of story and some of it is going to be put in the air, if not as story, at least in oral form. Even the epistles, which originated in script, were prepared for hearing. And so this subject will allow me to move in and out of that material. I am pleased also that it is a topic of some popularity and wide reading. Scores of books have appeared on narrative theology, metaphor, parable, storytelling and narrative theology, story theology, theology of story, speaking in parables, speaking in stories, and so on.

While storytelling is a great topic of recent engagement, it is not a new one. Great interpreters and great preachers have used their intuition throughout history to understand and harness the power of telling a story–and they did it without sophisticated training in narrative theology.

Harvard Professor Amos Wilder was asked to respond to a collection of excellent papers in a seminar on parables. While he praised the work, he also said something was missing. His closing comment was

> I have not yet read a paper that understood the story of the prodigal son any better than a preacher I heard, when I was just a boy, preach on that story in a little Baptist church. I have not heard a superior handling of it.

The man he heard preach had not been exposed to the academic theories of "narrative discourse" but had intuited something about life and the biblical material.

You may have heard intuitive preachers, too. I regret the passing of certain types of preachers so powerful in telling stories. I heard some of those preachers when I was a youngster. They preached to the poor, sitting on apple crates under tents in a wheat field. And by the power of their ability to tell stories, the whole scene was transformed. They weren't in the wheat field, under a tent, sitting on apple boxes. Instead, the streets were paved with gold, there was pearl all around, and the chandeliers were all the way from heaven. It was a marvelous scene, and these poor, deprived sharecroppers were laughing and having a great time.

I have also heard great preachers tell stories to the rich and have them weeping. Big house on the hill under the power of that preaching changed to a tent. All those closets of clothes fold into boxes of rags and the tragic, tragic picture as those preachers would describe somebody who had a lot of money and was looking for the market where life was sold. They would picture a man with a fistful of $100 bills running all over town:

"Hey, can I buy a home?" asked the man with money.

"No I'm sorry I don't sell homes, but I can sell you a house," said the real estate agent.

"Hey, can I buy rain?" asked the man with money.

"No, I am sorry I don't sell rain, but I can have water piped to your house," said the city water engineer.

"Hey, can I buy some time?" asked the man with money.

"No, I am sorry I don't sell one tick of time, but I've got a good clock here," said the clockmaker.

Oh, they could tell those stories and just move you. And as a boy I was always afraid to go home from church at night. For fear of something of the power for which they preached would wreak its vengeance on me. When those preachers spoke of death, you could feel the mist in your face, the fog in your throat, and get a little brown taste in the corner of your mouth. And when they preached on sin and dissipation—wow what descriptions!—"a wind-blown empty street," "a little blue front building in a small apartment overhead," "one little 15-watt bulb in that darkened room," and "a man leaning over a sticky table surrounded by cigarette butts floating in urine and stale beer."

Now, they could tell you a story.

For some of you, "preaching as storytelling" touches on your own craft in that it may simply mean reflecting about storytelling within the structure of the way you ordinarily preach. For others, it may mean simply enlightening and enlivening the basic style of your homiletics with some stories. For still others, you may be a little bit discouraged with the way you preach, and it may mean shucking all that altogether and picking up a new form. A form that thinks of the sermon as a trip to a certain destination and thinks not in terms of structure and outline but entirely in terms of movement.

I wish to give some suggestions that might be helpful to those who want to sharpen their craft at narration and storytelling. Most of my suggestions are drawn from the way certain biblical writers tell stories. I do not wish to imply that this is the only way to preach. It is not. One should not preach any one particular way all the time because you can't win all the races with the same horse. There should be some variety in them.

There are two good reasons why not all sermons should be narrative. First, sometimes the narrative or the story is not congenial to the experience you wish to create. Sometimes the experience is simply correcting misunderstanding or teaching some basic things that have been forgotten. There are all kinds of experiences to be created, and sometimes the narrative doesn't do it best. Second, there are times when the narrative is not congenial to the nature of the text. There are times when a narrative approach would distort the text, both its form and its substance. There are some passages that are just not that type. In other words, in thinking of the structure of a sermon, it is very important to think of the shape of the gospel.

What is the shape of the gospel? In the last century, Rudolf Bultmann and C. H. Dodd carried on a debate over the shape of the gospel. Dodd said the gospel is a story, a narration of the good news. Bultmann said the gospel is a word of address confronting the volition, calling for a decision. And it was a big debate. It turns out that both were right. And it is a little imperialistic to claim that one is the whole thing. We have stories—the gospels—and we have the word of address, as in Paul and John. We have both. There are some occasions when a story, or a discourse, or some long narration is simply not appropriate. When Jesus in John 21 said to Simon Peter, "Simon, do you love me?" it was not an occasion for the student to say to the teacher, "Well I would rather have an essay question if I may."

There are some occasions that simply call for a different kind of experience, a different kind of response.

Now we have some problems with storytelling at the outset. The very word itself has not been adequately and completely rehabilitated to be worthy of the grand enterprise of preaching. The word *story* in some parts of our culture is a negative word. It means untrue. In my mother's mouth, it had a verb form: to story. When I would say something like, "Well Mama, I must have lost the change out of my pocket. I didn't spend it on candy." And she would say, "Son don't you story to me."

Are you telling me a story? And with that echoing in the ear and mind, it is difficult to elevate the word and use it as a vehicle for preaching the gospel because it has that negative force.

In many areas, story is just a nonserious word. "Well, isn't that a nice story," they will say. In other words, "There was no substance to it." "He hitched up eight Clydesdales to a little red wagon." There wasn't really anything to it. Now, in the opinion of some people, that is what story telling in preaching is.

Other people regard story as an anachronism replaced in our culture by the instant replay. Now, the instant replay has in its favor complete accuracy. Just look at it again. Play back exactly what was said. Play the film back; see exactly what happened. But "instant replay" erodes the role and power of a story in culture because a story, if it is a good story and it's a good storyteller, is tailored and contoured to the audience. It's never repeated exactly. It's fitted in; a different nest is built before the egg is laid. It's just a different experience. The Bible does this. The Bible tells something . . . again and again . . . , but it's not instant replay. A different condition calls for a reshaping of the story so that it will address appropriately the new condition. You have to put the grease where the squeak is. And therefore the story isn't just said the same way. Some people believe that the story in our culture has been removed by the instant replay. I really don't think so but I can understand what is being suggested. The Bible uses—and good storytellers use and reuse—the basic stuff of the story in many ways.

I was at a family reunion some time ago at a relative's home and I was seated on the patio eating outside. I was seated on a very cold seat. All the other seats were wooden except this one, which was marble. Marble is cold. And I said, "This is pretty high class, but it sure is cold" and this person said, "Don't you recognize it?"

I looked at it, and I said, "I don't recognize this."

"Well you should recognize that."

"Well I haven't been on this before, so why should I recognize it?"

Finally I was told that the piece of marble was the bottom step at the old home place where we were born. And then I remembered the old rotten wooden steps, and somebody had replaced the bottom one with a piece of marble, and I recall one of the steps was still good. It was that marble.

And then this person said, "Turn it over." So I got help and we turned the seat over. On the other side was the inscription appropriate to the burial of someone named George Washington Duncan, who had died in 1792. A piece of marble had become a gravestone, then a step, and now a patio seat.

Now, that is the way a story is. It is the same; it's not the same. Is there room in our culture for this to continue? Some doubt it very much. I think the seminaries have created in some of us a prejudice against "story" because of the emphasis on preparing all of those papers (we are so script-oriented in seminaries). I try to create an oral world. Many seminarians graduate with an "A" average in the silence of writing papers. But when they take those silent paper writing practices out to their first pastorate, they are usually disappointed to find they have little to no meaningful impact.

Now, because of that script orientation and prejudice, the idea of a story, which belongs to an oral culture, is not valued: "Oh, well, that is just a lot of homiletical jargon. Oh, we will take that to your homiletics class." And nobody wants to claim the story, creating a kind of feeling that the story is just sort of a fringe. It's embroidery. It's a decorative edge. It's like the picture in the geography book. You remember that? There would be a whole chapter on Switzerland, number of cows, industry, and all that. There would be this picture of a mountainside with a little house at the top and some cows grazing and somebody up at the top of the hill yodeling. And you always welcomed those pictures for two reasons: One is that it cuts out a lot of the script. And second, you were never tested over the pictures. I know some ministers who get embarrassed by it but never get the point of somebody saying, "You know I remember that story you told–that sermon when you were here 10 years ago." They remembered the picture but forgot the number of cows in Switzerland.

Stories are not decorative embroidering on the gospel. The gospel *itself* is a story, and one will not do well using stories only to illustrate a heavy text. One does well as a storyteller when reaching the point wherein the story carries the gospel, like a seed carries its future in its own bosom. That is a high-heeled story, but some have been convinced that the story doesn't quite do it. "This is too important. I have to express conviction. I have to underline this. I have to ensure everybody understands this is really important." And how do we do that? Almost 99 percent of the time, the way we show it's really important is to dismiss the story. After all it's interesting but it doesn't really do it. And replace it with what? *Exhortation.* Just fill the air with "ought, must, and should" and then another helping of "ought, must, and should." Well, people get the idea, "You know that must be important."

But how do you convey that something is important? The classic example of that confusion is at the annual Thanksgiving service, when several churches get together. By getting together, they can muster up a crowd that is only slightly bigger than if only one church had it. And the ministers take turns preaching but all are on the stage for each of the services. The sermon's text is invariably the story of Jesus healing ten lepers, but only one returns to say thanks. And the preacher gets up, reads that text, and then says, "Where are the nine? Where are the nine? Where are the nine?" For thirty minutes he or she asks, "Where are the nine?" After a time of this endless exhortation, I find myself saying to myself, "Those nine are where I'd be if I had good sense."

The subject is very important, and I would like to register its importance to the minds of the people. Then how do I do it? Do I tell a story? Or is that too laid back and cool? Storytelling is difficult under any circumstance whatever the culture thinks. Storytelling is difficult because it is a part of communication, and all communication is difficult—extremely difficult. Suppose you have a class, a college freshman class; you are the instructor. And your subject—the task of your class—is to teach appreciation of Mozart. How are you going to do it? Here they are, 107 students coming into your classroom. Well, you play some records. Yuck. You assign some reading. Double yuck. "I'll get them. I will pull a quiz on them." It doesn't work. "I will reward those who memorize some facts. I will punish those who don't. I will move them to tears with stories of the tragedies of this man's life. Come on, please appreciate Mozart!"

Communication is difficult. How do you bridge that distance? It is a great distance between those who hear and those of us who speak. We think all of this is clear. It has been rolled out neatly and in order, but one thing we usually forget is the location of the person who's listening. Imagine a soldier stationed overseas undergoing hardship duty for thirteen months. Late at night, after midnight, he is listening to some music, this beautiful romantic music. He is lonesome. He is so far from home. He takes out a piece of paper (in the days before email) to write to his wife: "My dearest Peggy . . ." and writes a beautiful letter. It crosses the ocean. Peggy gets it, with one child in tow and the baby in her arms. The baby has a fever; she is on the way to the doctor. She stops at the drug store. The four-year-old is knocking stuff off the shelf. The baby is crying. Then she says, "Oh, yes, the letter." She opens her purse, tears open the envelope, and reads the letter. Later, when the kids are finally asleep, she reads the letter again. It's late and she turns on the radio and there is some beautiful music that she knows her husband likes. She misses him very much. And she reads the letter again. She doesn't need a lexicon or concordance or anything else to be in tune with her husband. It's clear.

But how many of you preach to people who are already in tune?

The distance is great. Just think of what is already in peoples' minds—how they are feeling already before we ever open our mouths, preconditioned. We are telling a story. It's a marvelous story, but what is being heard? At the University of Chicago I was asked some time ago to preach at Rockefeller Chapel, and I was told that there would be a young woman there, a business manager who would show me where I was to go so I wouldn't get in the wrong place and get lost in that big place. So she came out and introduced herself and squired me about, and I got through the service, and there was coffee afterward. I visited with her quite freely. At one point in the conversation she said, "Mr. Craddock, have we ever met before?" I said, "No, what's the matter?" She said, "You act like you know me." I said "Well, I am sorry. I didn't mean to intrude into your life." And she said, "Well it's all right; it's just you act like you know me." And then I knew what it was. I forget her last name, but her first name was Mignonne. I knew a Mignonne who was the sponsor of our youth group when I was growing up in the church. I attributed to this second Mignonne all the qualities of the first Mignonne and immediately was drawn to her. I didn't know her really.

When we tell a story, what is brought to the surface of the listener's mind? I will give you a sample. It's not biblical, it's not heavy, and you just think what comes to your mind as I say it. I am just going to say it and you just let it roll across your brain and see what's there. Ready? Here it is:

"Hopefully George will be released this weekend. Maggie can hardly wait. The old gang is planning for a party at Charlie's place."

Now, where is George? In prison? In the military? In a hospital?

Who is Maggie to George? A girlfriend? His mother? His sister? His pet?

Who is the "old gang?"

Is Charlie's place a bar? A restaurant? Charlie's home?

As you can see in this example, even the simplest story evokes a wide range of understandings.

To take what is profoundly important to me and move it into the public arena is like holding open house in a prayer room. The first thing to go if something is very important is my voice. For the life of me, I cannot understand the witness for Christ who is glib. It is extremely difficult to say something extremely important. To reexperience a story at the time I am telling it–now that is difficult. I have heard people criticize the apostle Paul for telling his story–that he was egotistical. But if you look carefully at the times he told his story, you will see he told it only when his critics prodded and pushed him into it. When he was compared unfavorably with the other apostles, he said, "Last of all, as to one untimely born, he appeared also to me" (1 Cor. 15:8). He was forced to tell it. When he was accused of preaching second-hand sermons, he told his own story. But he drew his breath in pain to tell that story because telling a story that's worth its weight is a weighty matter. Good storytellers are *reluctant* storytellers.

Telling stories is difficult because it also assumes something that is not always the case. It assumes not only the oral possession but also the social possession of material. In oral culture, stories belong to everybody. The material belongs to everybody. In a copyright-script culture, it just belongs to certain ones. I have this one and it is copyrighted and I may let you read it. But in a storytelling culture, the stories belong to the whole community.

I think something more important is that storytelling assumes that value is put on continuity. A story has continuity. It does not set a premium on discontinuity and radical junctures but on the movement, the larger story. We have gone through a period of existential influence in which the great accent was on the *now*. Now, this moment, now, now is the time and a general disinterest, disinterest in what happened before I was born. Disinterest in what happens after I am gone. It's only my life. This center. Nothing important exists outside of the narrow parenthesis of my birth and my death. And in that kind of culture, a story is not important, just little ego trips. I am talking about story in the larger sense in which my story is said in the context of *the* Story.

Some cultures understand how one's story is part of the larger story. I heard a lecture in Los Angeles by Scott Momaday, a Kiowa Indian and professor of literature in California. When he was a boy, his father awoke him gently one morning and said, "I want you to get up and go with me." His father walked with him hand in hand and led the sleepy boy to the house of an elder woman of the tribe. His father told him that he would return in the evening to bring him home. All day long the old woman of the Kiowa tribe told stories to the boy, sang songs to him, described rituals, and chanted the history of the Kiowa. How they began out of a hollow log in the Yellowstone River, of the migration southward. She told him of wars with other tribes, the great blizzards, the buffalo hunts, the coming of the white man, the clash and the war and the moving southward, Kansas, deprivation, starvation, diminished tribe, and finally Fort Sill, reservation, confinement. When it was about dark, his father came and said, "Son, it's time to go." Momaday said, "I left her house a Kiowa."

When youngsters leave our church buildings, do they leave a Christian? To be a Christian is to be enrolled in the Story. And anybody who can't remember anything further back than his or her own birth is an orphan. I just don't hear many of our church folks saying, "We were in the catacombs. We were in Bethlehem. We were in Nazareth. We were in the arena." Sometimes our stories fall on ears that find them strange and foreign. But the greatest difficulty in storytelling is whether we trust a story to "carry the freight."

Do you trust the kingdom of God, the message of the kingdom of God to something as fragile as a story, something as fragile as just the passing of vibrations of air over an eardrum? Well, only you can answer. But I have to tell you that the Story has a grand record. The Story has a great record in tough rooms, classrooms.

"Rabbi?"

"Yes."

"Rabbi, does God enjoy all that God did throughout our history?"

"No, God didn't enjoy it all."

"What do you mean God didn't enjoy it all?"

And the rabbi said, "When our people were coming through the Red Sea, God had to rescue them so God appointed a group of angels to take care of it. The angels looked down and saw the Egyptians chasing the Israelites, so the angels parted the waters and the Israelites went through. But when the Egyptians got in the Red Sea, the angels released the waters, and chariots, and men, and horses tumbled and drowned and the angels jumped up and down and shouted, 'We got them!' The angels danced around and danced around, and God came along and asked, 'What are you laughing and singing about?' They said, 'Look we got them, we got them, we got them!' And the Almighty said, 'You are dismissed from my service.' 'Why?' the angels asked. 'How can you dance and sing when some of my children are drowning?'"

A story has a good career in some tough cases. Jesus was often surrounded by critics and pundits wanting to put him in his place, to trip him up. What great syllogism will he pull out to put them in their place? Instead, he told a story. To paraphrase, there was a man who fared sumptuously every day. There was a beggar, Lazarus, lying in his gate. The rich man died and was buried and Lazarus died. Lazarus went to Abraham's bosom and the rich man went to torment (Lk. 16:19–24).

Wait, wait, wait, they must have said, this is not a good story. All we know about them is that one is rich and one is poor. But let's know something about their character—no, no, one is rich and one is poor. What is this? Well, one thing that is true is that in any situation where you have some who eat and some who don't eat, you don't have the reign of God. It's just a story.

You know for yourself the marvelous career of the story in the history of our faith. I know its power not because I have told the stories but because I have heard them. I heard it once up in the Smoky Mountains. Nettie and I used to go up to the Smoky Mountains to vacation a little bit. We lived in Oklahoma—that's not exactly the Smoky Mountains. So we would come back to the Smoky Mountains, she and I, leave the kids at grandma's house. We loved to stop at a place called the Blackberry Inn to eat. It's burned down since then but one side of this restaurant was solid glass and you could look out while you were eating and see the mountains. So we were in there one evening, relaxed, looking at this huge menu, trying to find the hamburgers, and an old man, well advanced in years, came by our table. "Good evening."

"Good evening."

"You all on vacation?"

"Yes sir."

"Having a good time?"

I am beginning to think, well, we were. And I said, "Yes sir."

"You gonna be here long?"

I was thinking not very long. I said, "No, we won't be here but a week."

And he said, "Well, I hope you have a good time, what do you do?"

That's not his business. We are on vacation. My wife and I got rid of the kids. I want to get rid of this old man. I said, "Well, I teach in seminary."

"Oh, are you a preacher?"

"Well, yeah."

He pulled a chair out and said, "I want to tell you a story."

I said, "Well, have a seat at our table here."

He said, "I was born back here in these mountains. My mother was not married and in those days that meant shame. And when we went to town the other women looked at her and looked at me and began to guess who I was and who my father was and the reproach that was hers fell on me. And it was painful. At school the children had a name for me. I hid in the weeds at recess. I ate my lunch alone.

"I started going to a little church back in there called Laurel Springs. There was a preacher–a craggy, rough preacher, full beard, big voice. He scared me but fascinated me. I would go just for the sermon. I was afraid somebody would speak to me in the earlier part and say what's a boy like *you* doing in church? And I was afraid. One Sunday after I had been going for some time, some of the people cued up in the aisle and I couldn't rush out as I usually did. I couldn't get by. I began to get chills, oh somebody will say something to me and I need to get out of here.

"I felt a hand on my shoulder and I looked out of the corner of my eye and it was that preacher. I saw his beard and I saw that face and I thought 'oh no.' That preacher looked at me and said, 'well boy, boy, you are a child of,' and he paused, and I thought 'oh no.' He said, 'boy, you are a child; you are a child of God. I see a striking resemblance.' He swatted me on the bottom and said 'go claim your inheritance.'"

He said, "I was born that day."

I said to the old man, "What is your name?"

He said, "Ben Hooper." And then he left. Ben Hooper? Ben Hooper?

Oh, yes, I remember my father telling about the people of Tennessee twice electing an illegitimate governor named Ben Hooper.

Ben Hooper told me a story.

No, Ben Hooper told me *the* Story.

4

Preaching as Storytelling

Sustaining the Power

I've never known a preacher (including myself) who has not experienced difficulty in sustaining a story. It is an old debate about whether storytellers are born or whether they can be cultivated and educated. I believe that regardless of whether we are *born* storytellers or *nurtured* ones, we can improve our skills of storytelling. But it is extremely difficult. It is a practical difficulty.

Sometimes behind that practical difficulty are some theoretical difficulties. We may not be aware of them sometimes. There is a suspicion, a lack of trust that the story can do anything, that it has any power. There's a fear that the story is just too fragile. I've met many skeptics who chuckle at us "naïve storytellin' preachers" who think "by telling stories they are going to make any positive difference." Telling stories, they say, has as much a chance to change the world as does throwing a light bulb to break up concrete. Now, you can believe that if you want to, but I have been present when someone threw a light bulb against concrete walls and they cracked and fell. Just a story did that.

Sometimes I think that our hesitation in using stories, especially powerful and effective stories, is *not* because we are afraid they do not have power. We are afraid that they *do*. Do you really want to be a party to *changing* the lives of people? Do you really want to make a positive difference? Is it frightening when somebody actually takes to heart what was preached and makes a commitment to change? There are preachers who are afraid of the power of preaching and therefore pull back with hesitation. There is in all of us a temptation to be ineffective.

There are two kinds of preaching that people will not listen to: poor preaching and good preaching. Some of us are more afraid of the second than the first. I heard a minister tell of visiting one of his parishioners in the hospital. She had been ill for some time. His custom was to pray with the sick person unless it was an awkward moment with a lot of strangers and a lot of noise. That was not the case in this occasion. Before he could ask whether he could pray with her, she asked, "Oh, pastor would you pray for me?" He stood at the foot of the bed and prayed for her recovery. When he finished the prayer, she sat up in bed. Then she swung her feet over the side. She put her feet in her scuffs. She reached for her robe. She put on the robe, stood up, stretched, and began to jump up and down. And then she grabbed him around the neck and exclaimed, "Thank you pastor, thank you! I am well! I am healed!"

He went out to the parking lot, got into his car, and before he turned the ignition key, he had a little prayer: "Please Lord, don't ever do that to me again!"

But I do believe that there is in many of us just a lack of trust in the power of the Word that is spoken. Jesus compared the Word to a seed. A seed carries its own future in its bosom. The farmer does not plant it in the ground and then scream over it. The farmer leaves it alone. So just think of all the ways (even when we are preaching on faith) that we reflect our lack of trust in the very thing we are preaching. Many of us operate out of caution, fear, and defensiveness.

One hot summer night when I was young, I was at a revival at our church that lacked air conditioning. I sat by the window at the back of the sanctuary. The minister was up front, preaching away on his favorite text: "Be not the first by whom the new is tried because it is better to be safe than sorry, for when you are in doubt, take the old paths because a bird in the hand is worth two in the bush." Like I said, it was hot and the window was open and a man I had not known before passed by and whispered to me, "Psst, Fred."

"What do you want?" I asked.

"Want to go with me?" he invited.

"Where are you going?"

"I am going to a place where there is a pearl that's worth all the other pearls in the world."

"There is no such place."

"There is. In fact, very close by there is a field with a buried treasure in it and I am going for it."

"Now you're just making stuff up."

"No, it's true. In fact, where I am going beggars and peasants are invited to sit at the king's table."

"Really? Now I know you are kidding me."

"I am not kidding you. They give parties for prodigals."

"You can't kid me. There's no such place. You must think I'm a fool."

After the service the minister asked me, "What was that disturbance?"

"Oh, somebody full of notions invited me to get out of here and get lost in some strange things."

"Who was it?"

"I don't know. But he had twelve other guys with him."

I confess that I am a hesitant, cautious person and it is easier for me to encourage other people to be adventuresome and to take risks. It's easier to say it and to preach it than to do it and to feel it.

The other morning, while walking down the street in front of my house, I saw a sparrow. I think that bird weighed about nine pounds.

"Aren't you kind of heavy for a sparrow?" I asked.

"Yeah, I am a little plump, and that is why I'm out walking. I've got to get some of this weight off."

"Why don't you fly?"

"What? I have never flown before."

"What is your name?" I asked.

"Fred," he said.

Now, it might help us to overcome the hesitation in storytelling if we think about what goes on in storytelling. First of all the storyteller recognizes that in telling a story you are not speaking *to* people so much as you are speaking *for* them. Let's remember that in preaching we don't just speak *to* the people. We speak *for* the people. We don't tell them what they want to hear—we have all been warned about that. But why not now and then tell them what they want to *say*? The unused treasure of preaching is the experience, the faith, the commitment, and love of the people, all of whom have a story to tell but they can't articulate it. They don't have an opportunity and when they do they fumble around and say, "I just can't talk about this." But you can speak for them. You can say something that they will say, "Yes! I have had that very same experience. That happened to me. Have you been reading my e-mail?"

Do you know what you are doing? You are evoking all of those stories. The mark of a good story is when its people begin to say, "You know, when you were talking, I was thinking of when I was once home on the farm." Now you are stirring the stories and the stories are coming out and you are invoking the stories. You are not using the old "banking system" of talking, of just tamping more in, and tamping more in, but you are calling more out. Good storytelling speaks for the congregation and evokes their own stories. And there is nothing more refreshing and more Christian than in the context of prayer, and music, and song, and worship, and fellowship in the house of God to have somebody stir up from the deep cellar of my own life the most important experience I can recall. And then when someone at the door says to you, "I really appreciate what you said this morning about so and so," and you never said anything about it, that's *good* preaching, because preaching is an act of the people, an act of the church, in the participation of it. But that is only if your stories are realistic.

I once heard a terrible thing in a sermon. The preacher had been doing extremely well. I was listening right along. Then he told about a time when he and his family were coming home late at night from a church gathering. He knew a shortcut along a county road. They took it and then had car trouble on the scarcely used road. What do we do? Does the family go with me to look for help? Do I leave them here and go alone to find help? What do I do? Suddenly there was a glow on the horizon. The family began to feel hopeful. The glow got brighter, and atop the hill were two lights: the light of love and the light of truth.

Now, doesn't that make you sick? If my family was sitting in the car and we couldn't find any help and here comes love and truth, I think I would be angry. I want a car to come over the hill to help! Nobody identifies with stories that have improper spiritualizing.

When you tell a story, everybody is relaxed. It's not confrontation time. It's not challenge time. It's relaxing. "Once upon a time . . ." and everybody relaxes. "I remember when I was about ten years old . . ." and everybody relaxes. And in that relaxation, you are drawn into the story and identification begins to take place. If it's a good story, you start identifying with the experience or one of the characters, and that is the power.

The great single power in storytelling (and in preaching for that matter) is the power of identification. You go to the theater. You sit in front of the television. What makes something very gripping? What makes it very gripping when you are at the theater? And you just say, I want to go back and see it. You go somewhere with friends, to a restaurant after the theater, and you can't even talk. You just stare at the cup in silence. What happened? You identified with that drama or with one of the characters. Nobody during the play came out and said, "I want to challenge you today. I have three points I want to say about this tonight." It was identification, and that's what happens in storytelling. That power takes over. In that identification, things long buried–known but not nourished, not dwelt on, not feeding the life, not doing their work–begin to do their work. And things that have long been in the head begin to move toward the heart–and that's when life is changed. In the process of storytelling, what we know gradually moves toward the heart and we become what we know. It's been true in my experience that it's a long trip from the head to the heart.

I grew up on the cotton patch in West Tennessee. And I recall one time, when I was about twelve years old, my uncle was driving a wagon and I was sitting up on top. We were hauling hay to the barn. Hot job, terrible job, I was just a kid but everybody worked. Sitting on top of the hay, my Uncle Jim driving the team and on the tailgate was my closest friend at the time, an elderly black man, Will. He was my teacher. He would come by the house and I'd go out there and he'd teach me things I never learned at school. For example, he taught me why grape vines are scared and have to hold on to the tree. Will said something to me, and out of respect I said, "Sir . . ." My next conscious moment was getting up from beneath the front wheel of the wagon with my head half paralyzed from the blow that my Uncle Jim had struck. And Uncle Jim's face was in mine, shouting, "Boy, if I ever hear you call a nigger 'sir' again I will kill you, so help me God!"

Eight years later I was in little old churches preaching as best as I could, "In Christ there is neither Jew nor Greek, bond nor free, male nor female, black nor white. We are all one in Christ Jesus." I knew it was true. But what if somebody had said to me, "Fred, we liked the sermon. There is a family visiting here, a black family, and they want to take you for lunch."

I knew. But I didn't *know*. The longest trip you ever make is from your head to your heart. And on the way in between you make casualties even out of your friends.

When you are telling a story and it is a grand Christian story and somebody who has known things all along says, "Oh, yes, well I remember once." What's happening? The trip is going on. That's the dynamic part because you see yourself creating the experience. We are not passing along *information*. A sermon is full of information. Understand what I said in the last chapter. The content is there; the substance is there. There is information to be sure. There is something redemptive about information.

But preaching is not *primarily* about transferring information. It is creating the *experience* of that information. And you have to decide, as the speaker, the nature of the experience to be created. For instance, if you are preaching on freedom, what is going to be the flavor, the size, the sound, and the shape of that experience? What is it going to sound like? What is it going to look like? What is it going to smell like? What is it going to taste like? Don't just say, "Today I will be talking about freedom." There is freedom and then there is *freedom*. It might be a loud sermon. You can preach on freedom while bombs burst in the air–Independence Day parade, firecrackers, drums, seventy-six trombones, and John Phillip Sousa marching down Main Street. Freedom!

You can also preach on freedom, and it could be as quiet as the humming of "We Shall Overcome" by six female voices outside a county jail. It could be as quiet as a whisper just inside of a cabin door: "Mr. Lincoln says we are free."

The way we put words together creates the experience. Too often powerful texts are used in sermons as information, such as, "And there was this beggar sitting at the gate." Now, wait a minute! Give me a chance to experience the beggar at the gate. Help me to see the rags, smell the odor, hear the coin in the tin cup, and see the hollow eyes. Let me get there. Because what Peter and John do is against the backdrop of this terrible need.

Don't *rush* to the destination—take the trip. For example, I've heard too many sermons on the flood and the preacher rushes to get to the rainbow in the sky. Instead, tell me about a flood. It's not just a boat floating out there with a giraffe sticking its head out of the ark. I mean what's a flood? Have you ever been to a flood? Have you smelled a flood, the silt, the mud, the scraping out the house, you can't get the odor out. The looters are coming. The National Guard is out. Whatever happened to this? We'll have to move. The wall is falling in. Washing all the furniture. Let everybody smell and see and experience a flood. Then when you say rainbow, whoosh. That is good news. Flood and rainbow is not just information—we are dealing with the promise of God.

Storytelling is the creation of the experience of the substance of the sermon. Now, where do we begin? Well we begin by listening. We begin by observing. Listening and observing; you remember the preparation of the servant in Isaiah 50? It is one of those servant songs of Isaiah—that marvelous passage:

> The Lord God has given me the tongue of a teacher, that I may know how to sustain the weary with a word. Morning by morning he wakens—wakens my ear, to listen as those who are taught. The Lord God has opened my ear, and I was not rebellious, I did not turn backward. I gave my back to those who struck me, and my cheeks to those who pulled out the beard; I did not hide my face from insult and spitting. (Is. 50:4–6)

Isn't that interesting? God opened my ear (literally, "dug out my ear") and I didn't rebel? What does that mean? It means it is a painful thing to listen, but I didn't rebel. To listen and to observe is the beginning place; the quickening and awakening of the ear. Now, this has to be very careful and very intentional: to be observant, to be open to the sights and sounds of the world around us. I once said to a group of students that it is my impression that God operates almost completely by whispering and therefore we have to lean forward to hear it. And a student came up afterward and said, "But don't you think God sometimes shouts? Whether you are paying attention or not you really get it." And I said, "Well, I suppose so." I don't want to limit God.

To hear and to see the ways of God in the world one does have to listen and observe carefully, and the place I would begin is in the listening and in observing carefully in the scripture. The first step always in the exegesis of the text, the interpretation of the text, is to *read* the text. Now I say that because I know it is possible to get up for a sermon, never having read the text carefully. Read the text. Read it out loud. Read it several times before you pull out the commentaries and concordances and lexicons. If you bring out all those books it makes you silent and quiet. Well what do I know in front of all these scholars? What do you know? Pretty soon they take over and it's their sermon. No. Just you and the text. Open up to the text. It's amazing what you discover just reading it. I have a sermon on file, a terrible one and I'm not using it anymore. My text is Luke 15, the shepherd leaving the ninety-nine and going in search of the one sheep that was lost. And in that sermon I say and the whole sermon presupposes that the ninety-nine were safely in the fold and he went out looking for the one that was lost. I read the text years later. It doesn't say that at all.

Where did I get the idea that the ninety-nine were safely in the fold? Well, my recollection is from an old hymn we sang in Sunday school opening. "The ninety and nine safely lay sheltered in the fold." What Luke says is, he left the ninety-nine in the wilderness and went looking for the one. Any good businessperson will leave ninety-nine in the fold and look for one. But only the risky, careless love of God will leave ninety-nine in the wilderness and look for one. That is high-risk love.

That's a different sermon. My old sermon is dead.

I used to preach a certain sermon on the prodigal son (Lk. 15). I would talk about this father's welcoming of this younger son and then I would pause between the points in my sermon to kick the older brother. I just really slapped him around, knocked him off the back porch as I just kept on talking about God's love for the younger one. Finally, one day in desperation, I read the text. And I realized both sons are treated the same. The father goes out to both. The father affirms his love to both. The father affirms his generosity to both. My "either-or" mind was trying to preach what needed to a "both-and" sermon. And I missed the text.

It is important to read the text, read the text, read the text. Open up the pores of the skin, get a piece of scratch paper and every conceivable thing that comes to mind, related-unrelated, relevant-irrelevant, every old memory, every question, every notion that is triggered, jot it down. It is what Paul Ricoeur calls the "first naiveté"–the first exposure to the text in total naiveté. How will the people hear this? I want to identify with my listeners. How will they hear this? I don't start off with Ernst Käsemann's essay on this text. I start off with the text and just think of all the possible things that come to mind–emotion, heart, feeling, and remembering this or remembering that–just jot it all down. Now, a lot of that will be thrown away when I get into the exegesis, and I don't just stop there and think, hey, I got a sermon. There is no shortcut to Nazareth. You've got to take the long route every time. But in my exegesis I go to work: some of that early stuff will still stand; some of it will be thrown away. And I will have to throw it away because a good story, a good piece of material, is a poor servant. It is a great master. It will take over your sermon. Have you ever attended some conference and heard someone speak and he or she told a really interesting story and then you used it the next Sunday even though it didn't fit? It just takes over. Now, some stories under the pressure and honesty of careful exegesis of the text will have to be tossed out because they do not fit the intentionality of the text, what the writer intended to say. That is why study is such a fearful business. Some of us wonder, "Why do I hate study? Once I get into it, it is not all that bad." The point is, any time study can upset your prejudice, your prenotion, your preunderstanding and nobody likes to have a bulldozer come in and scrape up their favorite landscape, so we "just don't really have any time to study. Man, since I've been in the parish, I just don't have any time to study." Buy a lot of books, stack 'em up there, show them to the board of deacons. Look at that. But the hesitation is the things I may have to give up or careful study may ruin a sermon, or may actually destroy one I've already preached.

I was with a study group in Israel. We had a fellow from Hebrew University giving lectures to this group. They were getting credit for it. In the group were seminarians and about twenty lay folks from churches in Oklahoma and Texas. It was during a time for a lot of tours in Israel, and there was a very large group just ahead of us as we came to this particular place in Jerusalem. We had to wait near the door. The person inside was a minister with a large group in there seated and standing in this particular place listening as he read from scripture, and then he gave a little talk. He said, "In this very place where I'm standing now, Jesus stood. And where you are now, the twelve apostles were." And he just gave them all that confidence and assurance. He knew—I am sure he knew—that by the decorations on the wall and the nature of the building it was probably twelfth or thirteenth century and had a Turkish influence. He said, "Oh, where I am today and where you are . . ." and just went on and on. Our group moved in and a professor from Hebrew University said, "As you can tell by the decoration this building was probably built . . ." and he started telling so and so. "There is a tradition that this building replaced an earlier one, which replaced an earlier one and perhaps Jesus was in a building at this place." A woman near me, bless her heart, said, "I wish I were in the other group."

We don't like to have things destroyed by information. But the way to begin is to begin with the story. How stories are told. How do the writers tell their stories?

Luke is a marvelous storyteller. I mentioned Luke 15: that story of the prodigal son. I preached on that and preached on that. The way that story is told; so absolutely moving that there is hardly a week goes by but what one identifies with that: Luke's story. When we were in Oklahoma, up the street from us lived a family, the parents divorced and there were some girls in the family, beautiful girls. One of them matured very early and was in all kinds of difficulty by the time she was fourteen. There was not much home life and she was truant at school. She was up before the juvenile judge. She was suspected of drugs and she was just everywhere. She was hanging on the tail end of every motorcycle that roared through town. She was just always in trouble. Finally the judge sent her to a detention home for girls in the southern part of the state. She was pregnant when she went. At the age of fifteen she had the child while she was there. We heard about it back home on the street. We also heard she was coming home. The afternoon that she was to come home all of us in the neighborhood "had" to mow our yard. And I was mowing my yard and watching up there. I was interested if she really was coming home because she had really only been gone six months or so. And would she have that baby. So I was mowing the yard and she didn't come. No car pulled in. She didn't come and I was down to about a blade at a time. Finally a car pulled in and she got out and she had that baby. Born in prison out of wedlock. There she had that baby. Some folk in the house came out and grabbed her and kissed her and gave turns holding that baby. And another car pulled in, and another car pulled in, and they were hugging her and holding the baby. And some were going in the house and they started parking up and down the street. You couldn't get a Christian car down the street. Just parked everywhere. Finally I got self-conscious and went in the house because it suddenly occurred to me suppose someone in that family sees me down here and says, "Hey, Fred, she is home and we would like for you and Nettie to come up we are giving a party for her and she has the baby with her." Would I go?

And they killed the calf and hired the musicians. And there was music and dancing and a party because a boy came home after wasting substance and ruckus living with harlots and living with pigs and denying his faith and his moral upbringing. And they gave a party. The party. Now, if you had lived next door to that old man and he yelled across the hedge and said, "Hey, you know that worthless kid of mine that left a couple of years ago? Came in last night. Like for you to come, we are having a party."

Would you go?

It's easier to preach on the prodigal son than it is to go to that party.

5

Preaching as Storytelling

The Form

In the previous two chapters, we looked at the difficulty of the transaction of telling and listening to a story. What happens in the congregation when the minister is telling a story and the people are listening? From my perspective, the first step in storytelling is the very first step in the exegesis of a text: open faculties of the mind, open emotions of the heart, and open direction to the movement of the spirit.

I am not talking about getting some stories from somewhere to spice up your sermons because your people are bored so you want something to liven them up a bit. Now, that may be true but I'm not talking about that.

When preachers tell me that they need to get some stories to spice up their preaching, I discover that their method of dealing with the text is usually the problem. The person goes to the text, reads it, studies it, and then boils the text down to a proposition or idea and then that idea is developed into an outline. That is disrespectful of the text. *Biblical* preaching asks not only what the text says but *how* it says it. Instead of moving away from the Bible to enliven your preaching, move in closer and see how the Bible does it. Be respectful, very carefully respectful, of the form in which the Bible gives you the material. The Bible is serious about form. The Bible has many forms. And if our preaching is dull, let's move back to the Bible to get some forms for our sermons. Why should I take something that comes to me as a parable or a paradox or a song or a doxology or a Christological hymn and boil it down into two, three, four, five, six points, disregarding the way I got it? The form in which it comes to me may be the form I want to keep when I pass it along.

The Bible uses a form of inverted parallel called a chiasmus. In chiasmus (it's a, b, b, a), the two middle lines match, and the outside lines match. It's a favorite figure of speech used by early Christians, especially when talking about Jesus Christ, because Jesus Christ in some Christological formulas fits that exactly: a, b, b, a. For example, a: he was rich; b: became poor; b: by his poverty; and a: we might be rich. Rich, poor, poor, rich. With God, suffered, died, with God; it fits. Why would I disregard that when I prepare my sermon?

I want a sermon structure that will be congenial and honest with the structure of the material as I receive it because the way my sermon moves may actually contradict what it is I seek to accomplish. I had more than one student preach an either-or sermon calling for decision, but the sermon had three points. It should have had two. The answer is yes or no. In three points, what is that other one? Maybe?

Now, the Bible is more serious about form than that. For example, the Bible has the form of Beatitudes: "Blessed are the poor in spirit" (Mt. 5:3). A beatitude is a form of material in which something comes, in which it does what it says, "Blessed are the poor." If I am going to preach on a beatitude, which to me is extremely difficult, how can I respect that form throughout my sermon so that what is being said is done by its being said? Because if I am not careful, I will convert the beatitude into an exhortation: "Let us be poor in spirit. The trouble with us is that we are not poor in spirit. Come on let's be poor in spirit at the count of three. One, two, three, poor in spirit!" That is not a beatitude any more.

A paradox, "For all who exalt themselves will be humbled, and those who humble themselves will be exalted" (Lk. 14:11). That is a paradox, but I can flatten that out into a strategy of how to get ahead. You know a lot of our sermons are un-Christian by just flattening out a text like that. Whoever humbles oneself will be exalted. You want to know how to get exalted? Humble yourself. Sounds pagan, doesn't it? It sounds pagan because we remove the paradoxical nature of the text. Sometimes it's important to understand what is said by noticing how it is said.

There are some ticklish points in the New Testament. For instance, the diatribe is a favorite form in James. You anticipate what the audience is saying and you answer it. But when you get to chapter 5, I question if that is a diatribe: "Come now, you rich people, weep and wail for the miseries that are coming to you" (Jas. 5:1). Is that a diatribe or is that an apostrophe? An apostrophe is a literary form in which you address people who are not present. Or address someone not present while speaking to those who are. I think he's talking to the poor about the rich. If it's a diatribe, he is talking to the rich. Come now you rich, weep and wail. If it's an apostrophe, he is talking to the poor about the rich. Come now you rich, weep and howl.

And the poor say, "amen, sic 'em, get 'em, yeah." The form is extremely important as to what is being said.

It is not absolutely necessary that I keep the form of the passage in the sermon I preach. Sometimes it's impossible. Some proverbs I can't just keep in that form to preach it. Service would be out too soon. When you say a proverb, what else do you do? But it is important to respect it and see if you can keep it. For instance, if your text is a prayer, that doesn't mean you have to pray your sermon. But if your text is a prayer and your sermon is not sensitive to the fact that that text, and hopefully your sermon, is addressed to God as well as to the people—if there is not a God-wardness in the flow of that sermon—then the sermon suffers from radical discontinuity with that text.

What's the form of the text? How does the writer tell stories? Now, some people think of the Bible in terms of the eye and look at the structure. I look at the Bible and think in terms of the ear. I listen to Matthew. Matthew has a way of raising his voice. Matthew shouts a lot. Matthew screams a time or two. Have you ever noticed how it comes on? It's just really hard and heavy. Now, the way that Matthew raises the volume is he sets his readers or his listeners in the Day of Judgment. When something is really, really important he pushes it right up against the Parousia, the end of all things, and looks at it in the light of that final day—when the Son of man shall come in the clouds of glory with all of his angels with him, he will divide us up on the basis of one question that he asks, one question: "How did you respond to human need?" I was hungry, naked, in prison, and how is that talked about? It's set against the judgment, people who are distortedly religious but don't carry out common responsibility.

> On that day many will say to me, "Lord, Lord, did we not prophesy in your name and cast out demons in your name, and do many deeds of power in your name?" Then I will declare to them, "I never knew you; go away from me, you evildoers." (Mt. 7:22–23)

See how Matthew does it? In Matthew, you hear doors slamming, gnashing teeth, screaming, worms turning, fires never going out, and the gavel coming down in the last court. That's Matthew. Matthew is loud.

In contrast, Luke is quiet. While Matthew argues, Luke just sort of prophesies. You can tell by the different ways they use the Old Testament. Matthew uses the Old Testament in such a way that it is obvious—"just as it is written"; and he quotes. And even in the English it is indented and in dark print. Luke doesn't do that. But even though I haven't counted the verses and the uses of the Old Testament, I would be willing to venture that Luke uses more Old Testament than Matthew, but Luke weaves it into the fabric of his story in an allusive way. It is similar to this, with Matthew using the material like a quilt: you can detect the pieces. But in Luke, it's a blanket. He is such a literary artist he has just woven it in there and if you don't know your Old Testament you will think he is not using it. But he is using it.

And Luke is quiet. Just take the birth stories. Matthew's birth story is loud. Wise men from the East, "Where is the child who has been born king of the Jews?" (Mt. 1:35.) Herod is shaking, his throne trembling, and he is hurling death warrants. The chariots are clattering, as well as the swords; soldiers are kicking in the doors; mothers are clutching their babies behind the cellar door, screaming and crying during the killing of the babies. Even at night you can hear a voice in Ramah: Rachel weeping for her children and buzzards soaring over the shallow graves of children. And Joseph escapes with the holy family at night into Egypt to hide from his enemies among his enemies.

Now move over to Luke 1: quiet. To paraphrase, an angel says to a little peasant girl in Nazareth, "Through the Holy Spirit you shall have a child" (Lk. 1:35). And she starts singing. Angels appear to shepherds. Angels are singing, shepherds are singing. Zachariah is singing. Everybody is singing. They are just singing and it's just beautiful. When I teach Luke in my classes I let the students hum the first two chapters. It's just beautiful. But that doesn't mean that Luke in his quiet beauty is any less powerful. Listen to what Mary sings. It's a protest song: "He has sent the rich away empty. He has filled the poor with good things. He's pulled down the mighty from their throne. He's lifted up the peasants" (paraphrase of Lk. 1:46–55). That is what she sang. And here are these shepherds keeping watch. Nothing is louder than a flute and a bleating of a lamb. And here come the angels and the angels said, "Now, don't be afraid. We are going to give you a sign." It's a beautiful thing. We are going to give you a sign. If I had been running the show I would have said, "Now, I know you don't believe this so I'm going to give you a sign. There are going to be some angels coming in here and hovering overhead and then you will believe it." That's not what it was. The angels were just taken as ordinary. The sign is that you are going to find a baby in town, in a crib, wrapped in swaddling cloth, mulling and puking in his mother's arms and that is the redemption of the world. A baby? Change the world? Julius Caesar couldn't. There he stood astride the world, one foot on land, one foot on sea, and went in triumph to Rome only to be cut down by his close friends. And this little baby subject to every little germ in the air is going to change the world? That's Luke.

When the baby is just six weeks old, the time arrives for dedication and the mother to be purified. It's the first male child and she has to be purified. The child has to be dedicated. She goes up to the temple scared to death. "Where do I stand?" she asks herself. "What do I say? What if the baby cries?" You can see her going up there. And then in the temple courtyard is an old man named Simeon: large, rheumy eyes, dried spittle in his beard, shuffling along, scaring all the mothers. Here comes Mary and this old man walks up and peeks into her blue blanket and says, "Give me that boy." And he takes that baby and she is nervous, afraid the old man will drop the baby and he says, "Now let me die. I have seen the consolation of Israel," and he said to her, "Because of this child a sword will pierce your heart. This child is set for the rising and falling of many in Israel" (paraphrase of Lk. 2:29–34). And here is Luke, humming and singing. And in his quiet way, he has spoken of world revolution, eschatological reversal, the redemption of the world and the final judgment, while he sings. Then somebody comes around and says, "I don't know what I can do to enliven my preaching." Why not use the Bible? How powerful and meaningful are the scenes in which Jesus is at the table in Luke; the dispensation of forgiveness at the table. What a marvelous series of sermons come from Luke when Jesus comes to dinner. Have you counted the times: in the home of Simon the Pharisee, invited to a banquet and everybody scrambling for the chief places, he tells a story of a banquet in the home of Martha and Mary. At the table Jesus tells stories that are worth everything.

And on into Acts. Every time you get a picture of the early church, they are eating, they are eating together, and then the test comes. Some don't want to eat together. Look at the marvelous story of Simon Peter in Acts 10. He's asleep on top of the house, hungry, and smells the aroma from the kitchen. It's snowing; he's getting ready to eat. And the sheet comes down full of all this nonkosher stuff. I'll never eat that, no. Three times, gonna eat it huh? I'm never gonna eat it. Look, if I call it clean, it's clean. A fellow is down there saying, would you come with us? You're Simon Peter? Yes, he goes up to Caesarea and there is this Italian soldier, Cornelius, and his household. And Simon Peter goes in there and Luke says, "He eats with them." He eats with them macaroni and pizza and all that. Now, the church in Jerusalem hears about it. The church in Jerusalem calls him on the carpet and they didn't say, "We understand you baptized some Gentiles." That is not what they said. "We understand you *ate* with them." And he said, "Gentlemen, I am just as prejudiced as anybody in this room but who am I to stand against God?" You see what the question was? The question was, "Did you eat with them?" because Luke understands that you have no right to try to convert anybody with whom you are not willing to eat. And Luke is just as quiet and soft. He will trap you. Warn your people before you preach on Luke. He will ensnare you before you know it.

My point to all of this is to invest enough time and read large enough portions until you begin to sense how a biblical writer tells a story. Maybe I should just keep telling it that way. Then what I do is I recognize that the message there is too complex to be captured without residue in one little story. So I want to make sure that my stories are lifelike—that the stories have depth, and height, and breadth and are not little, old, flat, one-dimensional, simple, clever, tricky, cute, little things. If there is a disease in the preaching that I hear most often, it's not that what the minister says is wrong. It's that it is just too small.

The Bible knows that there is an underside to everything. There is another side to everything and it is not all that simple. The Bible knows that the gospel is not addressed to people who are in a B movie, with the good guys and the bad guys, and you can tell by the sweatiness of the horse which one is the good guy and the bad guy. It's not that simple. You just read the stories.

A man came up to Jesus and asked how to serve him. When Jesus called on him to go and preach the kingdom of God he said, "Let me first go bury my father." He didn't say, "Let me go first have one more good fling." He said, "Let me go bury my father." Whenever the banquet was ready and the servant went out and said, "Tell them to come. Tell those invited to come. Everything is ready." One of them didn't say, "Well, I am sorry I can't come because I just washed the poodle and I have to walk it 'til it gets dry." He didn't say that. He said, "I have just gotten married."

The Bible knows the difficulties of faith. And it is sinful for us to reduce the whole thing. Let's just take the temptation stories of Jesus. When Jesus was in the wilderness, the tempter didn't come to him and say, "You know what I got down here behind this tree?" No, that's puny. The tempter said, "If you are the son of God, do something marvelous: turn stones to bread, stir the people by leaping off the pinnacle, free the people by taking political power, do something good." Read the temptation in Genesis. The tempter didn't say, "Do you want to sink?" No. The tempter said, "Do you want to be like God?"

That's it. The Bible knows that you are not tempted at a point of weakness. We are tempted at a point of strength. Temptations are a compliment to our power, not our weakness. It's our sermons that reduce the whole thing to a B western. The Bible knows it. Therefore, in the selection of stories or in the creation of stories, let's make sure that the story has enough dimension to it, that it does not reduce the quality of the message with which we deal.

For example, just think how the Bible considers children. Now it's easy to preach a sermon on children in which you just idolize children. Be as children. Now what qualities in children do we favor? Children do this and children do that. And children do so and so. The Bible doesn't do that. The Bible knows. The children are more complex than that. A child may burn down the living room and saw the family dog in half when you are not looking. Whatever. The Bible knows, so the Bible says sometimes, "Be like children." And other times, the Bible says to grow up and quit being children.

Take the matter of change. We say, "We want to get people converted. We want some change. Change, change." The Bible knows that change is an ambiguous good. Do you really want people to change? "I don't know if I can trust her. She seems to have changed." Do you really want people to change? Change is a painful thing. How many people really change? Not very many. Of those, who change for the better without pain? Almost zero. Change? The Bible knows how painfully complex it is. And it is not just a simple thing to yell at people.

I was parked one day at the curb, sitting, waiting on my wife; it was downtown. Next to me a car was parked. On the companion side was a young woman who looked to be in her midtwenties. She was sitting there crying and dabbing at her eyes with a tissue. Just a little dab and cry. I didn't know why she was crying but I had time and I had one course in psychology so, I thought, I wonder why she is crying. I think I'll figure out why she is crying. Maybe her husband is in the tavern around the corner. Maybe the family budget will not permit the new dress that she picked out. Maybe she has just gotten a letter from home that her mother is ill. Maybe her child is in the hospital. I went through the whole thing. Shortly, out of the building in front of me came a young man, who also looked to be in his midtwenties. He had in his arms a little boy with a fresh haircut. And he came out of the barbershop and the little's boy's head was just peeled. He put that little boy in the front seat and this woman, this young woman, grabbed the little boy and kissed him all over the head, crying, crying, and crying. Then she says something to the man. I didn't know what she was saying. He shook his head. She kept talking and he shook his head. Finally, he got out of the car, went inside reached under the barber chair, got a lock of blonde hair and came back out. Now if I would have stopped the car and said, "Now young woman do you want your child to stay a baby forever? Why are you crying?" She would have said, "Oh, no, no, no. But I've lost my baby." Now you think about that and it does something to the flavor of the words when you pronounce them. "We want some changes." Change is painful. The two most beautiful seasons of the year hurt: spring, those little petals that would just wilt from the heat of a child's hand pushing up through crust; and ice and snow for me to see. That hurts. You know how they stay alive? Little old hair like roots sometimes will push up a sidewalk to get some food and water. That hurts. And then in the fall—aren't the leaves beautiful as they turn to gold, red, and yellow? You know how they do that? They die.

We must not be small and silly in our preaching. There is another side to things. The Bible knows it. The Bible knows it sometimes in some ways much more than we do. We are tempted to say, "Forget. Let's forget the past. Forget everything and press on." The Bible wonders about forgetting. "If I forget thee, O Jerusalem, let my right hand forget her cunning. If I do not remember thee, let my tongue cleave to the roof of my mouth" (Ps. 137:5).

The Bible knows it is not simple. It's true with the case of John the Baptist. I used to preach John the Baptist and fuss at the Jews. Here came John the Baptist preaching, "The Messiah's coming, the Messiah's coming." And the crowds, Mark and the others say, the crowds came from every-where. They emptied Jerusalem from the country, from the city, from the north, and across trans-Jordan. They came to hear John. The Messiah's coming, the Messiah's coming. And then when the Christians took over and said, "The Messiah is here. The Messiah has already come and it is Jesus." The crowds begin to dwindle. I screamed and fussed at them and stuck my spurs in the side of the pulpit and yelled at those Jews, what's the matter with those Jews? And then I got to thinking about it. You know it is a pretty big disappointment if you have spent centuries looking for a Messiah, for somebody to show up and say he is here. It's true. You can make anticipation a way of life. And you know as well as I do it's easier to believe a Messiah will come than to believe one has come. That's why the second coming fascinates a lot of people. They are avoiding the first and its implications. It's true. As long as I say a Messiah will come, my hope can really be a postponement. I can say to the beggar on the street, "I am sorry but when the Messiah comes there is not going to be any begging." I can say to the cripple with his legs folded useless beneath him, "Brother, I am sorry about your legs, but you'll get better when the Messiah comes." I can say to the girl who has been assaulted, "I know it's bad but when the Messiah comes there will be justice." I can say to the couple who have been married fourteen years and still rock an empty cradle, "I know, but when the Messiah comes." When the Messiah comes. We are looking for a Messiah. And anticipation can be sort of a way of life. It's a lot easier than facing the realities of life.

My wife and I have a little place on a lake, about forty-five minutes from where we live. This lake is small and just has private homes around it. It's not open to public. Willows leaning lazily over in the water. It's great fishing there; the bass jump out of the water into your boat. That place has no vandals. We have never had a screen cut or window broken. We have not had any watermelon rinds or beer cans. And I have yet to feel my first mosquito or fly. You know where it is?

That's the kind of place we are going to have one day. And if you think I am going to trade mine in on what you have, you are crazy. So you just think about it. On the announcement that the Messiah is here, why isn't everybody really turned on by that? Because anticipation can become a way of life. And there is something judgmental about saying, "Now he is here." The number one miracle of the early church, of the church through the ages, is this: that anybody would believe that the Messiah has come and it is Jesus of Nazareth. Because it calls for the extraordinary reversal from a time of saying, "Where the Messiah is there is no misery," to, "Where there is misery there is the Messiah." Now that is a miracle.

But how glibly I used to just flail away at the Jews and anybody else who didn't believe. I used to say things like, "Anybody with one ounce of sense should be able to welcome."

Same way with Easter. Do you suffer from a post-Easter slump at your church? And you wonder how you can prop it up. Try reading the church page in your local paper for the Sunday after Easter. I did it in Oklahoma.

It's amazing what things churches will do to try to keep the attendance up. There was a magician at a church. Another church announced that a man was going to use a yo-yo and quote scripture and you could call out chapter and verse and he would quote it and never miss a yo-yo.

Now what are they doing? They are trying to make up for a fundamental failure to understand what the Bible understands. And that is the climax of the Christian year; it's not Easter but Pentecost. And if you have a "big" Easter followed by no Pentecost, you are dealing with an abortion. What is Easter anyway? It is sadness. Those lilies wilt. It is sadness because to the early disciples, Easter meant good-bye. Camelot is over. And John understood this and Luke understood this. John devotes nine chapters of his gospel to farewell. Chapter 13 onward is farewell, farewell, farewell. Much of the beautiful material in the New Testament is Jesus telling that group good-bye. We say, "Easter, glorious Easter, glorious Easter," but they did not. Read chapter 14: "Do not let your hearts be troubled" (Jn. 14:1). What is the matter with them? These disciples are like children sitting on the floor playing with their toys who look up and see mom and dad putting on coat and hat. And they always ask the same three questions: Where are you going? Can we go we go with you? Who is going to stay with us?

Now when you select your story, when you create the story, and when you tell the story, make sure there is a lot of stuff leftover after you have made your little point. It's just so big and the Bible understands that. When we flatten it out with our little light bulbs and saltshakers, cute phrases, it's not the same. Faith, the Bible knows what faith is.

I was once invited to a young people's prayer meeting. They said, "You will like it. We all trust in God and we have prayer." When I got there, they went around the room making their requests. And it was an unusual thing. These kids were all from affluent homes and they had trouble dredging up a request. I remember two or three. One wanted some new luggage for a trip. One wanted a dress. One wanted a boy named Mike to pay attention to her. Really, really, heavy stuff (Not!) and then what they did was they put pieces of paper "yes" and "no" in a container, moved it around, each person drawing one out. This was the answer to their prayer and they praised the Lord and went home. No sweat. They asked me to say something and I regret how I said it because it was not kind. But I don't regret what I said. They said, "Mr. Craddock, do you have any comment about our prayer service?" I said, "Well, yes, to me it is so regrettable that Jesus didn't understand that this is the way it worked." And one of them said, "What do you mean?" And I said, "You have no Gethsemane. You're holding a picnic in the olive grove."

The Bible understands faith is not just a simple process of "sayin' it and believin' it." The Bible says when you start believing that is when the problems start. It's because of you we are killed all day long. That's what the writers of the Bible say. Faith is tough. It has another sound to it.

My own faith has always had struggle in it—Gethsemane in it. It's never been easy for me. I went to the house where faith was born. It is not a sanctuary. It's not a chapel. It's not quiet. It's not a study with books of St. Aquinas and St. Augustine. It's a farmhouse. And a little boy is being told at breakfast one morning, "When the calf is born, it's yours." I had brothers and sisters.

"You mean it's just mine?"

"Yes, it's just yours."

"*My* calf?"

"It's your calf. When the calf is born, it's yours."

"All mine by myself?"

"It's all yours. Name it, feed it, care for it."

"I want to stay home from school."

"It's not going to be born today." Oh, my goodness it seemed to take forever, and one morning my father said, "I think today is the day."

"Really?"

"Yes, I think today is the day."

"I'm staying home from school."

"No, I'll take care of it. You go on to school."

"I am not going to pay attention."

"I know you won't. You go on to school."

Oh, it took forever for 3:30 to come. I dashed home and threw the books on the back porch. I ran out to the stall and in that stall stood that brown Swiss. Those big brown eyes of that momma cow. She was knee deep in glistening golden straw.

And beneath her was her dead calf, which had been born with two heads.

The next Sunday I went to church with my mother and the preacher said, "God loves us, God cares for us." My mother sang the hymns.

My calf was dead.

And the preacher said, "Christ is alive and with us."

My calf was dead.

I don't appreciate people talking glibly to me about trust.

Sometimes I feel guilty and think, "It's so simple. I've got it all messed up. It's so simple. It's just a matter of trust. And then when it gets so simple I think I am being a sucker." The teacher says, "Turn in your arithmetic lesson." A little girl starts crying. "What's the matter Mary?" asks the teacher. "I had mine in my book, but I have lost it somewhere, somebody took mine out of my book. I did it. You call my mother. I did my lesson; honest, I am not telling a lie." And the teacher says, "Mary, I believe you. It's all right." Now would you buy that?

A little boy goes to the grocery to get a loaf of bread. Comes back and gives the mother the bread. And she says, "Jimmy, what about the change?"

"Oh, I had it in my pocket. I was running, maybe it fell out of my pocket. I didn't spend it on candy or anything."

"Jimmy, I believe you."

Do you *really* believe Jimmy's story? Do you trust? Nobody likes to be a simpleton or a sucker.

When I was growing up, there was a boy in my hometown who was about my age. We mistreated him because he was what was then called "slow minded." The thing about him was he would believe anything we said.

"They're giving away watermelons down at the courthouse."

"Really?" he asked with a big smile and big eyes. And off he'd go to the courthouse.

"Did you know we're not having school next week because the school burned down?"

"It did? That's so sad."

He would just believe anything we told him.

"The President of the United States is going be here on Saturday in our town."

"He is? Where's he going to be? I'm gonna get there early!"

And he just believed all of that.

We had an evangelist come to our little church. The evangelist stood up there and preached, "God loves you, and cares for you, and sent Jesus to redeem you. Jesus wants to be your Lord and Savior."

And that boy believed it. He got up from his pew, he went forward, and he accepted Jesus as his Lord and Savior.

There were some people who said he was "slow minded."

Maybe he was.

I don't know.

6

Preaching as Storytelling

Additional Practical Suggestions

In this chapter, I'd like to move along to some practical matters related to the telling of stories. But first, let me remind you of my own firm conviction, lest you think that storytelling in preaching is mostly about "tricks" and "stunts." My own firm conviction is that one always starts with the text in sermon preparation. Regardless of the occasion or the issue, move quickly to the text, and live there, at first playfully and then with heavy examination, and then move back again playfully in a kind of naiveté, more examination, and then second naiveté.

The text is the "magnet," which you pass over all your material. The text determines whether the material will be included in the sermon or not. What "sticks" to the magnet should stay. If a story does not help to convey and enlighten that text, regardless of how remarkable the story, you have to put it aside and say to it, "I'll save you for later."

Have you had the experience of telling a story in a sermon and then later, when you are preparing another sermon, you wish you had saved that story? Most of the power of a story is not somebody's particular ability to tell a story. Most of the power in the story is in its appropriateness. Some churches still have maintained from the Elizabethan English the expression "meet and right." Let us worship God; it is meet and right so to do. That word "meet" is an old English word for the German *geeignet*, which means "it fits." It is fitting. For example, from the King James Version of the prodigal son: "It was meet that we should make merry, and be glad: for this thy brother was dead, and is alive again; and was lost, and is found" (Lk. 15:32). It is fitting. The Word of God is appropriate. There is no such thing as an inappropriate word of God. Therefore, the "fittingness" of a story is extremely important.

So we start with the text. We select stories, which by their nature have size and quality and dimension. Not little bumper sticker things–but big things. And then to move among them with the magnet of the text, not just appropriate to the text, but appropriate to the listener and appropriate to the experience to be created, the message to be delivered.

Now this appropriateness applies not just to the selection of stories for the sermon but also to the location of the stories within the sermon. That is difficult and many of us have regrets immediately after preaching: "I told that story too soon." "I told that story too late." Have you noticed sometimes you will hear a story that to you is very moving or very funny but when you go to tell it to someone else it just flops? And you say, "Well, it lost something in translation," or "Well, I guess you just had to be there." The difference is not your ability as a storyteller; it's that you have taken the egg out of the nest and laid it out on a limb.

What makes the story powerful is the taking of time to build the context in which it is told. Many marvelous things are said too soon in a sermon. The people need to be given time to get on the bus before you go roaring off. The way I was taught homiletics was to unload a lot of rich stuff right at the beginning to tantalize imagination, to capture interest, and to kindle thought. But I don't think that really works anymore, if it ever did. If the people know you are going somewhere, they will get on the bus.

This technique works even in telling stories to children. When our children were small, I would make up stories to tell them at night, because I got tired of reading the same children's books time and again. I couldn't skip a page. I was sleepy and tired and I'd been many times through the book about the nine friendly dogs. When I thought my children were almost asleep, I'd turn four or five pages. "You skipped some daddy." So I started making up stories. But first I prepared for the hearing of the story: hug the children; fix the covers so they are nice and comfortable; and talk with them about their day, what they learned, and how they felt. Then I would begin, "Did I ever tell you about the time when I was your age . . . ?"

Prepare for the story, set the context. But a lot of our preaching is like going to the child at bedtime and saying, "Well, I don't have time for the whole story but I want to give you basically the gist of it in three points." That is no good. Don't just *make* your point–help the listener *experience* the point. And that takes preparation.

Be very careful in the preparation of an introduction. The introduction should be the last part to prepare. How can you prepare an introduction to what you don't have? You prepare the sermon and then prepare the introduction. And that way, you will not too soon unload your strong material and stories that need context. Regrets about the location of material in the sermon usually have to do with giving it away too soon. If that story had been told at the end of that sermon, it would have been extremely powerful. But you wasted it just sort of getting people interested.

If I may drop a footnote here, this applies also in the placement of the text in a sermon. People have habitually thought that you read the text and go from there. Why? Sometimes that is just not appropriate. Did you know you could spend about twenty minutes dealing with some matters and getting them ready and then say, "And now let's hear the text," and people will go away saying, "I never really heard that text before"?

This technique works especially well with the parables of Jesus. You may think everybody's heard the parables. They haven't heard them. A lot of people who say, "Well here we go again," have never been there the first time. Why not just spend time getting them ready, and getting them ready, and getting them ready, and then say, "Now let's hear the story Jesus told." At least some of them will say, "Well, I've never really noticed that."

Now, where do we get stories? We get stories wherever they are. They are mostly in observation and experience. In observation, the stories of life, real good stories of things that happened are as available to you, as to me, as to anyone. Unfortunately, through negative adaptation, we can lose our capacity to pick up on the sights and sounds of our world. Or we notice things but we don't make any notes to ourselves. When we don't preserve any records, it's lost, and then we sit around in our study later saying, "Now what was that? What was that? What was that?"

When you make notes on your observations, be sure to write it in such a way that you can recover it later. For example, don't enter something like, "Bird sitting on limb." Later on you will look at that and think, "What's bird sitting on limb?" And it is gone. I keep notes of things I observe because I don't trust my memory and my experiences are too important to waste.

I also keep a journal. At the close of the day, I just enter my reflections and feelings about the experiences I've had that day. It is not a diary of such facts as "George came by at 9:00 this morning." It's what happened today and my reflections on the day. I write them so that I can access their context, and recover the experience of them, not just their information. These are observations, just listening, watching people, sitting in restaurants–they are everywhere.

An interesting thing happened to me once in New York City. I didn't get to New York very often and I spent most of my money on the hotel room. As a consequence, I ate in a little old place where I got a hot dog. There were only two customers. An elderly woman waited on us. She had to be in her seventies. Her name was Anna. There was an old man in a booth. I could just see the top of his head. I could tell he was an old man. Suddenly a conversation started between the old man and Anna. I don't know his name. She never called him by name. He said to her, "The boss wants me to stick around in case you get busy. I can help you."

"But it's not busy" she said.

"Well, you may get busy."

"I won't get busy."

"Well just in case."

"OK, you can stick around."

"And then when you close, I can walk you home."

"OK, now I know why you're staying," she said. "You'll not walk me home."

"Yes, I will walk you home. You need somebody to walk you home!"

"Yeah, you want to walk me home. Pretty soon you'll walk me home and then I will be great with child."

"What are you talking about Anna? You passed that time in your life years ago."

"You don't know about Sarah?"

"Sarah who?"

"Sarah in the Bible. Sarah in the Bible was older than I and she was great with child."

"Well how did she do that?"

"She believed in the man upstairs. And something else, Mary the mother of our Lord, before she was ever married, before she ever knew a man, was great with child."

"How did she do that?"

"She believed in the man upstairs."

And the old man said, "Well, if I were a woman, I wouldn't believe in the man upstairs."

The best biblical commentary in print cannot give that to you.

Your own experiences and observations are a great source of stories, especially if you have a sense of freedom. If you feel secure enough to be able to laugh at the things you do wrong, the mistakes you make, in the pulpit, out of the pulpit, things that happen to you that at the time you may flinch, later you laugh about. If you have that sense of freedom it gives you a sense of humor. A good sense of humor is the clearest evidence that the grace of God is at work in a person's life because they no longer have to try to be God's detective. God takes care of divine business and gets along well without me. God was working it before I came. God has given me the privilege to share in it. But it will keep going after I am gone. Possessing a good sense of humor does not mean being glib. It's simply to be free to accept one's place in the grace of God. And if you have that freedom to think about yourself and your own experiences, that will be a grand source of good stories.

The next question then comes along, "Should I tell things about myself in the pulpit?" The canon by which I measure whether a personal story is to be used is whether the personal story is not just mine, but whether it is every person's. The measure is to what extent in that experience I am "every person." And if I am "every person" so that the listeners can identify with the story, it can be told. If it was mine in a peculiar sense, remote from the experience of other people, it's for private conversation and not for the pulpit because there can be no identification. And the point of it all is for people to enter into the story.

What about using books and Internet sources of stories, anecdotes, and the like? There are some interesting books of stories. But the fundamental problem with these collections of stories is that they usually do not have a context. Since they are usually out of context they don't have the same power as they had in their proper context. The other practical problem is since they are floating around in a book or in cyberspace people may have already heard them. I don't recommend these books or Web sites of stories, especially if they are designed for the preacher, because if there are any good ones in them, you can be sure they have been used over and over again. (Of course, the collection of my stories in *Craddock Stories* by Graves and Ward does not deserve this negative assessment!)

I recommend going back and reading those books that you never got around to reading when you were in high school or college: the great classics; the old books; the good books. I know how you passed literature in college: You bought those digests and summaries and got through Shakespeare without reading him. Now, go back and read him again for the first time. In my own life beyond graduate school, I completed reading all the novels of Thomas Hardy, a master of the English language, material that is now over one hundred years old. Marvelous stories they are. I finally completed all those stories that I should have read in college.

Reading should not begin or end with titles such as *Stories for Preachers*. My discipline of reading *excellent* material such as the classics enlarges the capacity of my mind and the sympathies of my spirit. When I read, I'm not looking for "stuff I can use for Sunday's sermon." I am just a human being trying to expand my mind, heart, and spirit. The funny thing is, I will be reading and there it is: a jewel of a story or a profound statement from the author. The best material for sermons comes when I am *not* looking for it. It finds me. If I find it, it's usually not too good.

Another common and easily avoided problem is failing to give credit where it's due for the source of stories. I recommend that when you use material written by others, give them an oral footnote. The oral footnote should be very brief. If you don't know who said it, say something like, "A preacher once said . . ." If you know who it is, mention the name but don't spend a long time with it—just go on.

When you *create* stories, give clues to the listeners that the story was created. The clues to the listeners can include a number of things. For example, make it a total absurdity, such as my story about the nine-pound sparrow. Or the way you start it, such as, "Once upon a time." Jesus usually started them with two statements. One, "which of you" and you knew it was a parable; or "there was a certain man," and you knew it was a parable. Now, I am sure there were people who came up later and asked, "Jesus did that really happen?" Well, I don't know whether it did or not. They were accustomed to parables, accustomed to stories. But little clues that don't detract from the power of the story should be given to release people from engaging in the thing in the wrong way. Now we can all "create stories." The best way to do it is to start with children when you are not embarrassed to tell stories. And I suggest that you tell stories when you haven't completed it yet. Start telling one that you don't know how it is going to end. And under the pressure of finding an ending to that story you will create some very good stuff. That's the way many of you got through college and seminary. So just do it that way. I have myself started stories when the kids were small. I didn't know how it was going to go, but under the pressure of having to bring it to some conclusion, things came to mind.

I suggest groups do it, family groups. Our family had a little ritual during the evening meal. We would go around the table and answer this question, "What was the worst thing that happened to you today?" Our son John usually said the same thing, "The school bell rang at 8:30." And then we'd get around the table. The question then shifted to, "What was the best thing that happened today? And John would say, "The bell rang again at 3:30."

After we spilled our gripes, we looked at what really good happened today. And then we would start taking about that and stories would develop. You can do it in church groups. When I teach the parables, whether in a church or in a seminary, we don't start studying the parables of Jesus. We start with a parable. What is a parable? And we start creating parables. And the way you create parables is to set up a condition. And tell someone, "finish that." Just finish that.

I once started a parable with a group of church folks in Amarillo, Texas. "Let's just create a parable," I said.

> There was a certain man very, very stingy. The young people not knowing him very well, asked him to play Santa Claus in their Christmas program. In a moment of thoughtlessness he said he would. As the time approached he got nervous about it and the evening before the program he said to his family, "Why in the world did they ask me? They know I don't go for all this giving away stuff and Santa Claus. I don't go for this. Why did they ask me?" And he fussed around. And then he got serious and said to the family, "I hope you will be thinking of me and praying for me that I will do a good job." And the family said, "We will and you will." And so he went to the church with a suit on and it came to pass . . .

And I left it at that. That was in the evening. Next morning we got together after breakfast and I said, "OK, how did the story end?" We had some delightful stuff. People came up and said I couldn't go to sleep 'til I finished that thing. One fellow stood up and said, "And it came to pass that he went to the church and in the role of Santa Claus he gave away all his wealth. And his family had him committed."

Make up stories. It's a delightful thing to do so. This is one of the ways we taught the Bible to our children. Instead of just Bible verses, memorizing, like I did, which is not all that bad. I like to find somebody who knows a little Bible today. But sometimes I would tell a story and then say to the children, "Does that remind you of anything in the Bible?" And their mind would go searching around trying to find something, "Well, isn't that sort of like, or isn't that like, or isn't that like." And it was doing a lot of things. It was tying life and scripture together. It was an educational experience.

As to the telling of the story itself, may I make just a few suggestions? Use an economy of words, not too many adjectives, and leave something for the listener to contribute. If you overdescribe something it is insulting. Just think of that marvelous story to which I have referred several times. The story of the prodigal son—ring, robe, shoes, fatted calf—and you see the whole thing. You can describe a football game—officials in striped shirts, the uniforms, the cheerleaders, the raising of the flag, the National Anthem—and everybody is at the game.

But if you just go on and on and on, it's insulting because almost all of us have been to a ball game. We know. So use an economy of words. A reason for economy of words is not just that I've mentioned it but also that it's a way of avoiding dictating to your listener the conclusion they are to reach about it. If I throw in too many adjectives I am telling you how to feel and how to think about what I am saying.

I know this man, a neighbor of mine, who is one of the most marvelous, sincere, genuine, conscientious, dedicated, and committed Christians I know. OK, I am about to tell a story about him but I have already told you the way you are going to feel about him and think about him before I've told the story. Why blow that out? Why not just say, "I know this fellow who lives near me" and tell the story? We don't want to oppress and spiritually violate our listeners by drawing their conclusions for them.

Use images. People's minds are like galleries of pictures. This is where prejudices are lodged, misinformation is lodged, hatreds are lodged, and old grudges are lodged. And you mention something and they have a picture of that pop into their mind. The only way that's going to change and they are going to grow and become more Christian is to replace those pictures with other pictures. Therefore we need pictures and images. Can we see it? Can we see it when it's told? And that's very important because people have their own images and you want to change those images. I'm going to give you a word, two words actually. And I want you to just think what comes to mind. Don't say it out loud. Just think what comes to mind when I say this expression. I am sure you will have an image. If you are ready, I will go ahead and give you the expression now: "brick mason." What image comes to your mind's eye? One comes to mine immediately.

A contractor friend of mine in Oklahoma was having trouble finding brick masons and he went to the local vocational-technical school and hired two fellows who just graduated from school, to help him complete a house. One of them had hair down past his shoulders. The other one had long hair and a beard. They wore faded blue jeans that just hung on their bones. They drove an old battered convertible that had about nine different colors.

"I didn't want to take them," he said, "but I couldn't get anyone else. So I hired them and took them out to the job."

"How did they do?" I asked.

"Well, they did good work. As good a work I believe as I've had done."

"Good. Did they work hard and fast?"

"Yeah, they completed it ahead of schedule."

"I am sure you are proud to have a couple more good brick masons."

"Well, I let them go."

"Why in the world did you let them go?"

"I didn't think I could trust them."

That is what I see in my mind's eye when I hear "brick mason."

Let me mention one other word: "minister." The pulpit committee said, "That was a really excellent trial sermon, and you have answered the questions well in the interview. Your doctrine is in good order. You made outstanding grades in seminary. We feel like you are committed and could do a good job but right now we just don't feel that you are the right pastor for us."

And she said, "Why?"

It is important in storytelling also to use direct discourse rather than indirect. That is to actually use quotes, to recreate conversation rather than just describing it. Notice all the stories of Jesus. "Master, you handed over to me five talents; see, I have made five more talents" (Mt. 25:20). And the master said, "Well done good and faithful servant" (Mt. 25:21). "I was afraid and I went and hid your talent in the ground." (Mt. 25:25). "You wicked and lazy slave! . . . throw him into the outer darkness, where there will be weeping and gnashing of teeth" (Mt. 25:26–30).

"Then the son said to him, 'Father, I have sinned against heaven and before you; I am no longer worthy to be called your son'" (Lk. 15:21). And the father said, "Son, you are always with me" (Lk. 15:31). Notice conversation, conversation, conversation all the time. Don't stretch it out and make it descriptive. Reproduce the conversations. Also, it is important to allow people to identify with characters in the story without telling them to identify. It is a deadly sign that you haven't done a good job of telling the story, biblical or otherwise, if you have to reach a point and say, "Now let's identify with that person." This is the way it usually goes. There is a story. You are unrolling some material and then you pause and say, "Now aren't we very much like Simon Peter?" "Aren't we today very much like the Pharisee?" That's bad. I have tried to think of another way to say it. The reason it is bad is that you've been too dependent on the hortatory. In preaching, we call it application. Of course you want application, but the application comes bleeding through if you've done a good job. You can talk about Simon Peter in such a way that I am sitting back there and I am convicted because you held up a mirror to me.

But you don't hold up a mirror to me and say, "Don't you look like what you see in that mirror?" Let me identify. Don't tell me what I identify with. You see, that's a kind of a crutch. I don't want to do that. The Pharisees can be described in such a way that I squirm. I squirm. I squirm. It is important also in telling stories to remember that the key to the power of the story lies very much in its movement; forget structure–just the movement of it.

Stories move; stories that will be heard, not seen. That is usually my best counsel to anyone about sermons. Forget about getting an outline. Get the movement. How does it unroll? How does it move? Masterful storytellers master timing. You know I mentioned the storyteller; a good storyteller is reluctant. One reason they are reluctant is they have to pick the time and the occasion. You don't just walk up to them and say, "Hey, I understand you tell good stories. Tell me one." No, they have to build the occasion, and build the time, and build the way, and be ready for it. And usually there is a lot of hesitation.

As some of you know, my father was an excellent storyteller, my mother too, but my father created stories and he built in certain methods of delaying and timing it. We lived in a farmhouse. The only heat we had in the winter was the fireplace. Oh, there was a wood stove in the kitchen, but we gathered close to the fireplace. In the evening, he would put an old porcelain coffee pot down in the coals. He would warm himself and with his back to us, we would be sitting there supposed to be doing our arithmetic or something. And he, talking to himself, would say, "Whoosh, I hope I never see again what I saw today." And that is all he would say. And we were always a little bit afraid of him. We would ask my oldest brother, Walter, we would say, "Ask him what he saw." And Walter would say, "Well, Daddy, what did you see today?" He would say, "You kids still up? I thought that was your mother. Oh, well, never mind." Uh, we can't stand it, we can't stand it. And finally we would say, "What was it? You can just tell us part of it. What was it?" "Oh, well, I suppose . . ." and then he would start telling a story and he would get to a certain point, and he would smoke Golden Grain, roll-your-own cigarettes. It took him what seemed like thirteen hours! And then roll up some paper, and stick in the fire, and get it out the fire, and get that lit, and get a draw. Here we are–that timing. Now, it was part of his method, but he had to create the situation, move to it.

Picture an old man peeling an apple for his grandson: "Grandpa, will you peel this apple for me? Mama thinks I might get choked some on the peeling." "OK." And he pulls out an old Barlow knife that he uses for everything, holds it up, rubs it on his britches. After all, it is his grandson, and he doesn't want any germs. And he starts peeling, just starts peeling, real slow, and the curl begins to drop. And he says, "You know one time I peeled thirty-five of these before I ever broke a peel?" Now what is happening to the child? The juices are flowing. The stomach is saying, "I thought I was going to get an apple." The saliva is flowing. The body is getting ready for the apple, getting ready for the apple, and he just keeps going. When is he going to get through? Finally, the peel drops at his feet. I made it. And the child starts to lunge. "Wait just a minute" and then he lays it, "let me get the core out for you." And it's just taking forever. Now when the child receives the apple, it is the best apple in the world. Now contrast that to walking up to a machine, inserting money, pulling a lever, grabbing an apple, and eating it on the way to something when the stomach is saying, "I didn't ask for an apple." Now think of those two scenes and reflect on the movement of your preaching. Do the people get prepared to come to the conclusion when you come to the conclusion? It's not all that difficult. It's just a matter of saying, "I respect the listeners and I trust the listeners and I want them to take this trip with me." And when you get there, you will all get there and it's a delight.

Of course we want to be very specific and very concrete in our talk as I tried to discuss in my little book *As One without Authority*. We don't want to get lost in all of those long words that end in "-ity," "-ship," and "-ness": responsibility, stewardship, righteousness, and all of those similar words. We have to use them some, but can it be tasted? Can I taste it, smell it, see it, and feel it? Is it something very specific? You don't go out to a farmer and say, "I'd like to discuss calfdom." You don't say to a carpenter, "Well, essentially the chairness of that." No, it's just chair and calf. There is no such thing as holy matrimony. Holy matrimony is the distant summation of all the weddings. And if you describe a single wedding and picture a father getting a suit out of the closet and that whole scene and you start describing that wedding, every wedding in the house will be remembered and one man in tears back there will notice that he still has some rice in the cuff, and he remembers his daughter. But you told them holy matrimony. And nobody twitched at all. That's the way it is.

Mortality, we are all mortal, of course. But if you get up and say we have just received word that Mrs. Thomas's son Charles was killed delivering papers this morning, the church becomes the church. What can we do? What's the difference? Mortality, nothing.

Let me just mention an exercise. It's for the students but it is also all right for the experienced person to do. I think it would be helpful. In order to be sure that we are in touch and appropriate to the people–in touch with where they are and who they are—I suggest an exercise to the students to just once or twice a week take a sheet of paper and say what is it like to *be* and then put something in the middle of that page and write around it everything that comes to mind. Spend just five or ten minutes, once or twice a week, and it will give flavor, and pulse, and feeling, and power to everything you tell, scripture and otherwise.

What's it like to be fourteen? And if you will spend ten minutes with that—sympathetically, empathetically, with imagination, with recollection—the next time you preach you won't be saying, "The trouble with young people today is . . ." Instead, you have thought about what it's like to be fourteen.

What's it like to be fired? Nothing else now, just that.

What's it like to be alone?

One of the students, some time ago, asked me to go out and preach for him. He was away working for the kingdom. I think he was skiing in Colorado. Anyway, he wanted me to fill in. I went out. I like to go out to the churches and preach; small, large, whatever church is church. And I like to go and I went for him. And after the service an elderly woman came up to me and said, "Do you want to have lunch with me?"

"I would be glad to," I said.

It was a small village—no restaurant there. I followed her to her big-framed house. At one time, I'm sure there was a lot of laughter and playing, and I saw the pictures on the piano—an old upright piano. And I knew she had children and grandchildren everywhere, but she was alone in this big house now. She called it the home place.

"You go in there and read the paper or watch television. I'll be ready in a minute."

And she put on an apron. And I went in there and she went off to some distant place in the house. I could hear her in there just working. And I thought, "Well, maybe I can help" and I went in there and she was in the formal dining room. And she was pulling out her big drawer of this chest thing off to the side. I don't know the name of those things. She got out a linen cloth, had creases in it two inches deep. I bet it hadn't been used in years. And she put that on the table; big long table, big dining room.

"You really don't have to go to all of this trouble," I said. "We eat in the kitchen at home."

But she went right along. She pulled out napkins, cloth napkins, and put them in little silver rings. She opened this thing with a curved glass front and pulled out some stem glasses and some old china with roses on it.

"We just eat in the kitchen at home," I said again.

And she said, "Will you please shut up and sit down?"

"That was the next thing on my list."

She looked straight at me and said, "Mr. Craddock, do you know what it is like, day after day, to fix a meal for one?"

"'No ma'am, I don't." So in a little while we all gathered, she and I, around that table. And she assured me that the attendance that day was twice what it had been in months.

And we had a banquet. I will never forget that experience, and how it was a gift to me.

7

The Sermon as a Twice-Told Tale

What Is a "Twice-Told Tale"?

The title for this chapter and the four that follow came to me from a collection of stories by Nathaniel Hawthorne: *Twice-Told Tales*, first published in 1837. In a famous review of the book, Hawthorne's college classmate Henry Wadsworth Longfellow explained that Hawthorne called them twice-told tales: "We presume, from having been first published in various annuals and magazines, and now collected together, and told a second time in a volume by themselves."[1]

While Hawthorne's title is the *source* of the title of this material, it is not the *sense* of the material.

While it is true that the gospel has been revealed by God through the Holy Spirit, and therefore all of our preaching is telling it again, or "traditioning" what we received, that's not what I have in mind here.

Neither do I mean "twice-told tale" in a plain practical sense. Should a sermon be preached a second time? That is an important question and one with which I disagree with my revered teachers from seminary. They were adamant that preachers should *never* preach a sermon twice. I understood what they were trying to get us to do–to teach us the value of study. They wanted us to live out of a larger barrel than a smaller one.

But that is not good stewardship, as you know. If a sermon is worth preaching once, it is worth preaching twice, so long as there are appropriate modifications for time, place, and audience. In other words, if a sermon isn't worth preaching twice, it probably wasn't worth preaching once.

Nor do I mean "twice-told tale" in a pedagogical sense. All teachers know the value of repetition. Knowledge that is not repeated vanishes. Some things just need to be said, and said, and said, and said, and said before they are learned.

Nor do I mean "twice-told tale" in a cynical sense, that the first telling comes from the biblical scholars and then the preachers repeat it. Or to put it another way, scholars are the producers, and the preachers are the consumers. Now, there are some preachers who deserve the term "consumer." I don't mean that here.

Nor do I mean it in the sense that some contemporary linguists use the term. I don't understand a lot of what they say. But they talk a good deal about *reading* a text, the *art* of reading, the *difficulty* of reading, and the *density* of reading. And I notice occurring now and then the expression "twice told." In a sense, all reading is rereading. But I don't mean that.

What I mean by "twice-told tale" is in the Aristotelian sense. You may recall Aristotle's discussion of mimesis, translated as "imitation." Now by imitation I do not mean the production of an "exact" copy of something previous. Not that at all.

I pause here to drop in a footnote. The reproduction of things exactly as they are, even in the sanctuary on Sunday, is not a bad idea. There is great value in predictability, no matter however dull and boring you may think it is. Regardless of how much you want to frill it up, there is great power and meaning in the creed, the tradition, the songs, the prayers. Say it again *exactly* as received, because people increasingly come to the sanctuary where you preach to find sanctuary from a culture of ambushes.

Maybe it's my advanced age, but increasingly, I want to worship where I can expect a high level of predictability. I want to *know* the order of worship. OK, you can change the offering around now and then. But don't get too playful or "creative" because the world has disoriented me. I want you to reorient me just a little bit with that which is true. Let me illustrate.

A woman has just lost her husband of forty-five years. The children and grandchildren are sitting with her at her house. The funeral is over. There's a lot of food sitting around in the kitchen. The food is in a number of dishes with little pieces of masking tape on the bottom of them so you know to whom to return it. After a while the new widow gets up and begins to wash a few dishes.

"Mother, sit down and rest—one of us will do that."

A little later she goes and puts a few things in the washer and turns on the washer.

"Mother, that doesn't have to be done right now, we will do that, sit down and rest."

As evening approaches, she feeds the cat and the dog: "Mother, one of the kids will do that."

She then picks up one of the children's sweaters, notices a button missing and begins to sew on a new button. "Mother, we can do that when we get back home, sit down and rest."

My word to the family: "Please shut up and leave her alone. Your mother needs to do what she's always done, or she'll go crazy."

By mimesis I don't mean that *exact* reproduction. Indeed, is it possible to exactly reproduce anything, even an exact quotation of scripture? If you change the audience, the occasion, the time, or the place, it is not an exact quotation of scripture. If you want to say what the text says, you have to say something different. If I quote exactly Peter on the day of Pentecost, then I am not saying what Peter said. I have to say something else.

In *Repetition: An Essay in Experimental Psychology*, Søren Kierkegaard questions whether there is any such thing as doing something *again*. He tells of a return trip he made to Berlin. He went back to Berlin to see if there was any such thing as repetition. He said it was not repetition. There were some things in common, but it was a different trip entirely. Even coming home was different. When he got to the house, the servant had rearranged the furniture. There is no repetition.

Mimesis in the Aristotelian sense is not just copying somebody or something. Runners are not successful if they put their feet in the tracks of other runners.

What then is mimesis? Mimesis flourished in the world of literature during the Renaissance. Mimesis was about rediscovering the classics from the Greek and Latin. During the Renaissance these classics were resurrected, not reproduced. Sometimes it was totally unconscious.

The master of mimeses was Petrarch. Here is how he understood it:

A proper imitator should take care that what he writes resembles the original without reproducing it. The resemblance should not be that of a portrait to the sitter—in that case the closer the likeness is the better—but it should be the resemblance of a son to his father. Therein is often the great divergence in particular features, but there is a certain suggestion, what our painters call an 'air,' almost noticeable in the face and eyes, which makes the resemblance. As soon as we see the son, he recalls the father to us although if we should measure every feature we should find them all different.

But there is a mysterious something there that has this power. Thus we writers must look to it that with a basis of similarity there should be many dissimilarities. And the similarity should be planted so deep that it can only be extricated by quiet meditation. The quality is to be felt rather than defined. Thus we may use another person's conceptions though the color of his style, but not his words. In the first case the resemblance is hidden deep. In the second it is glaring. The first procedure makes poets, the second makes apes. (Letter dated October 28, 1366)

Again the same writer, Petrarch, in his writing called *Familiar Letters*, said, "Take care that the nectar does not remain in you in the same state as when you gathered it; bees would have no credit unless they transformed it into something different and better." Thus if you come upon something worthy while reading or reflecting, change it into honey by means of your own style. That is mimeses, imitation.

What he has in mind is that beneath your telling, your preaching, there is a "subtelling," a prior telling. Beneath your text there is a subtext. And it is that subtext that enriches, that haunts, and that resonates in the ear of the listener.

Now this raises some questions and a few obstacles. One of them is the ethical question. If the sermon is a twice-told tale, and there are these subtexts, these prior texts, this enriching material that haunts, and sometimes even surfaces in the sermon. If a sermon is a twice-told tale, who owned the "copyright" of the first telling?

We've got two ethical questions with reference to writing, one counterfeit and the other plagiarism. A counterfeit is to take your own work and claim that it belongs to someone else. A plagiarist is someone who takes someone else's work and claims it for one's own. I'm aware of the ethical issue involved here, and let me say briefly, so I can move on, that on the conscious level of the use of prior texts, all the rules of honesty and proper credit apply.

Another obstacle in the path of the sermon as a twice-told tale is the premium that we set on originality. When you set a premium on originality, to call a sermon a twice-told tale sounds very inferior. We like the idea of an original, although we know there's no such thing.

I remember as a child my grandmother who lived with us in her last years, giving my family at Christmas a quilt, which she kept tucked away in her little room in the process of making it. And it came out as a surprise and she with help from others, would spread it on the floor in front of the Christmas tree and give it to the family. The designs were beautiful, and there was not in the world another quilt like the quilt she made. And the quilt she made the year before and the quilt she made the year after were not the same.

But if you looked carefully at her quilt, you could see a little piece of my sister's dress, one of my old shirts, a piece of my brother's trousers, a little bit of one of my father's shirts. All year she went around asking, "Are you through with this?"

"Yes it's just a rag, it's no good now," we'd tell her and she would take the unwanted fabric. Then it reappeared in her beautiful quilts. Were the quilts "original?" Yes. No, not really.

If there were such a thing as original then we couldn't understand it. But still there persists a fascination with a notion of that which is *original.* That was my fascination with Jesus Christ: that he was without anything precedent, anything subsequent, just totally original.

I remember one of my New Testament seminary professors when we came to the story in Luke of the rich man and Lazarus. The professor sucked on his teeth a few times and said, "There are about eight to ten versions of this story in ancient literature. There's one very similar in the Egyptian Book of the Dead. There are stories like this found in the Near East, in the Orient, and in the rabbis prior to Jesus."

I went back to my little room devastated. I didn't want anything Jesus ever did or said to have ever been done or said; so much for my Christology. I told my wife, "There goes the kingdom. There goes the Bible, there goes the gospel, there goes the whole thing. I might as well be selling insurance." It was a terrible day. There is that appetite in so many religions of the world and in other areas of life: the desire to find the original.

How many religions, and philosophies, and theosophical traditions begin with what is called the *hymnobrief?* The message that must have come from heaven, we found it in this meteorite that fell to earth, fell from the ground. And in pulling it out we noted something strange and in this meteorite was the hymnobrief: a message from heaven.

The search for the book, the original in an ice cave that may be in the mountains of northern Tibet—it's a marvelous thing, of course, if you found it. But who could read it? The appetite was there when I was in graduate school at Vanderbilt. New Testament graduate students worth their salt spent their weekends figuring out what were the "original" gospels (such as Proto-Luke and Ur-Marcus). We were convinced that behind the gospels there was bound to have been the *first* one.

It haunts, the whole title, the sermon as a twice-told tale; it makes it sound at least rather inferior. But the obstacle in the path of thinking of the sermon as a twice-told tale that most concerns me is the third. And that is the question of the existence of the "first telling."

The first telling activates what Aristotle called the "joy of recognition." It activates what John Donne called the "central faculty of the human soul." And that is the memory. Not at the level of recall. Recall is the capacity to take something from the past and bring it into the present. But recognition is the capacity to take something present and locate it in the past, the joy of recognition: recognition not just in the sense that Augustine used the word "remember." As though the memory were like some great storehouse, some huge cave, the deposit of all that we had ever experienced, or sensed, or felt, or touched, or tasted, and it's just stored away there.

No, memory in a more active sense, a more working sense, initiates sense; classifying, ordering, reordering, rearranging, and putting together new constellations and combinations of the old. It is an active capacity of the mind. There is more than that involved than just the joy of recognition.

Think of what it's like to preach. Where does that subtext, that substructure, that prior knowing and hearing exist? What we are talking about is identity. We are in touch with the tradition; we are in touch with the past. It's not just the joy of recognition; it's the identity of my life as a part of that tradition. That to me is absolutely irreplaceable. And those who try through cruel ways to make the church forget by forcing on all the churches the model of conversion—"Forget everything that's past and start here"—that is a grave error, a disservice to the church, and very crippling.

When we moved to Atlanta, I received a letter from somebody I didn't know in Milledgeville, Georgia. It said,

> It is my understanding you have a relative, a maternal great, great grandfather, John Stevenson, buried in Whitfield County, Georgia. In case you are interested, you will find the grave out on the old Donville Road, behind the house owned by a woman named Marie Cox, about a quarter of a mile on a hill standing among six or eight old slabs.

Well, I'm not into genealogy, so I didn't do anything about it. It just so happened that shortly after receiving the letter, I was asked to preach at a church in Whitfield County. In my usual way of starting with a bunch of silly stuff, I said, "I'm at home here. I've got relatives buried here. John Stevenson is buried here, my maternal great, great grandfather." And then I went on with my sermon.

Afterward a retired school teacher said, "Did you say you were related to John Stevenson?"

"Yes," I said.

"Stevenson, John Stevenson," she pondered, "Why do I know that name?"

A couple of weeks later she wrote me and told me she had realized the connection. She wrote,

> My father died in 1921. He was an attorney here, and the last estate he settled was that of two unmarried elderly women named Stevenson. And he got for his services six chickens, some personal effects and $59. Among the personal effects was this book.

With her letter she enclosed *Fisher's Commentary on the Shorter Catechism of the Church of Scotland.* John Stevenson had come to fight in George Washington's army from County Antrim, Ireland. He didn't know much about America but he thought anybody fighting England was a friend of his, so over he came.

He brought with him that book, which was printed in 1767. Stevenson died at the age of 101. On his gravestone is inscribed, "In religion Protestant, in politics a democrat, in the revolution a Whig." In the front of the book is written, "This book belongs to me. John Stevenson is my name. Whoever tries to steal it, for shame for shame." As you can see, I come from a long line of poets. That book is very, very valuable to me.

Fisher's Commentary on the Shorter Catechism of the Church of Scotland goes into endless details and the questions and answers just drone away. But it's the signature and the connection, the joy of recognition, and memory. It's more than that. When I think of a twice-told tale in this regard, I think of that which thrills all of us. We call it liturgy or worship.

Worship happens when the sacrament tells us in dramatic ways what the Word says—and when the Word speaks to what the sacrament dramatizes. It's more than that; it is persuasion, *real* persuasion in the sense of the ancient rhetoric teachers. The most important persuasive force in your speech is your own character and your own value, the twice-told tale.

Isn't it powerful when the congregation gets it twice, once from the mouth and confirmed by the life? I'm not going to get into any pious statements about how you ought to live the gospel. We don't live up to it. Show me a bird who can say, "I look like my song." But it is still the case that the people who hear us cannot take them apart.

But what if the first reading—the prior reading, that subtext that enriches, haunts, resonates, and empowers your sermon—is missing? What if you are preaching the sermon as a twice-told tale to a congregation who has not heard it the first time? Is the sermon wasted if the first telling is not there? Can anything be effectively twice told if it has not been first told? On one level I think so. There are all kinds of twice tellings in our culture that the people who do it have not a single clue as to the source.

"Well, I understand you quit your job."

"Yeah, I saw the handwriting on the wall."

"Oh, you've been reading Daniel have you?"

"Well, I see the way this meeting is going, and I wash my hands of the whole thing."

"Been reading Matthew have you?"

Or as the sports announcer says when the Atlanta Braves take the field, "As a lamb that was led to the slaughter." But they have no idea about Isaiah.

I think of all the marvelous moving titles of stories that are really twice told: *The Sound and the Fury*, Faulkner-Shakespeare; *The Winter of our Discontent*, Steinbeck-Shakespeare; Adela Rogers St. Johns's marvelous, almost autobiographical story *Tell No Man*—the King James fragment from the Messianic Secret.

Now those titles are strong, regardless of whether you know their sources. One of the most powerful books in the last century was by Kenneth Woodin, *Weeping in the Playtime of Others*: a chronicle of the incarceration of children in America. It'll tear you to pieces. And you can be moved by the title and absorbed in the book and not know that its title came from a line from "The Cry of the Children" by the poet Elizabeth Barrett Browning. So on one level it is possible for the twice told to be effective without the first told.

But when we come to the sacred text, when we come to the pulpit, when we come to the sermon, is that the case? How much is really lost? Rabbi Lou Silberman was playing for some of us at a Society of Biblical Literature meeting an audio recording of a cantor reading the Hebrew Scriptures. We sat there mesmerized. There were some in the room that didn't know a word of Hebrew. And I remember, we were told later that what he was reading was a portion of Chronicles, not the most thrilling reading. But here was this cantor making the sounds of the Hebrew text and came to a certain place, and the voice trembled and quivered with emotion, and the voice wept. And what was the line? The line was "the vessels of silver and gold." The vessels of silver and gold? You get all choked up about that? Rabbi Silberman shut off the tape and said, "Don't you know, those were stolen from the temple?" Now, if you didn't know that, what would the trembling voice be? "Must have a cold. Must have asthma. Sounds kind of tired." But to the one with the subtext, the one with the prior reading, tears, mesmerized at the voice.

Jesus on the cross, "My God, my God, why have you forsaken me?" (Mt. 27:46). What does that mean to someone who has no clue about Psalm 22? Is it wasted?

I think of Luke's story of Ananias and Sapphira (Acts 5). Luke said they embezzled, and it cost them their lives. Is it necessary to know from the book of Joshua, chapter 7, the story of Achan, who in the Septuagint it is said, he embezzled that which was devoted to God and for it he paid his life? Is Luke's story wasted?

When Luke tells the story of Simon down on the coast at Joppa being called to preach to Gentiles (Acts 10), do you need to know about Jonah at Joppa? (Jon. 1:3) Or can I tell it twice even though they never heard it once? Or is something absolutely lost, painfully lost? I think of Luke's insistence (Acts 13:9) that the apostle Paul's name was Saul–Saul from the tribe of Benjamin. Can I understand Luke's portrayal of Saul of Tarsus, of the tribe of Benjamin, if I don't know of Saul of the tribe of Benjamin? Or is it important?

I think of the figure of John the Baptist. John the Baptist came in the desert preaching a baptism of repentance (Mt. 3:2–17). And he was wearing a leather girdle around his waist, he was dressed in camel's hair. He spoke about the kingdom almost being here–that there was one coming after him who would be far greater. John said he was not worthy to untie the sandals of the great one soon to come. He spoke of tomorrow, but he was dressed like yesterday: Elijah in the desert, the hairy cloth, the prophet in the wilderness (1 Kings 17). Now if you did not know the subtext, the prior text–2 Kings 1–if you did not know that, could you preach a sermon about this strange-looking guy who ate weird stuff?

You could join all the teenagers of Judea bored out of their gourds saying, "I don't know what I want to do. What do you want to do?" Just sitting around on the hoods of their camels wondering what they were going to do. "Well let's go out to the desert and hear that guy. Have you ever seen him? He's a strange-looking guy and eats weird stuff." John the Baptist is just sort of an object of curiosity.

But let's suppose that you know the prior text. And John comes in the wilderness. He stirs first your memory, then your hope. First comes Elijah and then the Messiah. Are you Elijah? Now which is it: a funny-looking, strange person or the announcement of God's new future? Is it the text or is it the subtext?

The question I'm asking is a simple one. The major obstacle to thinking of a sermon as a twice-told tale is when it hasn't been heard the first time. What is it to preach a sermon as twice told if I am preaching to a congregation that does not have even the echo of a prior hearing, a prior telling, and a subtext? That's the question that we will pursue in the next chapter.

8

The Sermon as a Twice-Told Tale

Funds in the Memory Bank

In the previous chapter, we looked at the idea of the sermon as a twice-told tale, which I regard to be preaching at its most powerful. I concluded by suggesting that the major obstacle to the consideration of this idea is the lack of a *first* telling. Whenever preaching can be buoyed along by a subtext, that prior hearing haunts and enriches the sermon. But what happens when many listeners have had no prior hearing? So this chapter focuses on the *content* of the twice-told tale.

It's hard not to join in all the stanzas of the common lament of biblical illiteracy: the lack of the prior hearing, the lack of the subtext, the lack of Aristotle's idea of the joy of recognition.

I once preached at a church in downtown Atlanta. In talking with a woman at coffee hour after worship, I learned she was twenty-eight years old and was a first-time visitor at that church. Indeed, it was her first visit at *any* church. She could not recall ever being in a church before in her life. Later, when I looked at my sermon text, I became aware that I had assumed everybody there knew and believed. In her case, and perhaps many others, that was a false assumption.

When I first began to teach in higher education, I taught "Introduction to the Bible." I enjoyed in those days divesting the students of their non-critical views of scripture. I liked to start the class by saying, "You thought Moses wrote the Pentateuch." And then we went through the JEPD (Jahwist, Elohist, Priestly, Deuteronomist) source theory. And many were quite agitated; some went out sucking their thumbs, bumping into the furniture, and calling home to momma.

But nowadays if you say to an introductory Bible class, "You thought Moses wrote the Pentateuch," students will raise their hands and ask, "Uh, prof, how do you spell Pentateuch? And who was Moses?"

The state of biblical illiteracy is as prevalent in churches as in colleges and seminaries. I regret the loss of the power of preaching in the rise of biblical illiteracy. Power comes when the sermon is a twice-told tale.

Even worse, a growing number of ministers *celebrate* the lack of a prior hearing, the lack of any kind of previous tradition. They make deliberate efforts at forgetting because their churches are founded upon no connection to anything, anytime, ever. They are entrepreneurial churches led by "visionary" ministers. I know of a tragic situation in a church in Georgia. The minister of that church is gradually deleting most of the worship service. The Lord's Prayer is out. The Apostles' Creed is out. They have not had the eucharist in two years. He's getting rid of all old loyalties because in his view, "authentic" Christianity begins now, with his group. It's a "community" church, not tied to any denomination of course, just open and sharing. Open to what? Sharing what? Apparently it only shares *this* moment, being open only to the triumph of immediacy over all mediated knowledge and tradition.

I went once with friends to a prayer service of one these "community" churches, and heard a sad string of testimonies. A bright twentysomething looking young fellow stood up to testify. He testified that he'd been in a denominational church all his life. His parents taught Sunday school and served on the church board. He said he was always there and even went to the youth meetings. Then he went away to college, was with a group in the dorm one night, and there "found" Jesus. He announced he was done with the tired and boring denominational church. And with one wave of his hand he tossed his tradition.

So much for the subhearing; so much for the prior text. I suppose that violation of the past is the most painful to me. There are all kinds of ways to violate the past. Rewrite history for some ideological economic ideology or make fun of the past, mock the past.

I remember hearing about a little town in Southern Oklahoma where during the town's "pioneer days," everybody's dressed up like it "used to be." And these young fellows, possibly nice in other ways, went out and hired an old Arapaho Indian and put him on a horse. They got a tired old buffalo that somebody had as a pet grazing with the cows. They put the Indian on the horse and put the buffalo out in front of him on the main street of this little town. They gave the old Arapaho a bow and arrows and tried to get the horse and buffalo to run and urged the old man to shoot the buffalo with a bow and arrow. And they gave him a few bucks for his trouble. They all laughed and slapped their thighs. They should be in jail.

There was a time when the Arapaho would have given those young fellows what they deserved. And a buffalo herd would have turned on them and stampeded, shaking the earth with their mighty strength. To make fun of their tragic fate is tragedy.

But I think of one tragedy worse. And that is to *celebrate* forgetting, to deliberately refuse to retradition *the* tradition in the name of "visioning." Some of these "visionary" pastors claim to possess a conversion paradigm as authority for their practices. They will refer to the great conversions of the apostle Paul, and St. Augustine, and Martin Luther, and John Wesley, and others. What they forget (or have never known) is that Paul, and Augustine, and Luther, and Wesley were in their conversion experience claiming a tradition to which they'd already been exposed to over and over again. Wesley had been preaching for a while when he was converted. Luther was into it up to his eyeballs in tradition when he experienced conversion while reading Romans.

One of the reasons the scripture to me is so dramatically interesting and powerful is that the scripture *itself* is a twice-told tale. Just think of what the Bible assumes on the part of the listener.

For example, Luke begins his gospel by writing, "I too decided, after investigating everything carefully from the very first, to write an orderly account for you, most excellent Theophilus, so that you may know the truth concerning the things about which you have been instructed" (Lk. 1:3–4). It's not a first hearing; it's a second hearing, and that allows the flow of power and beauty in the narration of Luke. In the first epistle of John, "I write to you, not because you do not know the truth, but because you know it" (1 Jn. 2:21a). Much of the Bible is the second telling and the third telling. It makes possible such extraordinary pieces.

Take for instance, the grandest sermon or series of sermons in the entire Bible: Deuteronomy, which literally means "second law" or the second telling of the law. Here is Moses, standing before Israel hundreds and hundreds of years after: Moses, standing up, addressing Israel, and preparing Israel for the life that is now before her. It would be like George Washington rising up to address a joint session of Congress today.

How is it possible to have the book of Deuteronomy? Because it is a twice-told tale. It assumes a commitment to the fundamental story of the exodus and Sinai. Just think of all the powerful things the Bible can do because of the assumption of that tradition.

There are the patterns of promise and fulfillment. However, there are many times we can't do that because the promise isn't in the "memory bank" of the listeners. For example, we preach Jesus as the Messiah to people who weren't looking for one. We give an answer to a question that wasn't asked.

Think of the other patterns that are there: the allusions to scripture, just little lines that you notice and that just thrill you: in Acts 8, the story of Philip and the Ethiopian eunuch. And when Philip finishes that mission, do you remember that line: "The Spirit of the Lord caught away, Philip" (Acts 8:39, KJV)? Does that remind you of anything? Elijah and the spirit of the Lord caught away (2 Kings 2:11). The boy Jesus in the temple, and the boy Samuel, in the house of God, "And the child grew in wisdom" (Lk. 2:40; 1 Sam. 2:26). The raising of the son of the widow of Nain and Jesus brought him back to life, and the line is "and he gave him to his mother" (Lk. 7:15). The prophet in Israel "gave him to his mother" (1 Kings 17:23).

Marvelous, powerful things are possible because the Bible itself is a twice-told tale: not just direct references but also clear allusions that are more or less surfaced to visibility. But beneath it all are echoes for the ear that is finely tuned and has a remarkable capacity to say, "I think I've heard that before."

I am grateful for my undergraduate days at Johnson Bible College, a little conservative school where you could work on the farm all summer and earn your room, board, tuition, everything for the year, and so I went. In my senior year, in order to graduate, we were handed sheaves of paper and pencils for a day-long ordeal of writing from memory the basic content, in order, of the New Testament. We were allowed to take breaks, but on that day we wrote from memory, in order, the content of Matthew 1 through Revelation 22.

What a grind. I grumbled my resentment and ground my teeth. But at the end of the day, I had passed. When I went away to graduate school at Vanderbilt, students with degrees from places like Yale and Harvard would come to me in the library and ask, "Uh, did Jesus or did Paul say or do this or that?" I'd give it to them from memory, and they'd say, "Wow, where did *you* go to school?"

Just think of the things the New Testament does within itself. Paul says, "I remind you of the tradition that I traditioned to you that the Lord Jesus on the night . . ." (1 Cor. 11:23), and what he evokes because they already had it. So many of you in your churches don't get to do that. You have to do the first and then the second. "I remind you of the gospel that I preached to you the first time. Our Lord Jesus . . ." so he goes, and goes, and goes, and goes. What is that? That's the second telling and that's the power of it. Just think of Paul quoting from the early Christian hymns. Some of the most powerful lines in Paul are quotations from the early Christian worship books. If they had the worship books they had the worship. What makes it so extremely effective is that when he quotes it they are saying, "That's right, we knew that. Yeah, that's in our book. We sang that last Sunday":

> Let the same mind be in you that was in Christ Jesus, who, though
> he was in the form of God, did not regard equality with God as
> something to be exploited, but emptied himself, taking the form of
> a slave, being born in human likeness. And being found in human
> form, he humbled himself and became obedient to the point of

death—even death on a cross. Therefore God also highly exalted
him (Phil 2:5–9).

And he sang all three stanzas in his Letter to the Philippians and everybody
says, "Well I knew that, I knew that." There is nothing as powerful as the
capacity to jab the person next to you and say, "I knew that."

I was in a service in which the minister's powerful sermon lifted us
higher and higher until we were standing knee-deep in the Kilimanjaro
snow—just marvelous. And then he said, "I'd like for us to close by singing
together this hymn." It was one none of us ever heard of. It destroyed the
moment.

Paul knows better. When Paul is taking up the offering, he says,

> You know it's in your book. It's in your book. It's on the left hand
> side, near the bottom of the page, where it says it, and you've sung
> it lots of time. He was rich, but became poor, that by his poverty
> we might be rich (2 Cor. 8:9). Now we will receive the offering. He,
> who knew no sin, became sin, that through him we might become
> the righteousness of God (2 Cor. 5:21). Oh, there are gods many
> and lords many but you remember how you said it. For us there
> is one God from whom all things, one Lord Jesus Christ through
> whom were all things (1 Cor. 8:5–6).

Yeah. Right out of their book. That was the power of it. They could say,
"Amen, that's right; that's the way it is; we sang it." Marvelous things happen when the text is known. Because the text is known, the Bible is able
to be rather playful. And preachers are able, where the text is long, to be
rather playful with the text.

Take Genesis 4, the story of Cain and Abel. Just think how layered
that text is in the tradition and in the preaching and in the teaching of the
church. Here is the story of Cain and Abel, brothers and children of Adam
and Eve. But what is this story? It's the story of the ancient tension between
the farmer and the shepherd. What is this story? It's the story of the beginning of violence and murder in the world. What is this story? Oh, it's the
story of the beginning of the tension between the Jew and the Canaanite.
What is this story? Oh, this is the story that tells us of the grace of God.
How God said, "Though Cain killed his brother, anybody who tries to harm
Cain has to answer to me." (Gen. 4:15, paraphrased) All those layers. How
is that wealth possible? Because of the text.

Sometime ago Rudolf Serkin, one of the great pianists of our time, the
foremost interpreter of Beethoven, was in Atlanta and I went. How can a
man in his eighties do that? And there were those magic fingers playing
through Beethoven. At the intermission, I began to talk to a young man near
me who had sat still as a mouse through the first part of the performance
with the music of Beethoven on his lap and he was turning the pages as

Serkin played. Turning the pages, turning the pages. I said afterward, "You must be a musician."

"Oh, yes, I teach music at the East Tennessee University, Johnson City."

I said, "He is an interpreter of Beethoven, I don't know anything about music."

"Oh, yes, world's foremost interpreter of Beethoven."

I said, "Well, but for somebody like me, how do we know that he is giving us the right interpretation of Beethoven?"

And he looked at me sort of like, "You are stupid." But then he patted the book on his lap and said, "No matter how Beethoven is interpreted, we always have the text."

I wrote that down: we always have the text. We always have the text and the layer and layer of interpretation and the power of the effective preaching of the twice- and thrice-told tale. This interpretation, that interpretation, this interpretation but always the text as the substructure.

The question is, what do we do? What do you and I do? What do we do in churches where there is reverence for the book without any knowledge of it–without any sense of its content? How can we preach a sermon as a twice-told tale when there has not been apparently its first telling? Now, let me make four rather practical suggestions that are predictable and for that I am pleased. You might call these ideas "twice told."

First, it's obvious we must enlarge our teaching ministry. Most churches have just one minister. And that minister rarely teaches. Can you believe it? The one person in the house, sometimes the one person in the town, with a theological education remains silent as the grave. And then in twenty minutes on Sunday morning assume what cannot be assumed.

We have to enlarge the teaching dimension of our ministry. We can no longer be smug or cynical about people not knowing the Bible. Or to do what I have done, I am sorry to say. I've driven by what's called a "Christian bookstore" and made snide remarks about the kind of books in there and I'd say things such as, "There you'll find a bunch of books written by Roy Rogers and Dale Evans, and probably Trigger, too." And with my knowledge of the Greek text of the New Testament, I continued on my way.

But where are the ministers when it comes to providing an alternative? If your education made you cynical, you missed something. Anybody who has an "A" in New Testament, but still hasn't gotten the point, has been a poor student.

Now it may be that some of us perhaps live out of the philosophy of Plato. Plato said that all knowledge is recollection. By that he meant recollection of a prior existence; the preexistence of the soul. And how do we know things? It's our memory of knowing them when we were in a prior life. We come from God. And we come into this world. That's why a child can speak so comfortably about God and Jesus. They just came from there. "Jesus is going to play with me today. I was talking to God. Can I have the blessing? Can I say the prayer?" Add thirty years on that person's life and ask, "Clyde would you have the blessing?" And a very surprised and confused Clyde stammers out something incoherent. What happened? When you first came from the other world, you had the knowledge of God and all things eternal and spiritual but then you get here and make a few car payments, mow the yard a few times, and the roof leaks, and the faucets drip, and you forget where you came from. That idea was picked up by many of the Gnostics: "Blessed is he who was before he came into being" and all that sort of thing. If you subscribe to that, then you don't need to teach. Just help them to remember what they knew already. But if we don't subscribe to the idea of the recollection of a prior life then it is up to us to enlarge the teaching ministry.

Some years ago in Israel trying to get someone to help me see some places, I was referred to a veteran of the Israeli army, who would help me. I met him, a very knowledgeable man. He had a little Volkswagen and we traveled around. One morning we were leaving the Hotel Samuel in Tel Aviv to start on our day's travels and he said, "Do you mind if we go to Jerusalem another way?" I was OK with that. And we started out on a back road and at a certain point he pulled the car over.

"See that hill over there?" he asked. "It was just covered with trees. And we were going to be marching along that lower side of that hill and they knew that, so they had gotten on that hill above us in the trees and when we came along the road they were going to ambush us and massacre us. But we got word of it and so we slipped around to the other side of the hill. We came up from behind and killed every one of them."

"Was that in the 1948 or 1967 war?" I asked.

And he said, "No. It was the Maccabean War."

"Well, pardon me," I said, "but you tell it as though you were there."

And he looked directly in my eye and said, "I was."

Jerusalem, if I forget you. Nazareth, if I forget you. Antioch, if I forget you. Rome, if I forget you. If the stories of our faith are such that you're too young to remember them, then you are not old enough to preach.

Second, enlarge the contextual work in every sermon. May I ask you to do this? Surely you can do me one favor. When you preach on a text, don't just narrow yourself down to the verse that has triggered your imagination. Instead, let the camera back up, and with a wide-angle lens get a sweep of the whole passage and then zoom in for the focus on the particular part. But not just the particular part–otherwise you spend forty years just notching the trees, but there is still no trail anywhere. Back up a bit.

For a third obvious suggestion, preach and teach from the same text. Now, some of you are perhaps already doing that. But in the Sunday school hour teach the texts of the morning and then preach the texts of the morning. And the most active interested listeners in the sanctuary will be the people who were in the class. And the most effective hearing of the Word of God is when it's a twice telling, a second telling. May I encourage that?

Fourth and finally, I also wish to encourage you to do something that is a bit more artistic in your sermon preparation and delivery. And that is to bring up matters from the scripture, from the tradition in your sermons that don't have any immediate relevance, don't have any immediate payoff, not leading to an exhortation. But you are filling the reservoir. You are putting the canned goods in the cellar so that when winter comes you go down there and bring it up and the congregation will feast as though it were May. Now that's one reason why the pastor is the preacher par excellence. Think of the things that guest preachers cannot do. We cannot make investments in next Sunday's sermon and the next Sunday's sermon and the next one after that. The pastor can use the tradition in a promissory way.

All the gospels begin with a promise of what is to come. Matthew after the introductory part has Jesus in the opening posture of his ministry, teaching on a mountain. That is what we are going to have: teaching. Mark, after the introductory material, has Jesus in the synagogue at Capernaum and there was a man with an unclean spirit and Jesus exorcises the demon. That's what we have coming in Mark: Jesus exorcising the evil spirits. In Luke, after the introductory matter, Jesus goes to his hometown, preaches from Isaiah 61 in the synagogue, and reminds the hearers about the prophets Elijah and Elisha. That's programmatic. That's what's going to come in Luke. It's an investment in the future of that very text. The gospel writers really knew how to preach. They knew how to invest.

Paul also does it in the letters: that little portion of the letter that we call the thanksgiving (1 Cor. 11:23–26). That thanksgiving is really pregnant and powerful because in the thanksgiving sometimes two, sometimes as many as eleven verses. All that is going to be unfolded in this letter is there. So that later on when he starts dealing with it, one can say, "Yeah, I remember that, he brought that up in the beginning."

So may I urge you to include in your teaching and preaching materials from the scripture and from the tradition that may not have an immediate but a delayed payoff. And if you want to really be refined and artistic, you can do that with just little phrases, even within the same sermon. I like the way Luke does it. For instance, in the book of Acts, Luke wrote, "And the witnesses laid their coats at the feet of a young man named Saul" (Acts 7:58). That's a promise of what's to come. And then later Luke says, "Meanwhile Saul, still breathing threats and murder against the disciples" (Acts 9:1). Very effective.

Or this: "Herod said, 'John I beheaded; but who is this about whom I hear such things? And he tried to see him'" (Luke 9:9). In chapter 13, the Pharisees came and said to Jesus, "Get away from here, for Herod wants to kill you" (Luke 13:31). And then at the close of the book, Pontius Pilate sends him to Herod and Herod was "glad" to see him. (Luke 23:8) Isn't that marvelous? That Luke can preach.

But I think probably the most effective investment in the future of your sermon is found in the gospel of John in chapter 18. You remember in chapter 18 the scene of Jesus in the house of Caiaphas and Annas, and they are working through the preliminary parts of his trial? And out in the courtyard, because of the cold, some servants and some of the police have built a charcoal fire. Around the fire are those who belonged within the courtyard–the servants and the guards. And they are talking. And there is one strange face and the flickering fire showing the faces and finally one of the servants said, "Aren't you with him?" "No." And they stand around. All of them just alike, except one. "Aren't you a Galilean, your accent, I believe you're a Galilean?" "No, no, no." And they are standing around the fire, all of them alike but one. "What are you doing here? Do you belong around this fire? Aren't you a follower?" He cursed and swore and said, "I belong in this circle! I don't belong in that circle!" Move to chapter 21. It was cold in the early morning and on the shore of the Sea of Galilee is Jesus. He has built a charcoal fire. "Peter, do you belong in the circle?" Isn't that something? Don't just use material looking back at tradition, but use pieces of it looking forward, and then when you get to the charcoal fire the second time, people say, "Oh, yeah. I remember he was at the charcoal fire."

If the sermon is to be a twice-told tale, we are going to have to *teach* it in order to *preach* it. And then preaching becomes what it is at its most powerful best and that is a twice-told tale. But preaching is not simply making deposits of information in the minds of the listeners. Preaching is also writing checks on what is already there in the minds and hearts of the listeners. And this refers not just to what they know of the tradition, but it also refers to what they know about life. When well done, people will say, "That's right, that's right, that's exactly the way it is, that is exactly how I feel. I have been there myself."

People will stop at the door after the service and say, "You know, I remember once when I was about eleven years old . . ." What's happened? You have awakened and brought out into the light of scripture and prayer and singing and worship in the house of God what had been buried there. And you have preached with power not simply because you made a deposit of information but because you wrote a check on what that person already knew: his or her own experience. For them to be able to say, "That's right, that's exactly the way life is for me." For them to be able to do that is to say in that sense the sermon is a twice-told tale. And it is in that sense of saying to the people what they have already experienced. To that dimension I want to move in the next chapter.

9

The Sermon as a Twice-Told Tale

Resonance with Human Experience

In chapter 7, I introduced the idea of the sermon as a twice-told tale. After introducing it, the last chapter dealt with the idea that preaching has special power and effectiveness when it rides upon a subtext, a prior hearing, a prior telling, and the obstacles that arise when the culture, including the church, lacks even the basic knowledge of the Bible and thus lacks a "first-told" experience.

I want to make a little turn in what I mean by "twice told." The sermon is a twice-told tale also in the sense that it has resonance with the experience of the listeners. It is twice told as evidenced by the "Amen, that's right" of the listener. Now turning toward the listener, I don't want to be misunderstood. I am *not* suggesting at all that the listeners are the *source* of the sermon. They are not the source. They are the ones for whom the sermon is shaped and whose ears, and hearts, and minds it seeks to catch. Let's look at the sermon as twice told in the sense that the experience of the text speaks to the experience of the listener.

Don Browning (following Hans-Georg Gadamer and Paul Ricoeur) has reminded us that there are three conversations that go on in a sermon.[1] One conversation takes place between the preacher and the congregation. Another conversation happens between the preacher and the text. The third conversation is between the text and the congregation. It's the third conversation to which I wish to move. I don't want to use the word "identify" as though the experience of the text and the experience of the listener are to be "identified." There has to be some critical distance between the two. One can consume the other. People can let their experience completely consume a text so that it ceases to exist. Or a text can consume the listener and they lose their identity. There has to be enough room between them to see the clouds. So I don't want to use the word *identify*. And still the word "resonate" is so prevalent that I hate to use it but I don't know another word. If you will, please permit that word to indicate a deep-to-deep, experience-to-experience, conversation here. In other words, the sermon that you preach does not just go out and keep going, and keep going, and keep going. No, it must strike a mind, strike a heart, and strike an ear. Then you get a response. In *that* sense the sermon is twice told.

What is assumed with the idea of resonance with human experience? One assumption is we communicate with each other because we are more alike than we are different. Even persons of different backgrounds, different ages, different cultural and ethnic origins, and different centuries can communicate because we are more alike than we are different.

Second, we belong to communities of understanding. I don't know why it takes the church so long to accept that. Scientists are in a world of understanding. No single scientist carries the burden. They borrow from each other's knowledge and understanding. There are communities of historians who borrow from each other. But in the church it seems so difficult for us to form those pools of peer learning and understanding. We belong to communities that communicate together because we have common interest, common orientation, and common faith.

Third, it is also assumed here that communication need not proceed out of suspicion and doubt. In recent years, we have heard a lot about the "hermeneutic of suspicion." Under this approach, the only way one can really get into a text, the only way one can really understand anybody or anything is to go at it with suspicion. I don't think so. It's important to maintain a reasonable level of objectivity, but I think there is a lot of deep thought, understanding, clarity, even discovery made in an atmosphere of *favorable* relationship to each other; an atmosphere of ascent, agreement, and cooperation.

Finally, I assume that in the words of Kenneth Burke, speech is never "neutral."[2] Whenever there is a conversation between two senders of meaning and power and influence and decision—that is, between you and you or between the biblical text and you. Wherever there is a conversation of that nature, there is change. It is never the same.

Now what is there to draw on when we begin to talk to folks and expect that there will be resonance or response? An "Amen," a sense of "Yes, that's true even though I don't know that text that you just read and you are talking about I know that that is true." What is the basis for that? The basis for that is that we have a common pool of experience. It doesn't always seem obvious at first. The things that people find deeply moving have to move across what seem like immeasurable distances.

I am continually amazed at people sobbing through a television show or a movie when it is about something from another planet. Several years ago at Christmastime, our grandchildren came with a video of *E.T.: The Extra-Terrestrial*, which I had not seen. We sat on the floor and watched *E.T.* Now, who would have thought that a little creature with three fingers would move modern America? What was going on? The movie moved from a starting point of galactic distances and nothing in common between the characters, and before it was over, we were sniffling, laughing, and saying, "Isn't that the way it is? I think I will come back and see this tomorrow. You want to come back and see this again with me?" My favorite part of that movie is when kids on bicycles fly through the air while self-important people with advanced degrees watch mesmerized.

So don't give up too easily when it seems that something you find in Leviticus is light years away from that church in North Carolina. It's not that far. It's not as far as *E.T.*

Don't be like the preacher who dreads that the text today is from Amos. Amos is a long way off and somebody else and somewhere else. The preacher starts to create all kinds of red-carpet ways to get to the text and the present together. It's almost as if the preacher is telling the congregation, "If you will sit there a few minutes I'll be through with all of this Amos stuff and I will tell you a funny story about Uncle Clyde falling out of an airplane."

How distant can anything be and yet when it comes to pain, and love, and loneliness, the distance disappears. We have a pool of common experience that will move across distances whether it is a story about something from outer space or prehistoric people, it doesn't take long until we move in and find ourselves closer to each other.

Once I landed on this twice-told tale idea from Nathaniel Hawthorne, I thought I should reread some of his stories. It's been a long time. What a joyful choice on my part. I recall reading somewhere something that Herman Melville wrote to Nathaniel Hawthorne. I paraphrase it here for you: "I find your stories wild and fanciful. But when I am well into them, I have a shock of recognition, for you have draped your wild and fanciful stories over the most common experiences and thought."

Flannery O'Connor could sit on her porch down in Milledgeville, Georgia, and write about southern semiliterate Protestant preachers and stir the hearts of Roman Catholics in Minnesota and Jews on vacation in the Catskills.

Do you understand what I am saying? You don't have to think of tricks or gimmicks. "Deuteronomy again? I thought we just finished Deuteronomy." It's not that far. We have a pool of common experience. For example, Edgar Lee Masters was a cynical poet from Spoon River, Illinois.

In *Spoon River Anthology*, he offered poems of all these people who have died and now they speak from the grave. Now what do we have in common with dead people talking in Spoon River, Illinois? Listen to one of them. Her name was Constance Hately.

> YOU praise my self-sacrifice, Spoon River,
> In rearing Irene and Mary,
> Orphans of my older sister!
> And you censure Irene and Mary
> For their contempt of me!
> But praise not my self-sacrifice,
> And censure not their contempt;
> I reared them, I cared for them, true enough!–
> But I poisoned my benefactions
> With constant reminders of their dependence.[3]

It turns out that it is *not* very far to Spoon River, Illinois. I can see and hear Constance bitterly reminding them of their dependence. And all of a sudden, I quiver with Melville's shock of recognition.

So don't get anxious if the text is Nehemiah. It's not so far; not at all. We begin at a distance but it isn't long until we find ourselves moving closer and closer.

Forrest Carter has that marvelous little book that's really about himself: *The Education of Little Tree.*[4] It takes place among the Cherokee in the Great Smoky Mountains of North Carolina. The time is the 1930s, with poverty everywhere. A Jewish peddler named Mr. Wine travels through the mountains selling thread and needles and takes orders for material. When he comes back the next month, he brings the material.

Mr. Wine notices that Little Tree has a thin coat against the winter cold. With his experienced and expert eye, Mr. Wine takes measure of that boy. It was almost as though he had taken out his tape and measured him. He buys some nice material and makes a coat. But how can he give it to Little Tree? Little Tree and his family are very proud.

The next month, Mr. Wine comes back and, to paraphrase, says, "You know you could do something for me. I have been packing around here something that is just about to break my back. I made this coat for my grandson who lives off in another state and I made it according to the size that I remembered him and I forgot how much he had grown. After I made it I remembered it was the total wrong size for him. And here I am with this coat and hauling it around. Would you try it on?"

Little Tree tries it on and Mr. Wine says, again paraphrasing, "Why look at that, the yellow coat fits! Would you do me a great favor and take this coat off my hands? It doesn't fit my grandson."

And Little Tree says, "I told him I would try to wear it." And that evening he ate supper in his new coat and was careful to eat over his plate to not spill anything on it.

What have we in common with a Jewish peddler and the Cherokee during the Great Depression decades ago? A common pool of experience. And yet we resonate with them now.

So don't give up too quickly if the text is from Isaiah. It's not that far away. This is the way common experience is. In his novel, *A Death in the Family,* James Agee tells what I believe is the story of his own life. The place and time is Knoxville, Tennessee, in 1915. His father dies in a car wreck. He was in his thirties at the time of his death. He leaves behind his wife and two little children. His widow goes to bed in grief and an aunt comes to take care of the children. There they are in a little row house in downtown Knoxville. And here is this little boy, Rufus. He's kind of awkward and is not good at sports. He gets beat up at recess on the playground and he's poor in his books. Nobody ever notices him. They don't know his name. His father's killed in a wreck. So the next morning, when he is on the porch, and the children are going by to school, he starts yelling to them, "My father was killed in a wreck last night!" His one chance to have some attention. He said, "I'm probably the only one in my class whose father was killed last night." The aunt comes out, "Come on inside." He starts getting ready for school. You don't go to school when your father has died. They have breakfast. He said, "This is the first time I have ever heard cornflakes. Daddy was always talking and we were having a lot of fun." And then he goes into the living room where his father always sat in the evening and smoked his pipe. And on the arm of the chair was an ashtray with those metal pellets in the bottom to give it weight and make it hold the ashes. And the little boy smelled the greasy place on the back of the chair where his father's head was and he took his finger and rubbed it around inside the ashtray and licked it. "His tongue tasted of darkness," wrote Agee.

Do you know what that's about? Most of you weren't born in 1915. Most of your fathers weren't killed in a wreck. Most of you have never been to Knoxville. It's not that far.

If your text is from Revelation don't get scared. It's not that far, not really.

I preached a sermon one time in a church in Denver. I was waiting for the minister to finish up gathering bulletins and turning off the lights. Everybody was about gone except this young woman. I learned that she was fourteen. She looked twenty-one. She was hanging around at the front door. She said, "Can I talk to you?"

"Well, I am not the minister. He is the minister," I said pointing to the man picking up the worship bulletins.

"I know," she said. "I want to talk to *you.* I want to ask you a question."

"All right," I said.

"Will I go to hell for not wanting to go to heaven?"

I was kind of surprised by that question, so I said, "Please tell me more."

"Well, every time I leave the house, my mother is yelling at me. And every time I come in five minutes late, she is yelling at me. And every time I go somewhere, she wants to know who is going to be there, and am I going to be with anybody, and what time. And she is always yelling at me and saying if you do this you're not going to go to heaven. If you don't do that you are not going to go to heaven. If you don't do this, you are not going to go to heaven. And what my mother doesn't understand is that I don't want to go to heaven."

Fourteen years old, oppressed by religion. But that was in Denver wasn't it? And that was somebody else, wasn't it? No, we are talking about *here*. We are talking about *now*.

Isn't that the way it is? Then why should I be afraid when the text for Sunday is a very strange passage from Ephesians? Shall I just tell the people, "Well, I'll read this but since it's so complicated we'll go ahead and just talk about the church budget and how we need to love each other." It's not that far, really.

I saw a classified ad in the newspaper when we lived in Oklahoma. It said a pastor was leaving the ministry and was going to sell his large and up-to-date library. The minister was a graduate of Harvard Divinity School. It was about 180 miles but I could not resist the temptation to pick up some good books for 25 and 30 cents each. So I drove over there. I was not disappointed by the amazing bargains! I got a whole shelf of those wonderful tomes for 10 cents each. I got stuff you wouldn't believe. It's still enriching my life. 10 cents, 5 cents, 25 cents—I just loaded up the car.

The Harvard-educated pastor was a cynical fellow, having just been fired from the church. He said it was the third time he'd been fired from churches. I asked about what had happened. He said,

> I started a Sunday school class for incorrigible kids. And I had gotten a good class going and we were studying the Bible. But one Sunday morning one of the church leaders was passing by the room where I was meeting with these kids and we were studying the gospel of Mark. We had the passage about Jesus casting the demons into the swine and they went into the sea. And I finished reading the text, one of the boys blared out, "Well that's the damnedest thing I ever heard!" A meeting was called, they fired me, and so I am hanging it up. I am leaving the ministry.

In one of his books was a little typed poem. I don't know whether it was his or someone else's but I kept it because I was fascinated by it. I didn't understand it really. It's a Yiddish poem titled "Der Ikker." It haunted me and I read it, and read it, and read it again. I kept it. I prized it. When our daughter graduated from the University of Tulsa and our son graduated from high school the same year, I decided to give them each a copy of the poem. And I hired a calligrapher at Phillips University to write it on scrolls of brown parchment paper. She made that curlicue writing and wrote this poem and I had her make two copies. It cost me $10 apiece and I stopped at the dime store to get some frames. And I wrapped them up and put them on their beds, "From Dad."

They opened my graduation present last because they thought, "That's kind of small, so old dad must have put some money in there." So they opened all the other gifts and then they both plunged into the gifts from Dad and opened them up and at the same time they both said, "What is this?"

"It's a poem."

And almost in one chorus they said, "This is *it*?"

"That's it. Read it."

If you go to their homes now, you will find the framed poems hanging on their walls. "Der Ikker," which is translated "The Main Thing":

> If your outlook on things has changed,
> This is not the main thing.
> If you feel like laughing at old dreams,
> This is not the main thing.
> If you recall errors of which you are now ashamed,
> This is not the main thing.
> Even if you know what you're doing now
> You'll regret some other time,
> This is not the main thing.
> But beware, light-heartedly, to conclude from this
> That there is no such thing as the main thing.
> This is the main thing.

I don't know exactly where that poem came from. It may be older than the Holocaust. It's Yiddish, German-Jewish. My land, what has that got to do with us? Everything.

What I am saying is a sermon is twice told in the sense that there is a resonance, a resonance between the experience of the listener and the experience of the text. We should not panic and either drop the text off because it's not relevant or too hastily collapse the distance between the two in an effort to make it say something relevant. Just let them talk a bit and you will discover that all that distance drops away and the real conversation begins to take place.

The pool of common experience: This is why I have always been fond of proverbs and aphorisms. They represent distillation in short sentences of ageless common experience of human beings all over the world: "Yeah that's the way it is." "A lie will take you far but it will not take you home."

That's right. "If you are bitter in your heart, sugar on your lips won't help." "Bad marriages can produce good children." "You have to fight fleas even when you are hunting elephants." "When smashing idols save the pedestals, they will be used again." "You can tell when the people have no voice even when they are singing anthems."

I love those sayings. Why? Because they do for me what I have to do as an exegete and preacher. They reach beneath, beneath, beneath and say, "Aha! It's true, that is true." Now the conversation is between the text and the listener; this is where I have been wanting to come. If there seems to be a distance between the Cherokee nation in North Carolina, and Knoxville, Tennessee, and Denver, Colorado, and a little Texas town where a defeated Harvard preacher is throwing it away and where you are, the distance collapses just as it does between the biblical text and your listeners.

So then what do I do? How can I handle the distance, the given distance, the recognized distance, the important distance between your listeners and a text in Hebrew or Greek, written thousands of years ago?

Well, I don't want to just read the text to authorize what otherwise would stand up there flimsily as a private opinion. I don't want to talk about the text as background for my exhortation. I heard way too many sermons from students who rushed to the library at the last minute, looked up a bunch of stuff in a commentary, and quickly piled it up in the front of their sermon as if to say, "Prof, I did my homework."

And then when they got to the body of the sermon, there was nothing there:

> Our text today is from the second chapter of Galatians. Galatia was one of the provinces in Asia Minor in what is today Turkey. There is some dispute as to whether this Galatia was northern or southern Galatia. It's a dispute as to whether or not it was the ethnic Galatia or the political Galatia. And there is really some uncertainty about that. The people who settled there were called Galatians. One branch of those people, coming from the north centuries before, had moved westward into another country and they called that Gaul. So we are talking to people who had cousins who are now called French. Now our text is from chapter 2.

That's marvelous but what does it have to do with anything? I want to encourage you to study, but does your study nourish? Does it speak the Word? That's what we want to do: not just authorize the sermon and not just give background to the sermon. It is the sermon if I will do with the text what you would do with James Agee's story, or Forrest Carter's story, or the experience in Denver, or the poem from Texas, or whatever. Live with it until you say, "Yes, now that is the way it is."

Do you remember the story of King Saul in 1 Samuel 28? Saul goes to the tent of a fortune-teller at Endor. This extraordinary man perhaps is now mentally ill. His mentor is the one who anointed him, Samuel, the one who also told him, "God has left you and you are no longer the king." Oh, what a terrible thing. Saul wasn't even looking to be king. He was out looking for his father's asses and found the kingdom, and was anointed king, and went home and said to his family, "I am the king" and they said, "Really?" And he wanted so much to be a king. He was a king without a crown, and he wanted the crown, and finally he got the crown, but he wasn't king anymore. Samuel's dead and the word is clear that in Saul's own house, a good friend of Saul's own son is the shepherd boy of Bethlehem, who is king. What do you do when your counselor is dead and your successor is already on the premises? He sought a word from God. There was no word. He tried everything and there was no word. He cast the lots and there was no word. He tried to pray and there was no word. And so he put on a wig, and changed clothes, and put on a mustache, and slipped out of his tent the eve of what would be his last battle. He had passed the decree that anybody practicing fortune-telling in Israel shall be put to death. And now he went to the tent of the fortune-teller at Endor: "Woman, I want you to call up the spirit of Samuel."

"I cannot do that—it's against the law."

"Call him up!"

"But sir, you. . . ."

"Shut up woman, call him up. I have to know."

Why would anybody turn from the doctors and go to the quacks? Absolute desperation. Do you know how long ago that story was written? I mean that story is in Hebrew. We are talking centuries ago. Does anybody know what his problem is and his state of desperation, his desire to know and not to know, and his ability to feel already his own death whistling through his soul like a cold wind?

For Saul, it's over. I understand that story.

I understand Hannah who, in 1 Samuel 1, told God, "Lord, if you will just give me a boy, I will give that boy back to you, promise, cross my heart, hope to die this boy is yours." She has a son; she names him Samuel. And when she weans him, she makes him a coat, and packs his little suitcase, and takes him to the house of God to give the child to God. Have you looked at her face for the two weeks prior to that trip? "I am giving my child to God. I'm giving my child away. I didn't mean it. It was a rash promise." Have you ever been in the kitchen just before that took place? I understand that story. Even though it's in Hebrew.

Do you remember Simon Peter at the church dinner in Antioch? Simon Peter who according to Luke stood up on the day of Pentecost and said,

> Repent, and be baptized every one of you in the name of Jesus Christ so that your sins may be forgiven; and you will receive the gift of the Holy Spirit. For the promise is for you, for your children,

and for all who are far away, everyone whom the Lord our God calls to him. (Acts 2:38–39)

Isn't that marvelous?

The church dinner at Antioch was under pressure from a group that came in from Jerusalem (Acts 15). Paul and Barnabas and a few others formed a separate table. You understand that? I understand that. Do you know what has happened to me sometimes? For all my growth, and inclusiveness, and moving forward, and being with seminarians so that I don't get old and out of date, I have found myself sucked into laughing and even telling an ethnic joke or some diminishing story. And I have stood in churches and said, "In Christ there is neither Jew nor Greek, bond nor free, black nor white, male nor female." But I understand that story even though it is in Greek.

I was lecturing in Antioch, Syria. A group of restless American Christians in the question-and-answer period said, "How long are we gonna be here? When are we gonna get to the Holy Land?" And I said, "We *are* in the Holy Land." They didn't understand. When Paul said,

> I don't understand my own actions. In my mind I serve God, but there is another law at work in my members. In my mind I say I will never do that. I do it. In my mind I say I'll do it. I don't do it. Wretched man that I am crucified between the sky of my intention and the earth of my performance? Who is going to deliver me?

I understand that. But it was written in a letter, not to me, but to a church in Rome, hundreds of years ago, and in Greek.

Live with the text. Live with the text. Live with the text.

And out of that living and studying, when you preach people will say, "You know, that is really the way it is. That really is the way it is."

Jonah the son of Amittai was asked to go to the town of Nineveh, which if you go on the Tigris River from Baghdad it's about two hundred miles up on the east side of the Tigris. The excavation is there to be seen. God wanted Jonah to go up there and preach. God apparently was concerned about Nineveh. Now the trouble with Jonah is he has two theologies. He has the theology of historical particularism: Israel alone of all the nations God has chosen. But on the other hand, he knows the God of creation. When he is on the ship and they are just about ready to throw him overboard, they said, "Who are you? Where are you from?" And he said, "I believe in the Lord God of heaven who created the sea and the land." And here is a preacher who has two theologies. One is a theology with a strong sense of "us" versus "them." But the other theology is a God of *all* of creation. Notice how the story surrounds him. God sends the sea storm, and God appoints a great fish, and then God appoints a plant to grow up above him. And then God appoints a worm to eat the plant. The King James Version says, "And

God ordained a worm." I like that. And then it says God appointed an east wind. And there is Jonah mad as a boiled owl, shaking his fist at heaven and God said, "You are concerned about the plant." "You are mighty right I'm concerned about the plant." And God said, "Well what about me? I have in that city 120,000 children who are just babies and don't even know their right hand from their left."

How does one work out the conflict of simultaneously having a theology of creation and having a theology of particularity? I understand how he felt, even though it's a long way from here to Nineveh. And it's in Hebrew.

And I haven't even started talking about Jesus yet. You know he was a Jew from Nazareth in northern Israel and probably spoke Aramaic.

Now I want to issue a warning at this point and the warning is this: when you do this, when you live this long with the text and live this closely to the people so that you can have deep speak to deep, I want to warn you, be prepared for it to affect *you* as much as your congregation. It may choke you up. It just doesn't get any more important than that. The sermon is a twice-told tale in terms of the content, the subtext, and the biblical material. It's also a twice-told tale in the resonance of human experience. And when told well, people will say, "I know that, that is familiar."

10

The Sermon as a Twice-Told Tale

The Form of the Sermon

I am not being light when I speak of preaching as a burden on the listener rather than the speaker. It's very difficult to listen–it's hard work. When I first began to restructure the preaching program at Candler, a major ingredient of that was helping students learn to *listen* to a sermon and to *listen* to each other.

Learning to listen is difficult. The Bible understands that it is difficult. For example, the Song of the Suffering Servant in Isaiah 50:4b says, "Morning by morning he wakens–wakens my ear to listen as those who are taught." Preaching, like music, begins in the ear. The passage goes on to say, "I gave my back to those who struck me, and my cheeks to those who pulled out the beard" (Is. 50:6–11). Painful. In spite of these indignities, Isaiah states, "The Lord God has opened my ear, and I was not rebellious, I did not turn backward" (Is. 50:5–11). In other words, God dug out my ear almost surgically because it was the *necessary* preparation to be a servant of God.

So far we've looked at the sermon as a twice-told tale in terms of the content and the subtext, the prior hearing. We then looked at the sermon as a twice-told tale in terms of the resonance with the listener's experience of the text and the experience of the listener making it twice told. In this chapter, we'll look at the form of the sermon itself; its shape and design. I don't mean anything mysterious when I refer to the form of the sermon. The form used to be called the outline of the sermon: the way it moves, the way it flows, and the way it fulfills itself and keeps its promise to the listener.

There are certain forms of sermons. There are certain patterns to human experience, which if honored in the form and pattern of the sermon will cause the listener to feel familiar even with a strange or new message. And the listener will therefore be more inclined to listen and perhaps be favorable toward acceptance.

Preachers and listeners alike know the importance of the form to the content. The minimum that we require of a form is that it does not violate the text. A text can be a blessing, such as, "Blessed are those who hunger and thirst after righteousness, they shall be filled." If the text is a blessing, then you want to honor that form in the sermon. It's not right to turn a blessing into an exhortation, such as, "We must hunger and thirst after righteousness. Now come on at the count of three: hunger and thirst!" No, the text is a blessing. Those who are hungry and thirsty for God will be filled.

If your purpose is pedagogical, then it's a contradiction if the form of your sermon is a diatribe against the ignorance in the world. You want to teach. You don't want to clean off the lot again. You want to build. So at a minimum what we expect is to not violate the text in the form of your sermon.

The form of the sermon has several qualities. First of all, clarity. In *The Company We Keep: An Ethics of Fiction*,[1] Wayne Booth talks about the fault, even the folly, of the writers of stories and novels. It was very popular in the 1960s and early 1970s for a number of writers to put out shapeless and formless pieces of literature. Those writers said things like, "Well who am I to try to give *direction* to other people's thinking?" Booth illustrates the point by quoting Donald Barthelme's story "The Party."[2] Here is the opening paragraph:

> I went to a party and corrected a pronunciation. The man whose voice I had adjusted fell back into the kitchen. I praised a Bonnard. It was not a Bonnard. My new glasses, I explained, and I'm terribly sorry, but significant variations elude me, vodka exhausts me, I was young once, essential services are being maintained. Drums, drums, drums, outside the windows. I thought that if I could persuade you to say "No," then my own responsibility would be limited, or changed another sort of life would be possible, different from the life we had previously, somewhat skeptically, enjoyed together.[3]

I'm guessing you're not wild over "The Party." It may remind you of some sermons you've heard. I use that exaggerated example, which was really published by a noted author in that day when many writers were saying and thinking things like, "Who am I to give shape and direction and pattern to the reader's thinking? We must just leave it open, totally open." Nonsense.

Clarity leads to persuasion. If you set a pattern, honor that pattern, and keep your promise that the pattern offers, listeners will be more open to considering the content. Form or pattern creates anticipation. You know what to anticipate when you hear these forms: "Once upon a time." "Dearly beloved, we are gathered here today." "May it please the court." "For your safety and comfort, please direct your attention to the flight attendants and follow these important steps."

Form also aids the memory. Sometimes ministers fuss about their inability to remember their sermon. It's very likely that the real problem is in its shape, its movement, or in its design. Remember that form is important to the listener's memory, too.

I once read with great difficulty a textbook on preaching that was written in 1693. This was a time in which the culture was primarily oral. Few people read or had books to read. The people who sat in church depended on their ear to capture and hold it. So in preaching in an oral culture, it was important that the shape of the sermon be easily portable. In the American frontier, the itinerant preacher lived in an oral culture. The audience didn't have a lot of books, didn't have time or inclination to study, and so it was a matter of being able to hold it in the memory and out of that came some of those now laughable sermon outlines. And while we might find them quaint or rustic, they could be remembered for years.

For example, the sermon on Samson: sin binds, sin blinds, sin grinds. That told the whole story of Samson. And years later, people could remember the sermon. The prodigal son: his madness, his sadness, his gladness. Under "his madness" were his caviling, his traveling, and his reveling. Under "his sadness" were he went to the dogs, he lost his togs, and he ate with the hogs. And then under "his gladness" were he ate the veal, he danced the reel, and he got the seal. Now I dare say that years from now you will remember that. And I have a suspicion that some of you will be using them soon in your own sermons.

In a culture that had to hold most things in the memory, these "portable forms" served a purpose. The form of the sermon, the pattern of the sermon, is an aid to memory. It orients, takes the raw material, and gives it shape and order and meaning. In the Bible, even a wailing lamentation is carefully ordered, predictably patterned.

Herman Melville's story *The Enchanted Isles* tells about a woman who is shipwrecked. Her brother and her husband have been killed. She was alone on this island and she ran in panic up and down the beach until finally she got control of herself. And this is what she did: She got some sticks and she would put a mark on the stick for every sunrise, every sunset. She had a stick and she put a mark on the stick every time she saw a seagull. She had a stick she'd mark every time she found turtle eggs. She had another stick and she marked it for the days that it rained. Do you know what she was doing? She was getting control of a life that was otherwise out of control. Form, order, and patterns orient people. And they are extremely important in that regard. This is why it is so tragically terrible the way some older people in hospitals under certain forms of insurance plans are moved around in the hospital according to where they are in their therapy. "Well, now that you are under this care, you go here," and they are just moved around, and it's so disorienting because for all of us, we are able to maintain minimum equilibrium simply because the world has fixity about it. They cut down a tree on a corner in Atlanta, along the way I travel, and it bothers me. There is something different here. I need form and order.

In the *Republic*, Plato said it is very distressing and disturbing to a society if you change the modes of music and exercise. It orients and sometimes disorients. If you want to disorient your listeners, change the pattern of your preaching. If you have a certain way you preach every time, change it. If you do, people say, "Were you preaching today?" Now it was not a change of substance, you are preaching the gospel. What you did was change the form. This is why as some of you who have been my students know I remind the students over and over again, especially the ones who have an inclination to experiment: a change of form is in the ear of the listener the equivalent of a change in the content.

For instance, here is a minister who has been at this church for twenty-six years and always preached the same way: a little humor in the introduction, and then read the text, and then said, "Now I have four things I want to say about this today." He did that for twenty-six years, and then he retires, and you follow as the new minister. You're fresh out of seminary and you've learned all kinds of things about narrative and this and that and you are poetic. And so you do this new kind of sermon and everybody is nice to you, sort of. Finally somebody says after the service, "Well I enjoyed your, ah talk, um, but, we like more Bible." Now if you examine your sermon and compare it to ol' Reverend So-and-So's sermons, yours may have forty-five more pounds of Bible than his. So what did you do? You changed the form. And the change of the form is disorienting and is taken by the listener as a change of content.

Wayne Booth[4] has argued that the form in which you share your material is an ethical matter if you are concerned about truth and the consequences on those who hear you or read you. What then is form?

In *Counter-Statement*, Kenneth Burke has an interesting discussion about form. Just these two brief quotations: "Form is the creation of an appetite in the mind of the auditor, and the adequate satisfying of that appetite."[5] Create the expectation, meet the expectation. He also wrote, "Form in literature is an arousing and fulfillment of desires. A work has form in so far as one part of it leads a reader to anticipate another part, and to be gratified by the sequence."[6] You are not going to find anywhere a better statement on form than that.

There is a certain pattern or shaping of human experience, or there are certain patterns or shapes to human experience, which if you honor in the sermon form will cause the listener to feel at home and familiar as though he has heard this before, even though the material is new, and therefore be inclined toward acceptance. Does this mean then repeating certain forms in preaching? Yes, I highly recommend repeating certain forms. Why? Because we are lazy? No. We don't have any imagination? No.

Have you ever noticed how people will listen to the same music over, and over, and over? Some people will go back and see the same play five or six times. There are people who will read the same novel many times. There is no more surprise. They know how it ends. They know all the characters. Why do they read it again? Because they've read it before.

Why do people go back to the same classics? Why has Shakespeare survived after all of these years? Well, the reasons can be many. Part of it may be Aristotle's "joy of recognition," which we talked about. It could be that the reading or listening to something that I already know and am familiar with brings to mind pleasant associations. The first time I heard that or read that I was with such and such a person at such and such a place. That probably is the case. Sometimes it is the way it is ordered and formed that gives order and form to my life. My life is all out of control but when I read this story it just seems to hold together. What I am suggesting, it may be that the form of that material corresponds in a way to the form of your experience. It fits. It's appropriate.

Now what does this assume? This assumes that there are certain patterns or forms to human experience; certain patterns of the way life is, the way people know life, and the way they wish life were that is common to us.

In *Contraries: Essays,* Joyce Carol Oates writes, "We are each haunted by different things, and we do not choose the presences, angelic or demonic, that haunt us: rather, we know ourselves chosen."[7]

In other words, we don't choose what haunts us—it chooses us. In her book she writes about ballads and folk music that seem to be imbedded in a community and shape experience and shape lives. It just seems to be a part of the fabric of who those people are. And in that writing I was persuaded.

Henry Louis Gates Jr. has that marvelous collection *The Classic Slave Narratives.*[8] In his introduction, he calls the reader's attention to notice in these narratives the same pattern over, and over, and over again. Why? He did a lot of research. Could this person have read or heard this person's narrative and then copied it? He persuaded me that the slave narratives were written by people who read and reread the slave authors who preceded them. "In this process of imitation and repetition, the black slave's narrative came to be a communal utterance, a collective tale, rather than merely an individual's autobiography," wrote Gates.[9]

Claude Lévi-Strauss studied moving among primitive societies.[10] He concluded that there are certain ways that people comprehend, experience, and convey life in rituals, in stories, and in certain patterns of behavior. It seems to me that the form of your sermons is a matter of corresponding to a fundamental pattern of human experience. "I like that because it fits the way I have experienced life. If not the way I have experienced life at least the way I wish life were." There are two kinds of people who know what life is about: those who have tasted it and those who have wanted it so badly they could taste it.

And so I was digging around to see if I could find some fundamental patterns of the way life is experienced. I found the following short list. As I mention each of these, would you take just a moment to think how many stories, how many things you've heard that just fit this pattern?

- Digging one's own grave. "Well I think she's just digging her own grave." How many stories use that pattern?
- A very small act that has a major consequence. A thousand stories told just in that form.
- Betrayed by one's close friend. Thousands upon thousands of stories fit that basic pattern. People read those stories and say, "You better believe it. That's the way it is." That's the shape in which people have experienced life. And why do you have so many stories with the same shape? Because that's the way life is.
- Being mistreated by the person you are trying to help. And when I read that and thought about that I began to make a list of the forms of stories, it's a short list, the forms of stories that are used all over the world, Europe, Near East, Far East, America everywhere you find these forms in stories that are told in every culture of the world.
- Two people die, one goes to heaven and one goes to hell. And the one that goes to hell sends a message back to the earth about how terrible it is.
- Cinderella. Some people have collected over 120 different Cinderella stories that are not obviously borrowed from each other. It is the way life is hoped, imagined, and experienced by people.
- The owner of real property has to go away on a journey, so the owner leaves the property in the hands of trusted servants. When at last the owner returns, the servants are called in to give an account.
- The king and the peasant change roles. The king becomes the peasant and the peasant becomes the king. How many delightful stories? All the way from children's stories to adult stories is just basically that pattern.
- A man has two sons; one stays at home and works hard. The other one goes out and fritters everything away. I once heard a sermon on that story form, and it sounded familiar but unfamiliar. The preacher was an Old Testament scholar. I quizzed him afterward, and he said that it wasn't from the New Testament but it sounded like it was the story of the prodigal son. He said it was the story of the prodigal son in an old Acadian story.
- Brother beast. I recall Rabbi Lou Silberman, one of my professors at Vanderbilt, telling about the Lamed-Vov legend. He claimed this story

exists in many forms. This legend, he says, is essentially that everywhere in every generation where there are Jews, God has one person who will bear the sins of the people through suffering and death. And the person who is the Lamed-Vov in a community at a given time doesn't know it.

Professor Silberman told one of those stories, which was set in the context of a pogrom in Poland. When in this Jewish community all the men had been either deported or killed, leaving women and children, except for one man. He was a big, hulky man, thirty years old but "retarded," and played with the children. You could see him squatting around, talking to the cats and dogs. Sometimes you'd see him leaning against a wall staring vacantly into space, foraging his nostrils with his index finger, just blank. He was as big as a man, he's thirty, but he's a child. But his very presence in the community reminded the women that all the men were gone. And he was no man. And they yelled at him and they got so frustrated one day, so angry one day, they chased him. He was awkward and stumbling in his gait. Exhausted, he stopped and leaned against a tree and one of the women reached down, picked up a stone, threw it at him, and it hit him in the temple. And he slumped at the foot of the tree. And these angry, frustrated women gathered around throwing stones and one of them said, "He had no beauty or comeliness that we should desire him." Another one said, "He was one from whom people hide their face." And another said, "By his stripes we are healed," and they felt the relief from all the hatred and anger go out of them. He was the Lamed-Vov–and dead.

God always has someone who bears in his or her person the sins of the community through suffering and death. Let us suppose that this is true, that there are certain fundamental shapes or patterns to human experience. If you honor these forms in the sermon, it will cause the listener to feel at home, familiar, even with a strange topic and therefore be more favorably inclined to hear and to respond. Let us just suppose that you listen, and think, and read, and make notes of those patterns that are at the heart of the world's literature and say that must be the pattern of human experience. So shape your sermons that way, not violating the text, not contradicting your own purpose, but shaping your message that way. And the listener says, "I don't know what it is but I've never heard that before, I know. And I am not familiar with that text. But there is something about it, something about it."

It's the shape. It's the shape. It's the form that makes it a twice-told tale.

May I encourage you to refrain from trying to be "novel" and "different" all the time? Stop saying to yourself week after week, "I bet *this* will get them." You know ministers do that sometimes when they are competing with their predecessor. So they go searching around on the dark side of Nahum looking for some sort of text to "get them." "I bet they have never heard this" and finally someone tells you, "We've never heard that."

But the most fatal error of all is to compete with yourself, to work on that sermon and preach the sermon. And before 3:00 p.m. that Sunday afternoon you are already in a stew and fretting about how you're going to top that. I know of nothing more fatal to your pulpit than competing with yourself. Don't try. Don't be *clever*. You want people to *hear* the gospel. And if there is a shape and a pattern to the way people appropriate life, then nurture it and honor it in your sermon. And they'll say, "I think that's right. I think that's right. That's right."

11

The Sermon as a Twice-Told Tale

New Words to Old Tunes

There remains one area to explore in this notion of the sermon as a twice-told tale. That area is the twice-told tale in the sense of the sermon as a linguistic phenomenon, the sense in which the language we use is a *second* telling of the gospel. In his essay on Matthew in *A Literary Guide to the Bible*, Frank Kermode looks at Jesus' ethical and moral demands on his disciples. Kermode uses the expression "the rhetoric of excess" to describe Jesus' teachings: "Unless your righteousness exceeds that of the scribes and the Pharisees." "You have heard it said, but I say to you . . ." Jesus told his disciples that they are to *exceed* in forgiveness, in love, in generosity, in caring, in fellowship, and in faith.

Kermode then goes on to say that this rhetoric of excess finds its literary support in the hyperbolic language of Jesus found fairly often in Matthew. And then he proceeds to call our attention to expressions that are buried in Matthew, such as the following: "First, take the log out of your own eye, and then you can take the splinter out of your brother's eye." "If a child asks you for a fish would you give a snake?" "You strain gnats, but you swallow camels." "It's easier for a camel to go through the eye of the needle than for the rich to enter the kingdom of God." The rhetoric of excess is also used in the parables and stories of Jesus, such as a king who called in his servants to give account, and he had one servant who owed him 10,000 talents, or about $10 million, about 150,000 years of labor. And the king forgave this $10 million debt. The servant went out and saw a fellow servant who owed him a hundred denari (about eighteen bucks), grabbed him by the throat, and demanded payment. Ten million dollars–eighteen dollars. The rhetoric of excess.

Let's talk about the use of hyperbole in preaching. There is a kind of opulence of language that is appropriate to preaching the gospel. We tend to preach among believers who have accepted the faith, who perhaps know the fundamental texts, who recite with conviction the creeds of the church. Among those people especially, it is not only legitimate but appropriate. I urge you to use exaggerated speech, for they have heard it once, the creeds, the basic texts, the sermons, the explanations, the lessons, and the exegesis. Now let them hear it again with hyperbole, the rhetoric of excess. Release all restraint and let it go.

This is not an obscure topic. I didn't pull it from cobwebs in the dark corners of the seminary library. I've heard exaggerated speech from *you*. "So I left him. Oh, he cried buckets, but it didn't change anything since he has cried buckets before." "She's a good batter. Last time she was at bat, she hit that ball a country mile." "My flight leaves in an hour and I still have a thousand things to do." "I'm now serving an older congregation–our average age is about 117." "I'm enjoying my new appointment although the salary is a little low. In fact, I just got a sympathy card from the IRS."

Some of you have heard me talk this way a time or two. I am not at all adverse to hyperbole in sermons. Some of you heard me in a sermon in which I was stressing the importance of words. It's not a matter of cheap words, words, words. Words are deeds! And what you say makes a difference!

I once visited my sister and I was put in the front bedroom upstairs. The next morning, the sun was coming through. It was a beautiful morning, so I got out of bed and opened the French doors and stepped out on to the balcony. My brother-in-law had gone to the front yard to pick up the morning paper and he looked up and saw me and said, "What are you doing?"

"Just standing up here on the balcony, enjoying the morning," I replied.

"But we don't have a balcony."

If I hadn't gotten a hold of a downspout, I would have been killed.

We know this kind of language. You use it, I use it, and the Bible uses it. Read again that marvelous little book of Jonah. In the repentance that went on in Nineveh, all the beasts of the field repented and wore sackcloth. I like that. Read again the ending to the gospel of John: "But there are also many other things that Jesus did; if every one of them were written down, I suppose that the world itself could not contain the books that would be written" (Jn. 21:25).

What is exaggerated or hyperbolic speech? Some folklorists say it is "a permitted lie." I don't like that expression. I know what they're trying to say, but it is based on the assumption that the fundamental normative canonical use of language is to convey accurate information. I don't buy that. I don't think I have bought it since the first time I heard a mother speaking to a child. The early and primary use of speech, as a mother to a child, is not to "inform" but to create a world for the child, a world in which little dogs laugh and the dish runs away with the spoon.

What is hyperbolic speech? Exaggerated speech? I do not believe as some cultural anthropologists say that it is a form of speech peculiar to primitive peoples, uneducated, or illiterate people. I don't think it is a "cultural lag."

The rhetoric of excess is quite at home in the arts. Vincent van Gogh said painting was "to exaggerate the essential and to leave the obvious vague."[1]

John Keats said poetry "should surprise by a fine excess and not by singularity–it should strike the reader as a wording of his own highest thoughts, and appear almost a remembrance."[2]

But what about theology? Now in theology it is our task to express that which is larger than our lives, the greater than, the high above, the far away, the deep beneath, and the transcendent. How do we express the transcendent? That's the task of theology. Well, we use a lot of different ways. One way is to use abstractions, to speak in tertiary language. We use a lot of words that end in "ness," such as the otherness of God. Abstractions are necessary in theological language to keep our preaching fit. Otherwise, it would just sink into a bog of sentimentality.

Sometimes silence is used to express the transcendent. You remember Ignatius talking about the silence of God; and then the silence of the bishop; and the authority of not saying anything.

Another way to express the transcendent is to use fragmented sentences, just bits and pieces. Paul sometimes starts a sentence and never quite finishes it. There are some things he starts to say, then gets fragmented and awkward, as if he's saying, "These ideas are so big that they're *bursting* my language."

Sometimes expressing the transcendent is done with ambiguity. This is quite popular today. The rhetorical function of ambiguity is to testify of something beyond itself, this ambiguity. After all, if you are totally clear, there is something reductionistic about that. There is something trivializing about it if you are just "high noon" clear. But if you are "late evening" ambiguous, there is something else here.

Glossolalia is sometimes used to express the transcendent. Sometimes I worship in churches in which they begin a kind of utterance, not words, but an utterance. And somehow there is a state of a presence of God. I have not myself done this, but speaking in tongues is a way of saying, "The ordinary bounds of my language are *bursting* and I have to just make these sounds."

Sometimes preachers do it by a change of the tone in the voice. We have drilled our students to get rid of it, but may I pause a moment to say that the history of that is to be revered. How can an ordinary person from Lee County, Virginia, or Crockett County, Tennessee, talk of God, and

Christ, and Holy Spirit, and the things to come? One way is to dramatically change the tone of the voice, to signal to the listeners I had moved into the big stuff. I make the announcements in the ordinary language: "The fellowship dinner is going to be at 6:30. There will be no youth meeting tonight. We can't find our youth minister." You say that in an ordinary tone of voice but then the text is read, God, I want to talk to you about Jesuuuuus. Now beneath our laughter, I hope you recognize that it is among a lot of preachers a way of saying, "This is just too important to say it in the same way I did the announcements." I am not advocating that we do this practice. I am simply saying beneath it is a reverence, like a red-letter edition of myself when I preach.

May I suggest that another appropriate way of speaking of the transcendent is to use hyperbole? There has been a lot of good material written on parables in the last twenty-five years, especially among American New Testament scholars. I belonged to the Parable Seminar for a number of years of the Society of Biblical Literature. I learned a great deal, heard a great deal, and joined in a great deal. I recall Robert Funk, who was in that seminar, saying that the parable is so appropriate to the preaching of the gospel because a parable is a "linguistic incarnation."[3] In the ordinary language of a story (such as "a man went out to sow"), there is conveyed the word of the kingdom of God. It's a linguistic incarnation. That's parabola. I would like to suggest that hyperbole is linguistic *transcendence.* Hyperbole is saying to the people who have heard it in creed, story, and homily: *this* has a second telling.

Hyperbole is needed given the subject matter of a transcendent God. Our subject matter presses the limits of language, bangs against it, and often finds it inadequate.

Do you remember the poet Elizabeth Barrett Browning? I think she was talking of her love for her husband Robert when she wrote her famous sonnet commonly known as, "How Do I Love Thee?" Here are the first four lines:

> How do I love thee? Let me count the ways.
> I love thee to the depth and breadth and height
> My soul can reach, when feeling out of sight
> For the ends of Being and ideal Grace.[4]

She could have just said, "Hey, Bob, I love you." But if she can say that about Robert, how are we going to speak of Jesus?

What is apocalypse going to be like? John said,

> I saw the new Jerusalem, like a bride coming down the aisle. Oh,
> I saw a new heaven and a new earth. The streets were solid gold.
> The gates were pearl. They were jasper carvings. Everything was

absolute total beauty. It didn't need any sun, or moon, or stars. It didn't have a temple. God was the temple. And underneath the throne came out the river of life, and on either side was the tree of life blooming and living forever. And the leaves of the tree were for the healing of the nations. (Rev. 21, paraphrased)

John could have just said, "The end of time looked really awesome." No, I don't think that describes it very well.

Isaiah, what will it be like with the coming of the son of God?

Oh, this is the way it is going to be. You will see a lion and a lamb lying down together and you will see a cow and a bear grazing together and you will see a little toddler playing over the hole of a poisonous snake without harm. That's the way it is going to be. The mountains will be leveled. And the valleys are going to be built up. And the rough places are going to be smooth and it will be a highway for the gate, right in the desert, and it will blossom. (Is. 11:6–9, paraphrased)

When Jesus was born, there was a choir of angels overhead in the shepherds' field, and the flapping of their wings scattered gold dust over the sheep and the shepherds. And there was singing—just singing, singing, singing (Lk. 2). And there were some fellows from way over in the East that came in and brought gold, frankincense, and myrrh. And there was a star in the sky—a puzzling thing—and it came and stood over where the child was (Mt. 2). But if you think that's something, you should have been there when he died. It was for three hours, dark as midnight. It was a frightening thing from noon until 3, dark! And when he died, that beautiful veil in the temple was ripped like an old coat, and the earth convulsed and rocks split and dead people came out of tombs and walked the streets (Mt. 27:45–54).

What else are you going to say? This is the central event in the history of the world. Thus hyperbolic speech, in my judgment, is not just permitted, it is *urged.* Not to satisfy the appetite of people who have heard so many sermons they have gotten hardened and calloused and are no longer alive to the ordinary in life. I don't mean for that reason. We don't use it to stir the congregations who are, in the words of Joseph Conrad, "Swallowed up in the immense indifference of things."[5] We do speak to people who have grown cynical and hard; it's true, but that is not the determining factor. The determining factor lies in what we are doing itself.

Another reason to use hyperbole is to avoid the reductionism in which we might get trapped into thinking we have captured in a system of thought the nature of God. In contrast, the use of hyperbole reminds us that we don't know *exactly* what we are talking about. And that is very important. We never want to give the impression in our preaching that we have walked all the way around God and taken pictures. What we are doing is we are just looking at that which is more than, greater than, above, beyond, and deeper than.

We use hyperbole to create a kind of playfulness. We should stay light on our feet. We should keep a quality of delight about our ministry and keep a playfulness in our talk about God. Not that we don't believe in the Trinity, and the Apostles' Creed, and the authority of scripture and all that. We have said that, we've affirmed that, we've held hands, we've prayed it, and we've sung it.

I remember a few years ago I had a student from Iraq. I called on him one day to discuss a passage about Jesus being greater than Solomon. "Professor," he confessed, "I'm sorry, but I have not read the assignment for today. But I know a story about Solomon from my own country. Do you want to hear it?"

I said, "Um, OK." And he told his Solomon story:

> There was a time Solomon wanted to feed the fish. Solomon had become so rich and powerful and so lifted up in his own estimation that he said to God one day, "I'd like to feed the fish." God said, "I feed the fish. You are not God, you are Solomon." Solomon begged God to feed the fish for just one day. Finally God said, "OK, feed the fish." Thousands of servants took crates of food down to the Great Sea, hour after hour, ton after ton, took it to the beach. Upon the raising of the arm of Solomon, they dumped it all into the Great Sea, carton after carton, ton after ton, and finally when it was all finished, a tiny fish raised its head out of the water and said, "When do we eat?"

Even though I would have preferred the student to have been prepared for class, I was grateful for the story. The story reminded me that we can get ground down in our heavy exegetical work. Maybe we need this young fellow from Iraq to tell us about Solomon wanting to feed the fish.

We use hyperbole to emphasize things, to underscore things. I love some of those exaggerations, such as "It was dark that night—it was darker than one hundred midnights in a Louisiana swamp." Now *that* is dark. Or to describe psychology: "You know what psychology means to me? It means a blind man in a dark cellar at midnight without a light looking for a black cat that's not even there." I like that.

Preachers used to ask, "Where will you spend eternity?" They all told the same story: "You want to know how long eternity is? I'm going to explain it to you. Imagine a solid granite mountain fifteen thousand feet high. And there is a swallow that once every five hundred years flies by and touches the granite mountain with the tip of its wing, once every five hundred years. Now imagine how long it would take that swallow to wear that granite mountain down to sea level. Well in eternity, that's before breakfast." And then when the preachers asked if we wanted to spend eternity in hell, we all said, "No."

What are we doing? We are emphasizing.

> If I speak with the tongues of men and of angels but don't have love, I am a noisy gong, clanging symbol. If I have prophetic powers, if I understand all mystery and all knowledge, if I have all faith so as to move mountains but don't have love—nothing. If I give away everything I own. If I give my body to be burned and don't have love, it's nothing. (1 Cor. 13)

Nobody can miss that point.

Why do we do it? I think sometimes we do it just to release ourselves from the bounds of facticity and historicity, to turn us loose, and to enter into another experience. Sometimes exaggeration will lead us into transcendence.

When our family was in Germany some years ago, we went down to Rottweil to the Fasching festival, which is sort of like Mardi Gras. There was a parade in which they reenacted the play of good and evil. Right down the street of this little city in southern Germany came the people dressed in those ancient masks, of the good angelic figures and the horrible faces of evil. The evil ones carried pitchforks and swords and the good came dressed in white with faces beatific. They clashed in the street and we watched. And those evil ugly things with distorted, exaggerated features were killed. And with the new lilt to the music from the band, the angelic host led us then to a large arena where we ate and danced. Exaggeration? Yes, of course, but I just lost all contact with things factual and practical and I was just lost in that and felt again the struggle of good and evil. I was a part of it.

Sometimes exaggerated language has a prophetic force. This is why some of the prophets of our time are cartoonists. They can exaggerate the features of a politician that represents the flaw, the weakness, and the error in the politician; exaggerate something about the face or the head or the ears, exaggerate some other parts of the body in this caricature. The exaggeration strikes a chord of prophecy. In former times, the king's counterpart in the palace was a court jester, a joker, a fool. The fool dressed like the king in exaggerated colors, wore a crown like the king only it was made of cloth and the tips fell down and they had little bells on the end. The fool had a scepter but it was limber and it would fall over. He had authority, but not real authority. And what the fool did in this distortion was to remind the king of the king's mortality, to get the king to laugh at himself. The fool's exaggerations were sometimes very persuasive.

There have been times in my life when I knew what was being said was obvious exaggeration, but I could not help but get caught up in it. Once was by an auctioneer in Marshfield, Missouri. I was there to preach at the church. I stayed in the home of a member who was an auctioneer.

He auctioned farmland, cattle, and machinery. His name was Case. He was a colorful fellow. On a Saturday morning he invited me to go along with him to a farm outside of town. When we got there, it started to rain. It was a boggy mess.

"This rain is going to kill your auction," I said.

"Oh, no, no better friend to a farm auction than the rain," he said.

"How do you know?"

"You watch. They will get out of their cars and just kind of tiptoe trying to find a dry place but after a while they will roll up their trouser legs and they will get careless, and then I've got them."

He began to auction this and that and finally they brought over six or seven Holstein cows. They brought one forward and tethered her to a wagon wheel. I could tell she was tired.

He started the rattle of the auctioneer, and got the bidding up to $65. The cow was saggy. I could tell she was old. The auctioneer took his cane and hit on that wagon wheel and said,

> Whoa, whoa, brothers and sisters look at this here cow. This cow has calves all over this county. Putting rolls in the cheeks of children. Have you ever sat down to a good cold glass of milk? Now let me see the hands of those who know for *sure* that good milk was not from this cow. Have you ever on Sunday evening said, "Well I am still full from that good lunch, but I think I will just have a glass of milk and crumble some cornbread in it and sit down and rest?" Have you ever done that? Do you know for sure that it was not from this cow? Now what is my bid for this here cow?"

He sold that cow for $350.

Why do we use the rhetoric of excess? One reason is to express feelings so deep, so rich, so profound, and so important that we can't think of another way to express them. For example, consider Ben Jonson's poem to his wife Celia in which he wrote,

> Drink to me, only, with thine eyes,
> And I will pledge with mine;
> Or leave a kiss but in the cup,
> And I'll not look for wine.[6]

Can you beat that?

William Ernest Henley from his hospital bed after losing one leg and facing the possibility of losing another wrote the poem that has come to be known as "Invictus." Here are the opening lines:

> Out of the night that covers me,

Black as the Pit from pole to pole,
I thank whatever gods may be
for my unconquerable soul.[7]

And John Donne wrote,

Batter my heart three-person'd God, for you
As yet but knocke, breathe, shine, and seeke to mend;
That I may rise, and stand, o'erthrow mee, and bend
Your force to breake, blowe, burn, and make me new.[8]

And consider several hymns:

My Lord, he calls me,
He calls me by the thunder;
The trumpet sounds within my soul,
I ain't got long to stay here. ("Steal Away to Jesus")[9]

Were the whole realm of nature mine,
That were a present far too small;
Love so amazing, so divine,
Demands my soul, my life, my all. ("When I Survey the Wondrous
   Cross")[10]

Could we with ink the ocean fill,
And were the skies of parchment made,
Were every stalk on earth a quill,
And every man a scribe by trade,
To write the love of God above,
Would drain the ocean dry.
Nor could the scroll contain the whole,
Though stretched from sky to sky. ("The Love of God")[11]

How else are you going to say it?

My God, my God, why have you forsaken me? I'm a worm. All
who see me wag their heads, they make faces at me. I'm poured
out like water. My bones are out of joint. My heart has melted like
wax. Dogs are all around me. They've pierced my hands and my
feet. I can count all my bones. My God, my God. Why have you
forsaken me? Whither shall I flee from thy spirit? Whither shall I
flee from thy presence? If I ascend to the mountains, thou art there,
if I descended into hell, thou art there, if I take the wings of the

morning and dwell in the outer most parts of the sea, thou art there, if I say to the darkness cover me, thy hand can snatch a swift and soon, from midnight shade is blaze of noon. (Ps. 22, paraphrase)

Have you ever had feelings that deep, wide, high, strong? If so, how can you avoid using hyperbole?

We use hyperbole–the rhetoric of excess–to praise God: "Oh, for a thousand tongues to sing thy praise." The psalmist in Psalm 148 uses words, such as praise the lord, all the earth, sea monsters of the deep, fire, hail, snow, frost, wind storms, mountains, hills, fruit trees, cedars, beasts of the forest, cattle, creeping things, birds, kings, princes, rulers, young men, maidens, old people, children, praise the Lord.

> In the year that King Uzziah died, I saw the Lord sitting on a throne, high and lofty; and the hem of his robe filled the temple. Seraphs were in attendance above him; each had six wings: with two they covered their faces, and with two they covered their feet, and with two they flew. And one called to another and said: "Holy, holy, holy is the LORD of hosts; the whole earth is full of his glory. The pivots on the thresholds shook at the voices of those who called, and the house filled with smoke" (Is. 6:1–4).

Opulence is *necessary* for praising God. The hearers know the text. They know the creed. They've said the confession. They need more, much more. Hyperbole is not only permitted; it is *essential* to the task and the nature of the subject matter of preaching. It is absolutely essential for life.

Hyperbole was essential to me as a boy. My brothers and I would watch falling stars on summer evenings on our little farm in West Tennessee. Blight had killed the chestnut trees some years before but stumps were still there in the wood lot. We stood on the stumps to see the falling stars better. We'd watch to see where they fell and we'd jump off the stumps, run quickly over to them, and put them in our pockets. We would race each other to see who would get to them first. We would fill both pockets in fifteen minutes.

I remember one night stars were falling everywhere, so we got my grandmother's laundry basket and we filled it in less than an hour. We dragged the basket full of stars to the back porch. We should have emptied it, but we were tired, so we decided to empty it in the morning. We shouldn't have done that, but we were just kids and didn't know that stars don't keep well overnight.

The next morning we heard Grandma call out, "Who's been putting something in my clothes basket?" We went out there, and there in the bottom of the clothes basket was a little smear of ashes and we all ran and scattered like a covey of quail.

In her last illness shortly before her death, she called me to her bedside, and she said, "I know what you were doing with my clothes basket." And

I got ready to receive her scolding. She said, "Go over there and open the bottom drawer of the chest and bring me the thing wrapped in newspaper." As instructed, I pulled a heavy drawer open and took out a bundle of newspaper and brought it to her. She opened it carefully. At the bottom was a little smear of ashes.

I looked over to her and asked, "You too, Grandma?"

She nodded yes.

"Why didn't you tell me?" I asked.

"I was afraid you would laugh at me," she said.

After a moment, she asked, "Why didn't you tell me?"

"I was afraid you would scold me," I said.

Perhaps out of fear of embarrassment, fear of being wrong, or fear of being scolded, we shrink the message until we produce little calculated homilies. Sometimes I come home from worship at church, and in a very secular moment I say to Nettie, "You know what I wish we had done this morning? I wish we had gotten in the car and started counting all the red and gold leaves between Atlanta and Hendersonville, North Carolina." I don't really mean that—at least not entirely.

I know I need to be scolded. I need to be corrected. I need to be instructed and exhorted. I need to be called to repentance. But I also need for you the preacher to take me by the hand and let me walk off the size of my inheritance as a child of God. I need every now and then to run my fingers through the unsearchable riches of the treasury of God's grace, to sing the doxology, and go home.

I need for you to assure me that life is *not* what the eloquent agnostic said it is: a narrow veil between the cold barren peaks of two eternities. We don't know whence we come or whither we go. We try in vain to see beyond the highest. We cry aloud and hear nothing but the echo of our own discordant cry. I need for you to tell me that that isn't true.

I need for you to respect the size of this grand book called the Bible and not reduce it to a series of unrelenting naggings. Instead, let me sense something of the size and opulence of the Word. Let your language get away from you. Because if you don't, I think I probably would rather be a pagan. Or maybe I would rather be a child nestled warmly under the cover, almost asleep, while my grandma reads to me: "Hey diddle diddle, the cat and the fiddle, the cow jumped over the moon, and the little dog laughed to see such sport, and the dish ran away with the spoon."

I have a million other things I could say about the sermon as a twice-told tale. But we don't have the space, or the time.

12

Preaching and the
Nod of Recognition

Preaching is the most complex and difficult subject I know. Sometimes I began my preaching classes by trying to get the students to understand how complex the subject matter is. And I create a situation such as this. A student sees a fellow student, a friend, and says, "Were you in Systematic Theology this morning?"

"No, I wasn't there this morning."

"You should have been there."

"Why, what happened?"

"Well, the professor lectured as usual for about forty minutes and then just suddenly for the last ten minutes began to preach."

And I said to my students, "What in your understanding was the nature of the shift?"

They began to talk about what made the shift. Some of the students say, "Well the professor started raising the volume of the voice."

Well, probably.

"The professor laid aside the notes–started speaking spontaneously, extemporaneously."

Possibly.

"The professor became more agitated . . . The professor became interested in the subject . . . The professor became more personal . . . The professor looked at us and wanted us to receive what was being said."

"Did you take more notes or fewer notes?"

"Fewer notes."

"Well, did the quality of the material go up or down?"

"Well, maybe down a bit."

"What really was the difference?"

One student says, "The Holy Spirit took over."

Well, possibly.

We talk about it for an hour and it's evident at the end of the hour that all of us in the room know what preaching is—it's equally evident that none of us knows what preaching is. It's a very complex matter. Part of the complexity, of course, is the subject of the Holy Spirit. I would not deny the Holy Spirit's involvement in preaching. The Holy Spirit is involved, but how?

It's a dangerous thing, if not heretical, to try to identify that part of preaching work that is done by the Holy Spirit. From the moment you identify what part belongs to the Holy Spirit, that part I cease to do. "Well, the Holy Spirit will do that." Any doctrine of the Holy Spirit that relieves me of any of my responsibility is false doctrine.

Part of the complexity of the subject of preaching has to do with a large body of fictions and prejudices that accumulate around preaching as they do around all human relationships and all communication. The common prejudice, for instance, that views the negative and critical as more honest than that which is positive. You have two students comment on the sermon and the evaluation. One student says, "I really appreciated what you said about Mark's view of the parables. That was helpful to me." Another student says, "I didn't get anything out of anything you said." Which one tends to receive more credit for being honest? Why this prejudice that if you're negative and cynical, you're honest, and frank, and going to the heart of the matter? Why is it that shadows are deep and sunshine is shallow? Why is it that a person has to be gloomy and melancholic in order to be profound? Well, it's a part of the prejudice.

Some of the complexity, of course, is related to the variables in the preaching situation. The listener brings so many variables that what we say and what is heard do not always coincide. Some time ago, I had dinner with a middle-aged couple whose first marriages had failed, and both had children by previous marriages. They had been married to each other about six months. I was a guest in their home. We were having dinner in the dining room. It was very nice, even had cloth napkins, sterling silverware, and stemware. Everything was beautiful. And I was enjoying the dinner very much. And then she said, "I don't like these forks." Now the forks were sterling and very ornate and beautiful, I thought. But it was of no matter to me. She could dislike her forks if she wanted to. But when she said, "I don't like these forks," he stopped eating, put his fork down, took his napkin out of his lap, and threw it in the plate, pushed his chair back, shoved it hard against the table, spilling the water, and left the house.

And there she and I sat. Well, being a "person of the cloth," I thought I should say something. I looked at my fork and I said, "They don't seem to be so bad." And she began to cry and said, "I don't know why in the world I said that, I don't know why in the world I said that, I'm so stupid to have said that." I said, "I don't understand." She said, "The only thing he brought to our marriage was a box of silverware, this silverware, which his previous wife had thrown in the yard after him when he left and said, 'And take your mother's damned silver with you!'" All of that was triggered by the word, "fork."

Now just think what you can create by saying an innocent little word like "fork." If you locate the Word of God on the lips, we know exactly what it is. If you locate the Word of God at the ear, who knows what it is?

It's extremely difficult to talk about preaching. Part of the difficulty is that preaching varies from place to place, time to time, group to group, because if there is anything true of preaching is that its effectiveness lies to a large measure in its fittingness, in its appropriateness. Whatever else you may say of the Word of God, however you may scaffold that term with scripture and theology, one thing is true of the Word of God: it fits. Therefore, it's difficult with the variety of context from which we come and to which we go to speak, to say something that applies to all of us because preaching has to fit. That's why the preacher par excellence in this country is the pastor, because the pastor is able to say the word that fits. Not visitors like me, but the pastor.

It's in the appropriateness where the power is. You can misquote not only by changing the words, but you can misquote by changing the listeners. And the same thing said here does not sound the same said there. It's difficult to talk about preaching. Part of the difficulty is that in talking about preaching, the assumption is that you're seeking to improve your capacity to preach. I think that's true and it's a worthy goal but it's not an unambiguous goal. Are you *sure* that you want to be an effective preacher? One of the most startling discoveries in some of my students just starting out is the sudden discovery that they can preach well. *Now* what do they do? Who wants that responsibility? That you actually can make a difference in somebody's life. Who wants to be responsible for the rising and the falling of many in Israel? To make a positive difference. Whoever turns on a light immediately creates shadows. Do you want to make that kind of difference? It's a frightening thing to discover that you can preach. And so we go to all the workshops and seminars to improve our preaching when one of the greatest temptations any of us will ever have is the temptation not to say *anything* while preaching, lest it make a difference.

And it is a temptation at the door following the service on a Sunday when someone comes out with something other than, "Enjoyed the sermon," when someone comes out and responds in such a way you know they were listening, it is a temptation, it is a temptation to take some of it back. "Well, I was just preaching, you know."

Preaching is a difficult subject to deal with because it involves the passion of the one who preaches. We don't preach ourselves. But we still must preach with passion.

There is a passion appropriate to the message. Anyone who preaches the gospel as though nothing were at stake—I mean laid back and cool—is the fundamental contradiction of the grossest kind. To preach the good news of the kingdom of God without passion? Unbelievable! But that does make talking about preaching different, very different, from preaching.

There are some ministers who believe that there is a sense of "professionalism" in the ministry that prohibits such intensity of spirit, such personal engagement with a message. I once had a student in a third-year New Testament Greek class. Since it was a third-year elective, the number had dwindled down to a precious few. I think there were seven in the group. It was springtime, and the class met at 1:00 in the afternoon, a terrible hour in the beauty of spring. This beautiful day in late March, the seven were gathering.

One of the students came in with tennis equipment: the racquet, the can of balls, the socks, the sneakers, the shirt, the shorts, all the same with the same little emblem and initials and all that. He was beautifully attired for tennis and sported a Greek New Testament. I resented it, of course. Everyone knows that anyone who comes into Greek class is supposed to come in with fear and trembling. He comes bouncing in, "Tennis, anyone?" ready to take a break and read a little Greek. I resented it so much that I said to myself, "I'll fix his wagon." So we were reading Romans. We had a difficult passage for the day. I said to him, "Please read."

He read and he translated it very well. I was very displeased. I thought, "I'll fix him," and I asked him then to identify and elaborate on the verb. There was at the heart of the passage in Romans, you recall, "I could almost wish myself to be damned for the sake of the Jew." You remember Paul's statement there. And that verb translated, "could almost wish," it's an imperfect, a strange form of imperfect. I said, "Identify that." He started telling us, "Some grammarians call it tangential imperfect, others call it inchoate imperfect . . . ," and he just went on and on and on like that. I grudgingly respected the excellent work of the tennis-attired Greek student.

We finished the class. The Greek-tennis student fetched his tennis racquet and the can of balls and was about to leave.

I stopped him and asked, "What did you think of that passage, about what Paul said?"

"What do you mean?"

"Well, what did you think of it? What did you think of Paul's comment, 'I could almost wish myself to be lost if it would save the Jew.'"

"I think that was very unprofessional. If you're in the ministry, you're a professional, and you should never get as personally involved as Paul was. See you later, Prof."

What do you think?

It's difficult to preach. It's difficult to talk about preaching but even so, I'll give it a shot. I want to say two things about preaching that will seem to be contradictory but they're not contradictory. I am referring to the "nod of recognition" and the "shock of recognition."

The first thing I want to say is this: preaching that is consistently effective generates in the listener a sense of recognition—a nod of recognition that is called in some traditions that nodding that produces an "Amen." Now recognition belongs to the larger world of memory. Retention is basic to memory. Some of that which is retained in the memory cannot be recovered. Some of it can be recovered with professional help; with free association handwriting, with psychoanalysis, with hypnosis. Sometimes we're able to dredge up from the unconscious that which otherwise could not be recovered and we actually do then say we remember. Some of that which we retain in the memory can be recovered in what we call "recall." Recall is that ability to recover what is remembered by bringing into the present what was previously experienced. It's absent now, but I can through recall bring previous experience into the present. That is recall. Recognition, however, is that recovery that works this way. It takes that which has been experienced and brought into the present and then I say, "I'm familiar with that." I'm not able to bring it into the present but once it is brought into the present, I then experience it as familiar. This is why some students prefer multiple-choice answers. If I can see different answers, "Oh, I recognize that's the right one." But if you ask me to recall it—that is, bring it out of the past—I can't recall it, but I can recognize it once it is there. Most of us are poor at recall, but most of us are good at recognition: That sense of being familiar in having previously experienced that which is brought to my attention. Consistently effective preaching creates a sense of recognition in the listener: "I have experienced that. I'm familiar with that. I *know* that."

In the theological sense, someone may pursue this. Well, maybe we have, as Rudolf Bultmann used to say, "a faint memory of Eden." Every one of us has some faint memory of who we really are; some recollection of Eden that goes with us all our days. That may be the way to develop the idea of recognition. Once I hear the gospel, it stirs in me that faint memory of Eden and who I really am as a child of God. And I recognize the gospel. It is my own conviction that when the gospel is preached, even people who are hearing it for the *very first time* recognize it, very similar to Luke's understanding of missionary preaching in the book of Acts. The missionaries went out and in chapter 14 of Acts when the missionary spoke the missionary tried to give the impression to the listener that this is not entirely new for God, that "he has not left himself without a witness in doing good—giving you rains from heaven and fruitful seasons, and filling you with food and your hearts with joy" (Acts 14:17). That is to say, there is some continuity between what I am saying to you and what you have already experienced.

As Paul said on Mars Hill in Athens,

> I know you have written over here "unknown god" but I want to talk about this unknown God. This unknown God is not totally unknown. Even your own pagan poets have said, "We are his offspring, in him we live and move and have our being," God is not very far from all of us that we might search after him, perhaps even to lay hold of God." (Acts 17:23, paraphrased)

What's Paul saying? I know what you have on your statue, *agnostos theos*, unknown god, but not really. Don't you recognize what I'm saying? But I don't want to deal with that. I don't want to talk about it in the theological sense of whether all of us have a recollection of Eden.

I want to talk about it in a more practical sense so that those to whom we preach, most of those to whom we preach, can recognize, need to recognize, and should recognize the message. If they don't, it's the fault of the preacher. When you go into a certain town, or city, or countryside to preach, you're not the first preacher who's been there. There've been many other preachers. There is already a Bible on the pulpit. There is already a church. There is already faith. These people have had banked up within them for years experiences of faith, and doubt, and righteousness, and sin. The confession of faith is their confession of faith. The confession of sin is their confession of sin. It's like a huge deposit banked up within them and the preacher who comes, writes checks on those deposits, and draws them out, and the people recognize that message and say, "Now what the preacher said this morning is exactly what I would have said if I were a preacher." It is a part of the power of preaching that the people are familiar with what we're saying. It is a mistake in preaching to try to disguise its familiarity. But that's a part of the preacher's ego—not to deal with the familiar. Somehow the familiar doesn't seem powerful, somehow the familiar is just a no-no and there is a veering away from what is familiar and a sense that the power of preaching is in its novelty: "I have to say something new, something different."

When I started out preaching at my first church, my goal every week was to find a text that they'd never heard a sermon on. And then develop it in such a way that they had never heard before. Every week, I was busy saying to myself, "I'll bet they've never heard this. This'll get them; I bet they've never heard this. They've never heard this one; they've never heard this one." And you know what, I was right. They complained to me later, "We've never heard that." You know what my problem was? My problem was believing the power in preaching was that it was brand new, that they'd never heard this. False. The power in the preaching is for the people to say, "Amen." And how can they say "Amen" if they've never heard it before?

And there I was, searching around on the dark side of Nahum for some obscure text, looking around in Leviticus to get a little clever something– and they have never heard this. And what I missed was the clear point that the best listeners are the most informed on the subject.

The more informed the listener, the better the listener. But that intimidated me. And so I would preach these "creative" sermons leaping off the pinnacle of the temple every Sunday and then I would fuss at the folks once in a while, "What's the matter with this church? I never get an Amen. I never get a nod." You know why I didn't get an Amen? It's the same thing many of us do–fuss at the people for not studying their Bible. You should know your Bible. Now how many of us would really be intimidated if we had a houseful of Bible scholars? Do we really want them to be informed? Not until we are confident that the more informed listener is the better listener and the power is in expressing for the church–not just *to* the church but *for* the church–the gospel. Preaching, therefore, is the first cousin to a pastoral prayer. It speaks for the people as well as to the people. I don't mean to say what the people want to hear. I'm saying what the people want to *say*. If I were a preacher, that's what I would say. That's what the church believes. That's what the church stands for, that's what the church is all about. That's right. Amen. You said it. That's true. Now there's the power–to speak *for* the church, not just *to* the church. So there I was in my young ministry competing with all my predecessors, trying to outmaneuver them by being novel. "This church is a hundred years old, but I'll bet this is new." Fatal mistake! Not only was I competing with my predecessors, but I was competing with myself.

Picture a situation. You're a pastor in a county seat town–pretty nice church–fairly busy, eighteen miles out at the far edge of the county is a church, small church. They have irregular preaching, once every month. They come in and say, "Will you come out and preach four or five nights for us? We'll have a revival. We always have a little revival in August. You say, "Well, I can drive out there at night, I can do my own work during the day and drive out there at night if that's OK with you." "Well, we'd like to have you come in time for supper some night." "OK." So when the time comes you reach into the file and get four or five of your better sermons, go out there, and just have a great time. They love it, the singing is good, you enjoy it, and everything is going great. Thursday night, just before you are to preach, some latecomers come in, fill up two pews. They're from your congregation in town. Your first thought is, "They've heard this one. Now what am I going to do?" About two months ago you preached this back in town. What are you going to do? "Song leader, the singing is so good–let's sing another one." And while everyone is singing you're sitting there working on that sermon. You think the thing to do is to disguise it, to get it in a shape that they won't recognize; those nine people who came in and interrupted everything by being present just when I was having a good time. So the introduction is made the conclusion, and the conclusion is made the introduction, and the middle part is garbled a bit. You preach in a sweat–miserable. The folks from your congregation who came out to say amen can't say amen. Then they say on the way home, "Well, I guess our minister's tired or not feeling well. That's about as poor as I ever heard our preacher preach." And the folks that were enjoying your ministry in this little rural church say, "Well, this was our worst night, and we had visitors too."

Do you know what I just described? I've just described a fatal accident; a minister competing with himself and tripping over ego. That's all it is. My, what good listeners those nine would have been if they could have recognized it. So they could say, "Amen, that's right, that's right." There's nothing so exciting and thrilling as learning what you already know. And they weren't given the chance. You listen to young people talk about music. They listen and they listen to the same songs, just listen and listen; after eighteen times they come out say, "I'll take it." "Why do you want it, you've already heard it." "That's *why* I want it."

It is a mistake for me to assume that the familiar ground is to be avoided. It is a part of the power of the preaching of the church for me to recognize that it is the preaching of the church, it is the preaching of the church from the scripture and from the church's faith. And I as the pastor am giving voice to that and the people are nodding and saying, "That's right, that's right, that's right."

Those portable outlines I mentioned in chapter 10, such as the prodigal son–his madness, his sadness, and his gladness–belong to the church. By the way, the last part is "he received the seal, he ate the veal, and he danced the reel." Now those were enjoyable because anybody in the congregation could share it. It's a cartoon in a way and I don't recommend this way to make everything fit. But there is something right at the heart of that, and that is, those sermons belong to the whole church and in the absence of a minister one of the most awkward of the elders or deacons could come up and share it. This is what the minister would say if the minister were here. How do you know? Because this is what the church believes. This is out of our Bible.

The young people come up from Sunday school class and they have these big pictures that they received in Sunday school class, and the picture is of Jesus and the woman at the well. And that morning they have studied John, chapter 4 in Sunday school and they come and sit near the front. Your text for the morning is John 4. Your sermon is on Jesus and the woman at the well. Does that bunch of kids bother you that they've just spent an hour with it? I would dare say that if you move right into the material, the best listeners in the room will be those young people, because they know it. They know it. That's our Sunday school lesson and they can't wait to talk to you outside and say, "We had that in Sunday school. We knew that story, that's found in the fourth chapter of John. We liked it." Marvelous!

People who knew exactly what you were saying will pay to you some of the highest compliments you will ever receive. I preached at a little church for one of the students. I preached on John 10, the good shepherd, "My sheep know me, I know the sheep. They don't follow strangers. They know my voice. They follow the good shepherd." Outside afterward a boy, about seven years old said, "I have something you can preach sometime."

"What do you want me to preach?"

"I have a dog and when we are all out playing ball, my dog goes out to play with us but when Momma calls us all to go home for supper, my dog doesn't go with the others, my dog always comes with me." He beat my sermon. That's a high compliment. He not only listened well but had the sense that preaching belongs to the church and I'm going to give something to the preacher to preach: good, because we all eat out of the same sack, we all partake of the same grace, we all share in the same message, and we all came out of the same fellowship. I came from the church. I go back to the church. And how stupid of me to disguise that fact with my clever stuff. The people, if the preaching is consistently effective, recognize the message and can say, "Amen." They are also able to recognize themselves in the message. To recognize themselves, they don't need a lot of help. They can do it immediately.

I was some time ago trying to explain or think of an analogy to illustrate the most marvelous rest. The best sleep there is in the world. I was trying to think of what is the best sleep in the world. And finally I said, "Well, it's like hearing the alarm go off and you look over at the clock, it's five minutes to eight and you say, "Oh, my goodness, I'll be late for class." You push off the alarm and run to the bathroom and get in there and just as you turn on the cold water to get yourself waked up you suddenly realize it is Saturday. You go back and the bed is still warm and you slip down in there and go back to sleep–best sleep in the world.

One of my students said, "Prof, but there'll be people to whom you're preaching that are not involved in schoolwork and so they can't identify with being late for class."

"What do you think I ought to do?"

"Well, when you're telling that when you shut off the alarm you say, 'Oh, my goodness, I'll be late for class, or for work, or for an appointment, or something.'"

Now the student had a very important point. And that is for everyone to be able to identify with the material. But the difficulty was the student was too imperialistic. The student wanted to do everybody's identifying for him or her. And therefore fix it so everybody could jump immediately into the story. And it made the story therefore unreal. Nobody ever shuts off the alarm and says, "Oh my goodness, I'll be late for class or work or an appointment or a doctor or. . . ." Nobody is late for all those things. If you just say, "Oh my goodness, I'll be late for class," everybody in the house can just change the word "class" to something else and completely find herself or himself in the story. If we trust the listener with the material, the listener will recognize "that is mine. That is mine."

It is amazing the hermeneutical leaps that can be made if we just trust them with the material; trust them with the text. It will take place. There was a young woman in one of my preaching classes who had no place to preach. She loved to preach; she preached pretty well but no church would have her–not even once on Sunday evening or anything. So she and three other students led worship services at a nursing home on Sunday afternoons.

One Sunday she asked me to attend and then give her some feedback. I joined about twelve or fifteen people in wheelchairs on a sunporch with plastic plants and stainless steel trays. She read Luke's account of Jesus and the little children. My initial reaction was, how inappropriate! To the elderly she reads a text about infants! After the reading she talked about Jesus' disciples wanting Jesus to tell the mothers to take away the children. "We're trying to build the kingdom here," they said. The preacher said, "I understand the disciples. Infants cannot teach, or lead, or sing, or contribute to the offering. In fact, they take the time and energy of those who otherwise contribute to the service. But Jesus said to leave them alone, let them share in the service, for these are the kingdom's children."

The elderly audience nodded their approval. The preacher was describing *them*! There was no need for the preacher to say, "Aren't we like those children today?" The nod of recognition was already there.

Trusting the listeners with the message can be consistently effective, generating in the listener a nod of recognition. Recognition of the message: "Yes, preacher, that's right, that's who we are, that's what we believe, and that's what God wants here." And the recognition of themselves in that message: "That's right, there I am; there I am."

Now, I know the problem. I know the question that this generates. Is that really enough? Is it really enough just to play the golden oldies? Everybody loves what they're familiar with: the familiar songs, the familiar text. Where is the edge? Where is the growth? Where's the new? Where's the prophetic indictment?

Good questions, very good questions. It is my conviction that buried within the nod of recognition is the shock of recognition. And without the nod of recognition, without the sense of familiarity, there will never be any shock–only anger, but no shock. Consistently effective preaching generates a nod of recognition. Within the nod of recognition is the shock of recognition. We'll talk about that in the next chapter.

13

Preaching and the Shock of Recognition

On a sabbatical from teaching one year, Nettie and I spent most of the time in a cottage in the Appalachian Mountains. It was a delightful time, but one Sunday morning, we were getting ready to go to a little church for worship in a nearby village when a brown wren had gotten in on the screened-in porch. Nettie, my wife, said, "You should get that wren off the porch. It's so frightened." It was flying from wall to wall hitting against the screen, so I propped the door open so the wren could go away, but it didn't. It flew against every side except where the door was. I tried to get around behind it to get it to go to the door and it would fly to the top and bang its wings against the side. Finally, I went inside, got a broom and went around behind it and finally got the wren to go outside. It went out the door, flew up in a tree nearby, and told a bunch of other birds that were up there, "Did you see that man with the broom trying to kill me?"

I think of that story whenever I'm trying to present the gospel and it is not clear. Effective preaching generates a nod of recognition, which is a feeling of familiarity, a sense of being at home. In the message I recognize the message as my message, what I have owned as a Christian from my Bible, in my church. I recognize within the message myself, identify myself in the story, and so I recognize what is being said and I can say "Amen." This nod of recognition is very important because for many people, their life is a disorienting experience. They have a sense of being not at home, not comfortable, and not familiar in a hostile world in disarrangement. It is one task of preaching to get the listeners to have some sense of order, and structure, and meaning, and familiarity in life.

In chapter 10, I mentioned Herman Melville's story of *The Enchanted Isles*.¹ The woman in that story was washed ashore after a shipwreck and discovered that she alone survived. The panic of having no one else on the island, of being with wild animals, calling out with nothing but an echo is absolutely frightening to death. Not knowing where she was, what would happen to her, how far to anything else. Totally alone. Her world was hostile and alien. She knew she had to get some order and structure, and you recall what she did: She got some sticks and she would put a notch in the stick every time there was a sunrise, and she would put a notch in a stick for every bird she saw. She put a notch in a stick every time she saw a turtle, she put a notch in a stick every time she saw turtle eggs, every cloud, every day, every sunrise, every sunset—notches, notches, notches. You know what she was doing? She was getting some order and some control in an otherwise totally disorienting experience.

If you were to preach to her, would you want to be cute and clever and say things that will "get her"? You want to give order, meaning, and structure, to give her a sense of recognizing something. You do not rearrange the furniture in the room of a disoriented person. You don't approach a funeral service by saying, "I think I'll experiment with a whole new clever type of funeral message." In this context, we make people feel at home; we preach creation, and providence, and restoration, and redemption so that the people to whom life has thrown so many curves can sit there and say, "I could sit here all day. I feel at home." I recognize that message, and the shape of the sermon, the form of the sermon is not full of curlicues and tricks. You see, the form of the sermon is very important for the form of faith and sometimes I want that form to be totally predictable. It's important to remember that a change of form is to the listener the equivalent of a change of content.

But the nod of recognition is not the sole task of preaching. If that were the sole task of preaching, the church would suffer from an excess of comfort. The church would be so relaxed and predictable there'd be no edge, no growth, nothing cutting, no prophetic intrusion, no shock—and so I hasten to say the rest of what I want to say.

Effective preaching carries in it and generates in the listener a shock of recognition. We all wish to create the shock in preaching, for people to be startled and see something afresh and anew. We all want that, but it's difficult. It's difficult because listening over and over to the same person on the same topic can create what psychologists call "negative adaptation." People grow accustomed to a voice. They grow accustomed to words. They grow accustomed to a place. They lose the capacity to see and hear.

For example, imagine a new clock that strikes at the top of the hour in just a horribly grating way. After a while you won't hear the clock anymore. It's negative adaptation. And creating a shock of recognition sometimes is difficult because people just get used to you, get used to the vocabulary, and get used to the setting.

Have you noticed the church tends to use the same words all the time? You can hear "love" thirty or forty times on any Sunday and finally the word just wears out. There are a lot of good words we just never use. They just don't seem appropriate for the sermon, such as "chinquapin." Did you use that word last Sunday? Or one of my favorites: "hypotenuse." It just doesn't seem to come up as frequently as "love." It is difficult to create a shock of recognition when we use the same words so often that we wear them out.

Part of the difficulty in creating shock of recognition is that people develop resistance to exhortations. Out of habit or frustration, some of us don't know what to do other than to turn up the volume and fill the air with "ought," "must," and "should." But those three words of exhortation aren't doing anything anymore. They're just ricocheting off the sanctuary walls and then falling down on the floor with the rest of the nouns that don't do anything. They join all the verbs that have quit working and all the adjectives just standing around with their hands in their pockets.

When we lived in Atlanta, I passed a used car lot on the way to work. They had cars for sale with the prices written on the windshields. One day I noticed on the windshield of a yellow Olds Cutlass Supreme the price of $300. After seeing the car there day after day with the $300 price, I stopped there and I said to the salesperson, "You've got a mistake on the windshield on the Cutlass Supreme. It says $300. I suppose you mean $3,000."

"No, $300 is correct," he said.

"How old is it?"

"Just a couple of years old, and just a few hundred miles on it."

"You're kidding!"

"No, it's yours for just $300."

"What's wrong with it?"

"Look at it for yourself."

I looked underneath. It still had that black, shiny coat underneath. I looked at the odometer–fewer than a thousand miles. No dents on the body. Upholstery good. I turned on the ignition switch. The engine roared to life just as powerful and smooth as you can imagine.

"What's wrong with it?" I asked again.

"Well, there's just one strange thing about this car," he said. "I can't explain it, but for some reason this car will not take you where you *want* to go. It will only take you where you *ought* to go."

I didn't buy it.

Would *you* buy it?

And yet we preach as though everybody in the house wants a car just like that–"ought" to go here, "ought" to go there. They don't want that car any more than you do. But in an effort to generate the shock of recognition, we try to sell the "ought-to" car and heap on more exhortation. It doesn't work.

Sometimes we try to overwhelm people with new things. I can appreciate this impatience. If I just do something different, we tell ourselves, we will get their attention. So we change the order of worship, put some balloons on the ceiling, and use a banjo instead of the organ some Sunday.

Now there is, of course, an understandable quality in the desire to get a shock. But overwhelming the senses doesn't do it. It just builds resistance, and hostility, and animosity. It's totally counterproductive. I encouraged students to understand that changing one variable is all that most people can handle at once. Not a bombardment of variables. For instance, when I was a guest in a pulpit and introduced as a professor in a seminary, those two variables were enough for the people to get accustomed to. To pile on top of that other variables is too much. I think it is sound and wise to say that if I were a woman going to a pulpit where they had never heard a woman preach, I think that in itself would be variable enough for a while. And then gradually add other variables but not just overwhelm to shock. That's not really what we want. We want to be *heard*. How is it achieved?

Sometimes it can be achieved by changing the form of the sermon. Instead of the usual structure, a narrative, a parable, something else. You remember, of course, that famous shift of form of Bob Funk and his discussion of parables called the shattered syllogism. The syllogism: all sinners are punished, Jim is a sinner, Jim is punished. The shattered syllogism: all sinners are punished, Jim is a sinner, Jim is forgiven. The shattering of the syllogism creates a new ear. Sometimes that is an effective way to do it.

This sounds extremely conservative, maybe, that a lot of marvelous things can happen in very familiar form. There are some forms for communication that are classic. And a thousand things can be done with the same form. "There was a certain king who was going on a journey and he called in a servant and said, 'I'm going away and I want you to . . .'" and then he entrusts some responsibility, or some prize, or something valuable with the servant and goes away and then comes back. Just think of all the things that can be done with that ancient form. There are children's stories:

> There was a certain king going on a journey and he called in his servant and said, "I have to be away and I want to leave with you my magic wand. As you know, if you make a wish and wave this wand it comes true but I don't want my wand to fall in the hands of wicked people, so I'm leaving it with you." And the king went away.

My, the children are waiting. Just think of the stories.

> There was a king who had to go on a journey and he called in a servant and said, "I have a new pet parrot that's now ready to learn to talk. While I'm away, I want you to teach my parrot to say

the things appropriate for a palace and for a king's listening." And he went away.

What you could do with that! Just think of all the things. Matthew loved that form. Just think of all the things that Matthew did with just one form, such as chapters 24 and 25. And the master went away and the servant said, "I don't think he's ever going to come back." In the middle of the night the master came back and the servants were carousing and beating on each other. They were punished. And the king went away to get married. Some of the attendants said, "He'll be back in a little while, just gone to get the bride." And it was later, and later, and later. About midnight the king came back but they were out of oil. The king went away and came back several times in disguise and they didn't recognize the king. And the king said, "I was here." "We didn't know that was you!" And the king said, "I was hungry, naked, in prison, a stranger, and alone." "But we didn't know that was you."

Just think of all the things done with one form. Ideally, the shock should come at the point of recognition—that is, in the very message over which I nod in agreement and familiarity. In that message comes the shock. In that very moment in which I nodded over the place in your sermon and said, "There I am. I recognize myself." There's the point of the shock. "Is that really me?" That's the best place for it to occur, and according to the scriptures, this is where it does occur. The shock of recognition is in the nod of recognition when we're dealing with that which the people have already owned as their own familiar territory.

In 2 Kings 23, there is the story of the reform of King Josiah. What was the basis of Josiah's reform? The refinding, the rediscovering, and rereading of the Law? Nothing new. Nobody came out with a clever new form and said, "You've all heard of the Ten Commandments and the Law of Moses. Well, I've got something new and relevant here. This is different from that old stuff. I mean, this is really good stuff. This is brand new stuff." No, no, no. They found the old stuff, and they read the old stuff, and they memorized in synagogue school, and they recited for hours. That was the basis of a reformation. The cutting edge was in the nod of recognition. "There's Moses again" comes the shock of recognition, and there is the Word of God.

"Jesus went," says Luke in chapter 4, "to his hometown where his friends and relatives were, and the Sabbath came." And Luke says, "Jesus always went to the services on the Sabbath." Very familiar, always there.

"How are you Jesus?"

"Fine."

"Good to see you again."

"You, too."

Time came for the reading of the scripture, Isaiah 61: "The Spirit of the Lord is upon me . . . to bring good news to the poor . . . year of the Lord's favor." Oh, how I love that passage, and he read it so well. And then says Luke, he told a couple of Bible stories. Any kid in the house could have told them. Elijah stories, everybody knew the Elijah stories. You know when Elijah was the prophet in Israel there were a lot of Israelites suffering from the famine–remember? Yeah, three-and-a-half years of famine. Oh, yeah. And who received the relief from God? A Lebanese woman. Well, yeah. Now, when Elijah was the prophet in Israel there were a lot of Israelites suffering from leprosy. Yeah, that's right, there were a lot of lepers. And who received the healing from God? A Syrian soldier. Well, yeah. Their favorite scripture, Isaiah 61, their favorite Bible stories they all knew them. Nod of recognition, that's our stuff.

Conclusion of service right after the benediction was the next line, "Kill preacher." They took him to the brow of the hill and tried to throw him over on the rocks beneath. Why? Because he told them what was in their Bible, what they already knew, what they recognized as their own, and to which they had a thousand times said, "Amen." If Jesus had come in with something he'd gotten somewhere else, they could have hit the parking lot after the service and said, "Probably went to school in California. I think next time we get a minister we'll get one from a different seminary. I don't know what's happening to our seminaries. What was that little book he had in the pulpit? I didn't recognize any of that stuff, did you?"

"No, that's a lot of new stuff, I don't know what they're coming out with nowadays. As far as I'm concerned, what we need to do is stick to the book. Let's stick to the Bible."

If Jesus had come out with stuff they'd never heard of, brand new from somewhere else, they could have shaken it off before they cranked up the chariots in the parking lot. They could have said, "I don't go for the new stuff." But what did he do? He read to them from their Bible. He told them their stories and while they were saying "Amen" they suddenly realized, "That is God's word."

For the shock of recognition to be effective, it must be in the nod of recognition. Otherwise, the shock is associated with the messenger and not with the message. When the problem is the preacher, the solution is simple: get a new preacher. Or quit going till this one leaves. But if it is in *my* book, in *my* faith, in *my* familiar ground, it is absolutely inescapable. Like giving a piece of cellophane tape to an infant, it just won't come loose.

What I'm urging, therefore, is that the shock of recognition comes in that material, which sometimes we handle so cavalierly. We call it the Bible. For the nod and shock of recognition to come, two things need to happen: One is that I neither caricature any of the stories nor lampoon any of the stories. For example, if I want the people to recognize themselves and then be shocked in that recognition that we, in many ways, are as the Pharisees, I can't picture the Pharisees as villains–eyebrows knit together, eagle-like noses, pinched faces, frozen smiles, glaring around every tree and every building, trying to trap Jesus—and then say, "Aren't we like the Pharisees today?" No, we're not. And the Pharisees criticized Jesus and said to his disciples, "Why does he eat with publicans and sinners?"

Now instead of the preacher getting in a hurry to make a point and say, "Aren't we like that today?" why not stay in the story and deal with it as it really is? Those Pharisees had a point. I don't know a parent in the country that hasn't said exactly the same thing: "Birds of a feather flock together." "You're judged by the company you keep." "Evil companions corrupt good morals." As a parent, I've been with the Pharisees much more often than I've been with Jesus. Some of the friends my kids brought home, my goodness! I start thinking of verses not from Jesus but from the Pharisees. Now once I get inside and see the logic, and the wisdom, and the sound conventional knowledge that says, "Evil companions corrupt the morals, birds of a feather flock together"—once I get inside of that and then let Jesus respond, the nod of recognition can become shock of recognition.

The second thing needed to create a shock of recognition is that I give the details. For some reason or another in much of the preaching we hear, the story isn't shared. There are passing references to it. A minister says, "Well, the point I'm trying to make is exactly what Mark made in the story of Jesus healing Bartimaeus" and then goes on. Now, who got anything out of that? The people who don't know the story got nothing, and those who do know the story didn't get to enjoy recognizing the story. Nobody got anything. The power is in the details. Many a marvelous passage receives a little bit of comment in the introduction of the sermon and then goes on, making a point. It's almost as if the preacher stays just long enough in the text to find a thread to preach on and then just leaves it. No, no, no. The recognition is in the details. That's where we live, in those details, not in "If you people will hold still for just a little Bible here, pretty soon we'll get to the interesting stuff. I want to tell you how my Aunt Myrtle fell out of the twelfth-story window and survived." And there are several minutes given over to the marvelous story of Aunt Myrtle's death-defying fall and thirty seconds referring to the text.

If there is to be a nod of recognition, if there is to be a shock of recognition, it comes in that material so that the message, and not the messenger, is the point of contact. Share the details. Stay in the story longer. Consider how Matthew 25 is commonly preached:

> The master called in three servants and to one he gave five talents, to one two talents, to one one talent. The one with five doubled it, the one with two doubled it, and the one with one buried it in the ground. Now aren't we like that today? We're afraid to venture anything, afraid to try anything, afraid to call, afraid to sing, afraid to teach, afraid to do anything. We ought to be bolder, we should not be afraid.

Now wait, wait, wait, wait. Stay and move inside that story awhile:

Don't you think the praise of those first two servants is a little hasty? The one with five made ten. How do you make ten out of five? You run the risk of losing five. How do you make four out of two? You run the risk of losing two. Is that wise? And it wasn't even their money! Can you believe it? It's almost like putting all five on red and spinning the roulette wheel. Now, one said, "Master, I knew you to be tough. You like to gather where you haven't hewn and harvest where you haven't sown. And I knew that, and my primary concern is, when you came back I will not have spent it, I will not have lost it, but you would have every penny of it just like you gave it to me and here it is, thank goodness." And the master said, "You wicked servant!"

Now if I stay inside the story long enough so that people experience that third person, recognizing themselves, there's the shock. But to get there, you need to stay inside of the story.

For another example, consider how Matthew 2 is usually presented:

In the days of Herod the King, wise men from the East came to Jerusalem saying, "Where is he that is born king of the Jews?" The wise men found Jesus and worshiped the king and being warned by God in a dream, they went home another way. Wise men always go home another way. We should be wise and find new ways to do church.

Now that's OK, but look a little more from the inside of the story. Have you read that story carefully? Do you realize what that story is? It's a Herod story. Notice the setup. In the days of Herod the king, wise men came to Jerusalem and said, "Where's the king?" Herod thinks, "Two kings?" And then follow six little stories of Herod:

1. Herod, the king
2. Herod, the troubled king
3. Herod, the deceiving king ("Go find this child and, when you find him, come back and tell me so I can worship him.")
4. Herod, the deceived king ("They went home another way.")
5. Herod, the vengeful king ("and he killed all the boy babies")
6. And then, Herod the dead king ("and when Herod was dead, the real king came back from Egypt")

Matthew tells six Herod-the-king stories and puts beside them the story of the *real* King.

Isn't that delightful? People everywhere cannot get enough of stories that challenge the establishment, and go against the king, and go against the pretenders, and go against the ones who think they have it all figured out. Matthew 2 is the whisper of Bethlehem over and against the shout of Jerusalem. Why should I just read it long enough to illustrate a point for my sermon and leave the rest of it lying there saying, "Hey, hey there's good stuff here." Linger longer within the story.

When you first read what may be a familiar text, people might be sitting there saying to themselves, "Well here we go again. I'm familiar with that." And sometimes preachers will go too fast to the familiar. For example, in sermons on John 15, preachers will often preach something like, "Jesus says, 'I am the vine; my father is the vine dresser. Every branch that bears no fruit, he cuts away; every branch that bears fruit, he prunes. I am the vine, you are the branches. Abide in me and I will abide in you.' Thus, we must all abide in Christ. We must abide in Christ. The important thing is, are we abiding in Christ?"

Granted, "abiding" is an important word in John. But notice what the text says: "I am the vine; my Father is the vine dresser." Do you know what vine dressers do? They walk into the field with that big crooked blade and start whacking. Some of the vine is cut away. Some of it is cut back. In the Greek, the difference between *cutting away to burn* and *cutting back to prune* is just the difference of a prepositional prefix. Now, if you're experiencing the knife of God, how do you know whether you're being punished or pruned for something better and more fruitful? How do you know?

What a powerful text. But you have to stay there long enough to sense that that church was experiencing the knife of God. God is the vine dresser, but what's happening to us—being killed in the name of God, thrown out of the synagogue? What did we do wrong? It may not be that you did anything wrong. You may be pruned, not punished. It takes a while to stay in the text long enough to get inside the reality of being pruned.

Or look at John 9: the blind man at the pool. Who sinned, this man or his parents? Neither, so that God may be glorified and Jesus put the clay in the spittle and sent him to the pool of Siloam. He went to the pool, washed, and he could see. Many sermons use this text to preach this basic sermon: "There's a lot of blindness in the world today. But I tell you the ointments of this world will not heal. Jesus heals blindness." Well, that's true. But get inside that text. Here is a man who's blind. Has been blind from birth. Without any request of his own, without any knowledge of who does it, without any knowledge of Jesus whatsoever, and without any statement of faith on his part, suddenly he finds himself able to see and his troubles begin. He thought he had trouble when he was blind. Now his real troubles begin. The neighbors don't believe him, his family says, "He's of age, don't bother us."

The clergy come around probing and, with nothing left but their anger, throw him out of the synagogue as an outcast. So Jesus comes into a person's life and that's when the troubles start. Finally, at the end of the story, Jesus comes back and vindicates the blind man, who then comes to faith. Isn't that a marvelous story? The first coming brings troubles into this world; the second coming brings vindication. People will see themselves and say, "Come to think of it, it's since I've been trying to follow Jesus Christ that I've had the hardest time. I've had the greatest difficulty, the greatest demands, and the greatest problems." That's true. I see that. I understand that. It's not true what people say: "If you just believe, everything is OK." When I started believing, it got worse. Ah, now I'm inside the story.

To linger in the story that is so familiar is to locate the strangeness in the familiar and the shock of recognition in the nod of recognition. And what I firmly believe to be true is that the people want to have that intruding shock. They want some word from outside of themselves. That doesn't seem like it sometimes when so many of the folks that we know–friends of ours, church people with us–express life as sort of like a visit to the spa: sitting in the sauna, reading pop psychology in little paperbacks on self-improvement.

But I know what many of them really want. They seem to be playing hide-and-seek. You played hide-and-seek as a child. The object was not to be found; but not really. If the game goes on, and goes on, and goes on, and you're not found, you know what you do–make a little noise, or stick out your foot, or stick out your hand, and then you get caught and you say, "Aw shucks, you found me!" Some of our friends that make their trips to the spa and sit in the sauna and read the paperbacks say, "Have you read this one lately on how to be your own best friend and help yourself look better and be marvelous and all like that with nothing?" While that seems to be the case, if you look into their lives carefully there's a foot out, there's a hand showing, and they want desperately to be found.

In the nod of recognition, "I've heard that story, I've heard that scripture, I've heard a lot of sermons on that text, here we go again," they want there to be the shock; the sense of strangeness in the familiar place. And it can be there. But it means to linger awhile in the text, to walk all the way with them from Jerusalem to Emmaus.

Walk the whole seven miles and I can almost guarantee that when you get to Emmaus, they will say, "Did not our hearts burn within us when she opened up the scripture?"

14

Preaching the Same Sermon
Every Week

I want to talk to you about preaching the same text every Sunday. Now, when I say that is my topic, I don't mean to be resurrecting an ancient practice that you may have read about, and that is, how many sermons can you preach on the same text? That was a kind of homiletical game in the ancient church, and you'd have somebody preach on one verse from one of the psalms–fifty sermons. Another preacher would hear about that and try to preach sixty sermons on the same text. They would preach on letters, parts of words, sounds, and minutia. I'm not talking about that.

I don't wish to resurrect the ancient argument about "a canon within the canon." To focus on the text that is within the larger cannon because in a practical, functional sense, I think most of us gravitate to a certain quarter of scripture and do most of our preaching there. I recall in seminary doing an evaluation of the sermons that remained upon the retirement of a minister who had preached for forty-six years. And of the sixty-six books of the Bible as texts for his sermons, twenty-two of the books had been used over forty-six years. Now I'm sure he did not deliberately say, "Well there is the canon, but *this* is my canon." There is a tendency to gravitate to one quarter of the Bible. If you like the gospel of John, they get a lot of the gospel of John. I don't intend to make a value judgment. It's just what happens. I don't mean to resurrect that argument.

I do not want to discuss with you the literary critical discussion that is involved in the phrase "surplus of meaning." The literary critical approach to scripture often uses that phrase. Every text has a surplus of meaning– never exhausted, always with another angle and perspective. There's more there than you actually see at one time, especially in a very complex text. I'm not getting into that literary angle.

I do not want to say that I think we should impose the same message on every text. This is the practice of getting around to what I was going to talk about regardless of the text. No, not that. And I certainly don't mean to be criticizing the listeners, the auditors of our sermons. You can preach the same text every Sunday and they won't know the difference because they're not paying attention anyway. I don't believe that. I have experienced too many cases of folks who resisted preaching. They wouldn't have resisted it if they didn't know what was going on, if they were not paying attention, because there are two kinds of preaching that people don't listen to: one is poor preaching and the other is good preaching. And you can understand why, because if I submit myself as a listener to good preaching, it may actually change my life; change the way I earn my living, spend my money, relate to my family, and behave in the community. Do I want to have a radical makeover? It's like being asked to lie down on the operating table. What will I be like after the surgery?

I don't think it's true that people are not listening. There are people who will make you think they are not listening. There are people who try not to listen, rolling up papers, making grocery lists, texting. All of those are efforts to resist the Word, of course. But I think it is wise in our preaching to just turn the gospel loose, and let it go, and realize that the listener is as interested in the topic as we are.

I suggest it makes a big difference in the ambience, the mood, and the tune of our preaching what we assume about the listener. I assume that everybody in the house is keenly interested in the text and the subject of the day. Somebody may not be. I'm telling you what I assume. If I assume they're not, I begin to have negative thoughts and I begin to use the pulpit as a barricade over which I throw hand grenades that'll "get 'em." That's terribly destructive.

What I mean by preaching the same sermon every week is simply to ask you to reflect on this simple notion. There is a text of scripture that is so central to your theology and to your beliefs, so life-giving in its nature, so pregnant with meaning that all of your preaching flows out of that text and the implications of that text for your life and work. I propose that you identify that one distilled truth—just one brief text—one distilled truth out of which every one of your sermons come. And by which every sermon is informed and disciplined and inspired.

Sages of every generation have blessed us by distilling life into just single expressions, single sentences, single affirmations, aphorisms, maxims, proverbs. When listeners hear the expression, they say, "That is it. That is what life is." I was reared in an oral culture. A lot of material, wisdom, information, misinformation, and folly were passed along orally. My mother would give me a proverb or a saying for practically everything. Whatever happened to me—fall out of a tree, get hit with a rock—she had a saying. Sayings such as, "it takes one to know one," "it's the bit dog that always hollers," "it's the creaking wheel that gets the grease," and on, and on, and on. She drove me nuts with those things.

Jesus used them. There are about 112 aphorisms from the lips of Jesus in the gospels. Here are some aphorisms you may have heard before:

"A prophet is not without honor except in his own country."
"Whatever you sow, that's what you'll reap."
"Do unto others as you would have them do to you."
"The girl who cannot dance thinks the band can't play."
"When smashing idols, save the pedestals—they'll be used again."
"Do not muzzle the ox when it treads out the grain."
"I saw them eating and immediately I knew who they were."
"There is staying in my going and there is going in my staying."
"A city set on a hill cannot be hidden."
"Never buy the hide off of a bear that's still in the woods."
"Do not cast your pearls before swine."
"If they do this when the wood is green what will they do when it is dry?"
"If you are bitter in your heart, sugar on your lips won't help."
"Whoever knows what is right to do and does not do it, to that person it is sin."
"Faith without works is dead."

I want you to think "distilled." Just the stain that's left in the bottom of the cup after you've boiled the water off. I'm talking about that little nugget that says, "That's it, that's it, that's it!" Now there is the risk of over-simplification, of course. But sometimes we're called on to state it, to say it. Although you'll spend the rest of the day, I should have said this, I should have said that, and I should have said this, but just say it. And he came up to Jesus and asked, "Rabbi, what is the greatest commandment?" We have beaucoup commandments, pages and pages of commandments. What is the greatest? "And Jesus said . . ." Sometimes you're just pressed to *say* it.

Paul did it when he wrote to the Romans in chapter 13. The whole law is summed up in this, "You shall love your neighbor as yourself" (Rom. 13:9). That's the whole shebang. Sometimes you just have to do it.

Now quite early in the life of the church this kind of activity was going on. Put it in some brief form. We have a lot of it in the New Testament and quite a bit outside of the New Testament. Take, for instance, in the pastoral letters first and second Timothy and Titus: there is a cluster of teachings called "Faithful Sayings." By their rhythm you know they're little memorized, concise, distilled summaries: "Faithful is the saying and worthy of all acceptance that Jesus Christ died for sinners." "Faithful is the saying and worthy of all acceptance if we died with him we shall live with him." That's it.

Paul did it with his Christology, his theology, and his soteriology. He sometimes would give us a little, clear statement. I think many of them are not his creation. I think he's quoting from the life of the church. Sometimes he said,

> I delivered to you what was delivered to me. I passed along the tradition that I got and gave it to you. This is the tradition I received. Christ died for our sins according to the scriptures, was buried, and on the third day was raised according to the scriptures.

That's the tradition. That's it. Any questions?

Sometimes you just do it, and Paul did it. Second Corinthians 8:9: "He was rich but became poor that by his poverty we might be rich." Rich, poor, poverty, rich. Second Corinthians 5:21: "He who knew no sin became sin that through him we might be the righteousness of God." Isn't that powerful? First Corinthians 8:6: "Yet for us there is one God, the Father, from whom are all things and for whom we exist, and one Lord, Jesus Christ, through whom are all things and through whom we exist." That's it. That's an audacious thing to do. Just say it. Most of us don't like it that briefly. "Well, some of the scholars say, but on the other hand, you know there's a lot of difference on this matter and I'm sorry we don't have time to. . . ." Would you just please say it for me? "Well no, I can't do that–I'm not sticking my neck out."

> Let the same mind be in you that was in Christ Jesus, who, though he was in the form of God, did not regard equality with God as something to be exploited, but emptied himself, taking the form of a slave, being born in human likeness. And being found in human form, he humbled himself and became obedient to the point of death–even death on a cross. Therefore God also highly exalted him and gave him the name that is above every name, so that at the name of Jesus every knee should bend, in heaven and on earth and under the earth, and every tongue should confess that Jesus Christ is Lord, to the glory of God the Father. (Phil. 2:5–11)

Any questions? That is it. I'm trying to get you to think just that way.

The values of such an exercise are many. It's easy to remember. And there's nothing wrong with somebody remembering something you said. And you will be much helped and encouraged when you go back to the church you had as a student or back to the church you had years ago. You're standing around, everybody's having lunch in the fellowship hall, and they're glad to see you and all that. And somebody comes up and says, "What was it now, twenty-two years–no, twenty-four years since you've been gone? Well, I remember something you said in that last sermon" and gives you a quote, an excerpt. You just said it. It's not that you're poetic; you just hit it right on the head. Another value of this discipline is that you have a lot of people listening to you who don't know how to put it into words. That's one reason they don't want to go calling on Tuesday night: "Everybody who can do some calling, please come out Tuesday night at 7:00 and we'll have prayer and go calling and come back then and have prayer again with some light refreshments." And out of your membership of 576, three show up on Tuesday night and everyone says, "I'll drive but you'll have to do the talking." "Well, I don't know. I'm not a good talker."

Well, nobody's a "good talker," including the minister, when it comes to the matters of God. I'm highly suspicious of a good talker. Whenever the words concerning God and Christ, salvation, cross, and resurrection slide smoothly from a tongue, I am immediately suspicious. But if the words come from way down deep and almost cannot be spoken, I will listen.

Folks don't know what to say when they invite others to church: "You'll like our church, you'll like our minister." "You'll like our choir; we've got a good choir." "You'll like our building, it's real nice." That's the best they can do. If you ask them to witness for Christ, they say, "Tell me what to say."

One reason some groups who are labeled "fundamentalist" do so well in witnessing is they're given something to say. Five steps to heaven or eight ways to hell or something like that. You know it's just memorized. And before we start feeling superior to them, think about how we sound: "Well on the one hand, it can be this way. And yet on the other hand, but it seems to me, of course, there are others who have this, you know." And we leave them in a twilight zone. That's why they go to your church on Sunday morning but they go to another kind of church during the week because they have to supplement their diet at another table.

I'm not speaking against what those churches teach them to recite. And I don't like rote recitations. All the same, could *we* please just say something clearly? And say with confidence: "*This* is it." And whenever people hear it, they'll say, "That's it!" One of the values that you can bring is to say the Word for wordless people.

I recall when my mother died in 1980. She died in the home of my sister, where she had lived for eight years. It was a most grievous thing for my sister. She was in the kitchen cleaning up dishes and fretting about what to do with the leftover food well-meaning people had given to her. They brought in all kinds of food and they put that piece of masking tape on the bottom of the dish that tells you whose dish it is.

She's doing all those dishes, and saying in exasperation, "What in the world are we going to do with all this food? Would it hurt their feelings if I gave some to the neighbors?" She's crying and fussing about it all. I went over to her and said, "Sister, it's time for sweeping up the heart, and putting love away." That's a line from a poem by Emily Dickinson.[1]

She looked at me and said, "What did you say?"

"It's time for sweeping up the heart, and putting love away."

She stopped and thought for a moment and then said with an expression of recognition, "Yes." That afternoon she must have voiced those words around the house at least a half-dozen times. That just sort of said "it" for her.

There are people in your congregation who crave to be able to say, "Now that's it, that's it. I just didn't have the words. I couldn't get it together, but that is it." To have this concise expression of truth is highly portable. Take it with you wherever you go. It gives coherence and consistency to what we do and say. It is healthy for you to reflect, "*Who* am I? *What* do I believe? And what am I *saying* in the pulpit? What text of scripture gathers it up and causes me to say, 'Now that's it. That is it'?" If your board of elders came to you tomorrow and said, "We want you to preach on one text for the rest of your ministry here," you would be able to say, "That's it. That's the text." What is the one text that you can put on your gravestone, the one that you preached on the rest of your life?

To help us focus on that, I would make two suggestions from scripture. First, if we were to ask Paul, "Paul, you wrote a lot of letters and I sort of agree with 2 Peter; there are many things in them that are difficult to understand. But would you tell us what is the heart of the matter? What is the center of it?" Paul's not here to give an answer. So I posed that question to Hendrikus Boers, my former colleague, who was a professor of New Testament at Emory. Boers taught Paul's letters in seminary and graduate school for thirty-five years.

"Hendrik," I asked, "What verse in all of Paul's letters is the heart of the matter?"

He acted like he expected me to ask it, because he had such a ready answer. He said, "Romans 2:11, 'God shows no partiality.'"

Hendrik explained that was the heart of it for Paul because that was where his struggle was. Before he became a Christian, that was his struggle. During his persecution of the church, that was his struggle.

"Do you mean to say there's no distinction between Jew and Greek? What's the point of being a Jew? Being the people of God? Going across the desert? Being mistreated and stomped on like a bunch of frogs? Having your gabardine spat upon in every city where you live? And then you come to the end of that and here comes Jesus and somebody stretches out the arms and says, 'There's no difference.' No sirree."

According to Hendrik, and I agree in this matter with him, after Paul's conversion near Damascus, he didn't just immediately go preaching to all these Gentiles. He spent years working through what finally came to be his theme statement, the center of his understanding. With God, there is no partiality; or as the New International Version translates Romans 2:11, "For God does not show favoritism." Now, once he came to clarity on that matter–however many years it took him, he then had the means for dealing with the issues that divided his time: Jew-Gentile. That was the ground for dealing with the next issue: male-female. That was the ground for dealing with the next issue: slave-free. And the next: rich-poor. And you read his letters and he is working out the practical implications at the meal, at the Lord's supper, at the fellowship, in the mission, in the organization, in the worship of the church. He is working out what it means to say, "God shows no partiality."

I'll give a second example, this time from Luke. What would be the heart of the matter with Luke? I believe that the text on which Luke would preach every Sunday of his life is Acts 11:18: "Then God has given even to the Gentiles the repentance that leads to life." Luke uses "repent" and "repentance" more than all the other writers in the New Testament. Paul just says it five times in all of his letters. Luke says it all the time. For instance, when Matthew says, "For I have come to call not the righteous but sinners" (Mt. 9:13), Luke has it, "I have come to call not the righteous but sinners to repentance" (Lk. 5:32).

In the parable of the lost sheep, "there will be more joy in heaven over one sinner who repents" (Lk. 15:7). In the story of the lost coin, "there is joy in the presence of the angels of God over one sinner who repents" (Lk. 15:10). When Jesus was asked whether the eighteen people killed when the tower of Siloam fell were worse sinners than others that it fell on, he said, "No, I tell you; but unless you repent, you will all perish just as they did" (Lk. 13:5). And those Galileans who were slaughtered as an act of worship by the governor, "unless you repent, you will all perish as they did" (Lk. 13:5). Luke talks about repentance all the time and once the church was started, its very first sermon was, "Repent, and be baptized, every one of you" (Acts 2:38). When Paul went up on Mars Hill in Athens–to that marvelous monument, to the nobility of the human mind–and he stood up there among those statues and those people and said, "While God has overlooked the times of human ignorance, now he commands all people everywhere to repent" (Acts 17:30).

At the close of his gospel, Luke instructs, "repentance and forgiveness of sins is to be proclaimed in [Jesus'] name to all nations" (Lk. 24:47). Paul didn't put it that way. Luke put it that way–*repentance and forgiveness of sin.* And he says this is a gift of God (Acts 11:18). God has given the gift of repentance to all people for life. And it's very striking that Luke makes a point of saying this is not just for poor people but for wealthy people, too. He didn't have it in for the wealthy, but he had courage to tell them that when you die and all your furniture is piled out in the front yard, and strangers are crawling over it, and the auctioneer auctions it off for practically nothing, whose is it anyway? What's the point of your life? He just called for repentance–the educated as well as the ignorant, the rich as well as the poor.

Now we must not withhold the gift of God–repentance–from people who are doing well, thank you, and pick on the others. Luke was a good preacher. I recommend you read Luke—you know, if you get laid up with the measles or break a leg skiing. And Luke has a way with this message of repentance, of just puncturing all the falsities of life. If Luke were alive today, he would say, "This is what I preach: God has given the gift of repentance to all people for life."

I hope you can appreciate what focusing on a text does. Focusing on a text does not shrink anything; it enlarges things. It's not a case of saying, "Honey, I shrunk the text." That's not it. The more confined and focused your point, the more liberating and enlarging it is. You're in that marshy bog of general ideas when you preach in such a way as, "And as we all go forth today unto the victories for the kingdom in this contemporary society of our modern world in which we're living at the present age." As long as you're in that bog, there's nothing. But if you take that same amount of water that's just out there in that bog and put some *boundaries* to it, it becomes a river. And with that restraint is its freedom. With that restraint is its power. At the risk of oversimplification, if you can say, "*This* is what I preach," it will set you free. It sets you free for gathering other material. It's almost magnetic; it just gathers things. And the method by which you preach it, it's just free. Your sense of humor is set free, your imagination is set free, and your tongue is set free. It's knowing what you're talking about and believing it's important. And then you're free.

Aristotle said, "If you have a point of great importance and passion, spend some time lingering." You don't have to go whammy all the time. Linger. In the sixteenth and seventeenth centuries in England, many people spent Sunday afternoons under their umbrellas as they walked in the country. They called it "marveling." We're going to go marveling this afternoon. Would you like to go? Listening to you preach could just be going marveling. You're not chasing rabbits. You're not wasting time. You know exactly where you're going. That's why you can linger, and loiter, and marvel.

Great authors know how to linger. How does *The Adventures of Pinocchio* start? The storyteller says, "Centuries ago there lived—'A king!' My little readers will say immediately. No, children, you are mistaken. Once upon a time there was a piece of wood." Isn't that marvelous?

I was interested in what Charles Kuralt said in response to a reporter's question about Kuralt's work on the Lewis and Clark expedition. Kuralt was engaged at the time of his death in research on the Lewis and Clark expedition to the northwest. He lamented that the American people didn't know much about something so important. So he was researching it. The reporter asked Kuralt if he was writing a biography of Lewis and Clark. "No," said Kuralt. What he wanted to do was to write a poem that school-children would memorize so that it would pass into the consciousness of the American people.

What if that happened in our sermons? That our work just passed into the consciousness of the folks who listen? You know, there was a time when folks like you and I gathered like this and talked about "How else can we say the gospel? What other ways can we communicate it?" Around the turn of the last century, a lot of preachers decided to start writing Christian novels. The most famous one was by Charles M. Sheldon, *In His Steps: What Would Jesus Do?* But there were dozens and dozens written by people who didn't know how to write a story but they were absolutely captured by the idea "How can we get somebody to hear the Word?"

Now what about you? What about me? What really sets us free to do it is to have one clear message. If I don't have that, I'm just a wordsmith, a technical writer, and a speaker. I've given a lot of time to think about what my text is. What is the text that I preach on every Sunday?

If you'll allow me the freedom to change my mind, I'll tell you what it is right now. It is Luke 6:35b: "[God] is kind to the ungrateful and the wicked." That verse is most extraordinary and it sets me free because it identifies with both God and ourselves and sets before us what is required if we are to be like God. If you are ever in Cherry Log and talk to the folks who've listened to me preach in that little country church there and ask them, "What did Fred preach?" I hope they will say, "He preached that God is one who is kind to the ungrateful and even to the wicked."

15

Wanting Out

Some friends of ours had a son graduating from high school. We all went together to the commencement ceremony. The speaker used an "open door" as the governing image of his keynote. "Young people," he said, "you stand before an open door." It was a good speech, better than what we usually hear at commencements about "launching out on to the sea of life," "standing at the crossroads," "having your foot on the first rung of the ladder of success," and that sort of thing. The speaker talked about passing through the open door to economic security, higher education, a fulfilled life, and happiness.

The problem for me was that I knew some of the graduates and their families (or in some cases, lack of family). I knew that for some in that graduating class, the door was *not* open. They would not "pass through" the door to fulfillment, happiness, higher education, and economic security. They might *crash* through that door someday. But for them it was, at least temporarily, closed. And it was a bit depressing to me because that speech had such a lilt and lightheartedness to it.

A closed door is depressing. The only thing more depressing is to hear the closing of a door behind me, when I'm in and can't get out. To hear the slamming clang of the iron door and to know there is no exit and to be trapped there. I may have wanted in at one time; but now I want out.

No doubt persons have come to you for pastoral care and have told you, "I feel trapped." The person in a bad marriage: "I feel trapped in this marriage. When I consider the pros and cons, I suppose I should stay married and not get divorced. I have to think of the children. But our 'marriage' is nothing but a long period of painful toleration of each other and heavy, swollen silences and nothing to say. I feel trapped."

147

Or the person in a terrible job: "I hate my job, but I need the money. We're drowning in debt. I have to keep it. What am I going to do?"

Or the person afflicted by chronic disease: "I feel trapped in this wretched body, by this terrible disease. I have much to give, but I cannot 'go' because the body says 'no.' I'm trapped!"

Or the person living in unrelieved poverty: "My grandparents were poor, my parents are poor, I'm poor, and my children will be poor. There's no way out of this. We're trapped."

Some feel trapped in caring for a sick relative. Think of the number of people who get up in the morning and clean up for a person in the family who is still a child or a child again. They give care to all the basic needs of their relative and then go rushing off to work smelling like bleach. The caregiver rushes home at noon, not spending the lunch hour with friends but cleaning up, and fixing, and doing. And then back to work, returning in the evening for the same thing. And every once in a while the caregiver has the fanciful notion, "If she were to die, I would be free." This notion is immediately followed by heavy-as-lead guilt for even thinking such a terrible thing. "I love her, but I'm trapped."

I wonder whether anyone would come to you for pastoral care with the presented problem of, "I feel trapped in church. How do I get out of this?" Most churches have a lot of entrances, but no marked exits.

The book of Hebrews is a word of consolation, delivered by somebody unknown to persons unknown who were leaving the church. For reasons sometimes clear, sometimes not, they're leaving and have left the building for the parking lot. The writer of the epistle is a preacher and he preaches this one last sermon from the parking lot. He goes out to the parking lot and just as they're moving away, he climbs up on a stump and cries out, "One last time, let me plead with you."

And in the parking lot with the departing congregation he cajoles, he begs, he threatens, he teaches, and he warns:

> If you're looking for somebody greater than Christ, there isn't anyone. Not Moses nor Joshua. He's above them all, the one unique son of God. What are you looking for? He's the only one. I know you've suffered; we've all suffered. But you haven't suffered yet to the shedding of blood. Pull yourselves together. If you wouldn't quit your assembly, if you'd attend more regularly, you could encourage each other and we'd have more lifting up of our weakened knees and our failing hands. Come on, people, don't you remember what we've been through? We've worked together, prayed together, shared together. I want to warn you. Think about Esau. Esau sold his birthright for a mess of pottage, and afterward he sought to get it and it was refused him though he sought it with tears. Once you have tasted the Word of God and the fresh breezes

of salvation and entered into the very presence of glory; once you have received the Holy Spirit, seen the goodness of the life to come, and shared in the richest fellowship on Earth; once you've had all that, if you walk away, there is no second repentance. You cannot come back. I know you're not that far yet, but I want to warn you; now come on back, let's get it going again. We can do it! Remember the heroes, Abraham and Sarah, Isaac and Rebecca, Jacob and Rachel, and all those who suffered, and waited, and longed just to have what you have. Don't go.

Hebrews is a sad sermon in some ways. It reminds us that churches don't have very good exiting ceremonies. It's hard to leave the church. In fact, you *can't* leave my church's roll. Even if you move to California, we keep you on the roll. All right, you're not in service every Sunday; we still keep you on the roll. In our church we discovered recently even *dying* doesn't get you off the roll. We had a new minister come in and took on the painful assignment of cleaning up the church roll. We thought we had a little over nine hundred members. Now the new minister says we have almost seven hundred members. What right does the new minister have to take them off the roll?

I've seen just one person "unjoin" a church. The congregation didn't know and the minister didn't know what was happening until it happened. We had no ritual or order of service for anybody to unjoin the church. She was in her late twenties. I knew her. She had been in my class once when I taught in the university. She was a very bright person and had been very active in our church. At the close of the service, there was a hymn of invitation to discipleship and she came down the aisle. Since she was an active member, I assumed she was rededicating her life to Christ.

She asked the minister if she could speak to the congregation and he thought she wanted to say a word of rededication. "Sure, go ahead," he said. She turned around to the congregation and said, "I'm turning it in. I want you to know it's not you people and it's not this church. It is Christianity. I have tried it. I have made every sincere effort, but I want you to know that with the same sincerity I joined here four years ago, I wish now to have my name removed from the roll of those who are called 'Christian.'" And she left. The minister stood there fumbling with his bulletin and the rest of us stood around in silence—we had absolutely no idea what to do.

There's just no exit, is there? The church has a hard time with Hebrews. About eighty or ninety years after Hebrews was written, the church had such a struggle with its harshness about no second repentance. The prevailing doctrine was, "If you leave, you can't come back. There's no second chance." And the church struggled with what to do with people who left and then wanted to come back. In an early Christian book called *The Shepherd of Hermas*, it warns that there can be but one postbaptismal repentance. The sense of it was, "You can leave and come back once but after that you can't leave and come back anymore." No exit, not even for ministers.

Have you spent any time looking for the exit for yourself as a minister? Some never do. They're perfectly happy, adjusted, and wonder what all the complaining is about. Other ministers don't spend any time looking for the exit because they never come all the way in. They sit near the door and put a little block in the doorway so it won't lock on them. They can get out any time because they never really come in. There are a lot of people like that. They do everything that way.

We had students come that way to seminary. They never "unpacked." They'd say things like, "You know, I didn't have to come to this seminary. I was accepted at another school. I could have gone to another school. This is not the only school. I could have gone to another school. I was accepted. I had a scholarship to another school. I could have gone—"

"Then why didn't you go to the other school?" I always wanted to ask, but never did.

Some people are that way about their marriages. "Well, I just keep a few things alive on the side in case this doesn't work out, you know." Many people are that way about their jobs. They don't get settled into dentistry or engineering jobs or anything else. They take those tests at those career guidance places. "Hey, I show good in math; what am I doing here?" "Hey, it shows I can really work with people—maybe I ought to do this other thing." Just sitting near the door, never really inside.

And some who come plunging all the way in, all dramatic, powerful, and righteous, even those people sometimes reach a point of looking for the exit. I didn't at first, though I created many problems for myself. I had no call to the ministry that was dramatic; I had no whammy experience. Nothing like John Wesley's, Martin Luther's, St. Augustine's, or Billy Sunday's. It was gradual and slow through the prayerful influence of my mother. I think that was it. But it was sincere.

I knew the language of commitment in my nonpermissive house. We weren't reared with any kind of it-is-OK attitude. We weren't allowed to set fire to the living room or anything like that. We knew that you could say, "Till death do us part" about anything and stick with it.

That was the language with which I gave myself to ministry. The first time I let it be known was at a Christian summer camp in my high school years. It was a beautiful closing of a week together, a very moving week. We were around a lake, everybody holding a little candle with a little piece of cardboard around it so you wouldn't burn your hand and say an ugly word during the consecration ceremony. As the service closed we sang, "Are Ye Able?" And as we sang that song, we had written a resolution on a piece of paper and laid it in a bowl at the foot of a cross that had been erected out by the lake. And then we went back to our room in silence, having taken a vow of silence until morning. It was a very moving thing. That night in the silence of my heart, I said "yes" to God and to the ministry.

As I laid on my bunk that night, I imagined the most impossible dreams for myself. We're talking 1948–49, and there was so much idealism afloat and I was thinking about that expression, "Give your life for Christ." I took that seriously and literally: "Give your life for Christ."

I pictured myself in the most impossible situations, giving my life for Christ against a gray wall facing a firing squad. "Will you deny Jesus Christ? If you will, you can live. If not, you shall be shot."

And I stood firm in my faith. "Ready, aim, fire!" My body slumped, the flags were lowered to half-mast, and the widows wept in the afternoon. A little marker was set up there and people came with their cameras and said, "Jimmy, stand over there and let's take a picture of where Fred Craddock gave his life for Christ."

I had all of these grandiose scenarios running through my mind. "Are you able to drink the cup?" I was asked. "Yes! I can drink the cup! Give me the cup–I can drink the cup!" "Are you able to give your life?" I was asked. "I absolutely will give my life!" I promised with all the earnest seriousness that you can imagine.

Away from the candles and the natural beauty of church camp, I went off to Bible college. When I came back during the Christmas break, the minister said, "We'd like for you to preach while you're home. We picked an opportune time for you–the Sunday after Christmas."

For the first time in my life I saw the inside of a pulpit. The outside of the pulpit was always so beautiful to me as a boy when I gazed at the carved wood and the Christian symbols and the tapestry. It filled me with awe and I imagined myself there someday. Then, at the appointed Sunday after Christmas, I noticed for the first time ever the *inside* of a pulpit. There was a piece of an angel's wing from the Christmas play, a glass of water with green scum floating at the top, an alarm clock, a bunch of old bulletins, and other papers; just a bunch of useless stuff! I remember wishing that I was still out there looking at the beautiful side of the pulpit.

I was soon to learn that the church that I loved, and to which I gave myself completely, can hurt me to the core. Congregations can devastate the minister. Sometimes they know, and sometimes they do not know, that they've hurt the minister with a deep-to-the-bone kind of hurt. And add to that the isolation, the loneliness of those remote churches, the economic privation, the impossibly low salaries while trying to start a family, and the price the family pays when they didn't ask for this life. It's tough.

"Are you able to drink the cup?"

I imagined drinking the cup in one dramatic, heroic "gulp." That never happened for me. Instead, I've sipped at that cup for over sixty years. A little drink at a time–nobody noticed. Nobody noticed because "drinking the cup" was grading papers, writing lectures, daily study, going to faculty committee meetings, and dealing with deans. Why didn't I get a chance to drink the cup for the entire world to see?

"Are you able to give your life?"

There has been no firing squad (yet), no writing of "one big check" of my life. Instead, I've been writing checks for $0.87, $1.12, and $2.50 of my life, giving away little nibbles of my life in church committees, Sunday school, teaching classes, lecturing about preaching, preaching, and studying.

Where's the exit?

And then prosperity came. By prosperity I mean I began to make a living wage. I was then overwhelmed with guilt because I had a theology for liberating all of that poverty and pain. I had laid it all at the foot of the cross. I identified with Jesus. But look here, we can pay our bills!

It never occurred to me that prosperity casts a shadow, too. Now what do I do with things going well? People said they liked the sermons and now I'm at risk of the sweet embrace of people who say, "Wow Fred, that's good stuff." And when I rose up on my hind legs and fussed at them some Sundays, they didn't listen. They just said, "Why don't you take a day off, Fred. You look tired." They wouldn't even let me be prophetic.

Where's the exit? Does anybody know where the exit is?

There have been so many times when ministering didn't come out like my dreams by the lake. Sometimes doing things for people is like releasing a caged bird in the name of liberty—and the cat eats it. It happens to almost every minister, especially those who actually care about people. For example, a marvelous young priest in Atlanta gathered up kids from the southwest side of the city, where life is just a grind. He got the money and the bus and he picked up those children from poverty and took them to see the pretty things in Atlanta. They went to Cathedral of St. Philip, they went to High Museum of Art, and they went to the Eastern Orthodox Church, which is a poem of light and color. And those kids spent a whole day looking at all of this cultural beauty and they had hamburgers on top of hamburgers. They laughed and had a wonderful time. When the day grew late, the priest gathered the kids on to the bus and took them home.

That night, a thirteen-year-old boy in the group set fire to his own house and the two next to it. But why? "I didn't know till today how ugly they were," he said. That result was obviously *not* the one the now less-idealistic priest had in mind. When your best efforts to love and care backfire, where's the exit?

There's a story in the second chapter of Matthew that says the vultures were circling over the shallow graves of children because of the terrible Herod and do you know what triggered it? Some men came into town and said, "Where is the King of the Jews? We have come to worship him." And by the time the sun set, mothers were weeping. That's not what they had in mind.

I have painfully learned that the moment I begin to love and to care, old hate is going to put on helmet and boots and come marching against me and charge me with what isn't true. That's just the way it is. I sympathize with people who say,

"I am willing to help, but I don't want to commit myself."

"I'm willing to give, but I won't make a pledge."

"I'll teach a Sunday school class, but only if a substitute will take care of it three Sundays a month. I don't want to get trapped in there."

"I'll serve on the committee, but I won't be chair."

"I'll attend, but I won't join. I don't want to be trapped."

"I'm willing to love, but I don't want to wear the ring."

Do you see what I mean? I don't want to get in there, and hear that iron clang behind me, and feel trapped. Like the youth sponsor who spent most of Saturday getting together nine dozen hot dogs, fourteen jars of mustard and catsup, and got the place decorated—and one teenager showed up. "I think I'm done as youth sponsor. You'll have to get somebody else." I can understand that.

I think about a nurse who worked very hard in school to earn the privilege of joining her honorable profession. She entered nursing with all the zeal, heart, and dedication of Florence Nightingale. Then she ends up on the ward of tubercular old men with one-half of one lung who tie sheets together to go out the window to a liquor store. She drags them off the hospital lawn to put them under oxygen lest they die. She works sixteen-hour shifts, has varicose veins as big as your thumb, and she's practically dead on her feet. She nurses them back to health so they can escape out of the window to go to a liquor store. She wants to quit every night. I don't blame her at all when she says, "Where's the exit?"

Somewhere between the dream and the reality falls the shadow. I look to the writer of Hebrews and ask, "What do you have to say to us?" And all he has to say is, "I warned you, if you leave you can't come back. Now please don't leave. We can still do this."

And so I looked elsewhere and I remembered Paul. If there was any-body I could not blame for looking for the exit, it was Paul. That church at Corinth, for instance. They fussed at him about everything. "You know," they said, "he's not one of the original twelve. He's not even number thir-teen. You can count the others—they're the apostles. And then there's . . . Paul."

Paul's response to that sort of thing was along the lines of "Believe me, I know I'm like one untimely born. I came last of all. But I have labored more abundantly than all of them."

"And Paul's not married, you know," they said. "Just exactly why is he not married? You know when Peter and John came to our church and they had their wives with them and it was all so nice and we went out to dinner. But that Paul is always by himself. Why is he not married?"

Paul's response? "I have just as much right to be married as anybody. I have chosen to be single to be able to give more of myself to Christ."

"He doesn't preach very well, that Paul," they said. "His body language is weak, and his boring monotone puts people to sleep. Do you remember when Apollos came and we held that preaching festival? Now that Apollos was a *preacher*. He could climb the silver stairs and leave it all as clear as dew. But here comes Paul and we can barely understand what he's talking about. He's not a very good preacher."

Paul's response? "You like somebody to boast about their preaching? I'll boast, but not about my preaching. I bear on my body the pain, suffering, and crucifixion of Jesus. I carry the death of Jesus in my body everywhere I go. Will that do? Is that boasting? Is that enough?"

"He doesn't even take a salary," they said. "Just where exactly does he get his money? What's he got going on the side?"

Paul's response? "Look, if I preach free of charge, that's my decision. But if I preach Christ, that's not my decision because I have to. Necessity is laid on me. I have to preach about Christ, people, I *have* to!"

Paul didn't look for the exit because he was firm in his belief: "I have to do it." Now, personally, I don't much like the expression "I have to do it." It makes me feel pressure and makes me feel like I'm supposed to feel guilty. I don't like it, but I'm beginning to like it. I'm beginning to like that expression because it looks like that might be the very key to his freedom— *inside* the ministry, *inside* the church, and *inside* the will of God. "This is my necessity," Paul said.

In other words, Paul didn't have to get up every morning and decide whether or not he was going to be a minister. It was a settled matter. That may be the key to his achievement. I don't know. I do know that people who *have to* do things get a lot more done than the rest of us. Someone who *has to* do something can really do a great deal.

There she was: a single mother with three little girls just as pretty, prim, and clean on the way to school every morning as anybody's. I happen to know she got $387 a month—that's all. I asked her, "How in the world do you make it on $387 a month with three little girls?" And she said, "If anybody had said to me that I'll have to do it on $387 a month, I'd have said that they were nuts. But you never know how much you can do until you have to."

When I went to see Frank in the hospital, he was wrapped like a mummy, burns all over his body, just his nose and eyes showing. "Frank, how do you stand the pain?" And he mumbles through that gauze, "If you had told me I would go through this I would have said I cannot. But you never know what you can do until you have to."

And you can go to some congregations that "church consultants" would have written off because they did not appear to have the right ingredients to achieve much of anything. They don't have anything. They're not big enough to do anything, and yet year, after year, after year, I marvel at them and wonder, "How in the world do you do this?" You never know what you can do until you have to.

As long as you get up every morning and think, "What shall I eat, and what shall I drink, and what shall I wear?" and wrap your minds around all of those luxurious options, nothing of much good is going to happen. But if you feel the *anache*, the sense of "I have to do this," it'll set you free and give you the one fundamental joy for which the human spirit is capable: a sense that your life amounts to something meaningful.

We have friends for whom I have such pity because they get up in the morning and say, "I'm kind of bored, what do you want to do today?"

"I don't know. Wanna go to the movies?"

"Nah, we've been to the movies a lot. Wanna go out to eat?"

"Not really. I don't know. What do you want to do?"

"Sometimes I like to go shopping when I'm kind of down. Wanna go shopping?"

That's their life day, after day, after day.

But not you. When you get up in the morning, the world is your parish. The needs are there, and they need you. And people ask you before you're clear-eyed, "Is there any word from God today?"

There's one prayer I pray every morning: "God, thank you for a way of life and for work that are more important than how I happen to feel about them on any given day."

I confess that I have spent some time looking for the exit. But when I reached for the door, I asked myself a question, "When you get outside— where are you going?"

16

Thirteen Ways to End a Sermon

There's an old joke about how preachers end a sermon. A child asked her father, "Daddy, what does it mean when the preacher says, 'And finally . . .'?" And the father says, "It doesn't mean a thing."

"Thirteen ways of ending a sermon" does not imply that a sermon should end thirteen times. The conclusion of a sermon should not be like pinning the tail on the donkey or saying, "I have my sermon now I just need a good way to wind it up." Each sermon should have only one clear and prepared ending.

A lot of good sermons take a nose dive at the end, which gives a clue that the sermon was probably prepared in the order in which it was delivered: introduction, body, and conclusion. Preparation time ran out so the conclusion didn't receive adequate attention. I urge you to prepare the ending first. The end of the sermon should be first in conception, even if the actual wording of it and framing of it comes later. In conception, I know exactly how this is going to end. I know what my purpose is. I know what my message is. Now how do I get there?

It's possible to have a false ending to a very good sermon. For example, I heard a sermon some years ago, when "Tie a Yellow Ribbon Round the Ol' Oak Tree" was popular. It was a good sermon, told from the viewpoint of a wayward child who had questions about whether there would be a welcome on returning home. The whole sermon dealt with the wayward-ness, the attraction toward home, the question of welcome, getting on the bus, turning the last corner, and going over the last hill and seeing a big tree near the house all covered with yellow ribbons.

It was well done, but the closing of the sermon went something like, "Therefore let us all be good stewards and let us be sure to tie the yellow ribbons on the old rugged cross." That ending destroyed the sermon, because the sermon was to be heard as a prodigal returning home. My best guess is that ending was tacked on as an exhortation that everybody ought to witness. The whole movement of the sermon was on that bus, topping the hill, turning a corner, seeing the yellow ribbons. Suddenly, we're jolted from riding on the bus with the prodigal to the ones tying yellow ribbons on the cross. After all of these years I still don't know what the point of that ending was.

Preaching is a contract between the preacher and the listener, and we want to honor that contract. And the contract is simple: that which is promised is delivered. The way the sermon begins is a promise to the listener that this is going somewhere–and then it actually does. Many sermons start well–enlightening, exciting, dramatic–but then just trickle out.

When a sermon trickles out, the contract with the listener is broken. When you deliver what is promised, that's good movement. But to deliver what was not promised is boring. There is no anticipation in the sermon. Here's the material dumped in your ear, on your lap, but it wasn't promised. The listener wasn't ready for it.

What makes us think our grandparents were such good cooks? Perhaps it was when we ate with them at their home, we saw the food being made, heard the food being prepared, and smelled the food as it cooked or baked. Our body was prepared to eat when the eating started. Maybe that's why I go sometimes to Waffle House. The food is made right in front of me. I smell and see what I'm going to eat. What is promised is delivered.

Sermons can be delivered but not promised. If you just start in and go without a promise of an ending, you are not asking the listener to get engaged. I would rather run ahead of you and be sitting on the porch before you get there. If that exercise is not built into the sermon, I have been cheated as a listener.

To deliver what has not been promised is boring. To promise what is not delivered is cruel. So the whole matter of the end of the sermon is related to the movement of the sermon, and the movement of the sermon should carry a sense of an ending.

I urge you to read Edgar Allan Poe's little essay titled "The Philosophy of Composition."[1] In it, he describes the way he wrote "The Raven." He knew where he was going; he had made some fundamental decisions, the experience he was going to provide the reader, and it was going to be based on several things: a dark night, a raven, and one single mysterious word uttered by the raven, "nevermore."

It is important for me to stay worried, I use that word carefully. Stay worried about leaving too much work for the listener to do, or doing too much of their work and insulting them in the process. Sometimes we press the sermon so far that it's like hitting the ball over the net and then running around and hitting it back and calling it a tennis match. Do I have the audacity to trust these people with the ball that's hit over the net? They may hit it back, they may miss it, or they may walk away. I can't stand that, so I run around and hit it back. "What I'm saying is . . . ," "What this means is . . . ," "What we ought to do is . . . ," and so on. Just leave it there.

The final preliminary remark I would make has to do with your own physical strength. My concern in later years is the amount of reservoir strength available for preaching. If you are not taking care of yourself, having rest on the day before and a good night's sleep, the end of the sermon will sound like you are winding down. You did not have adequate energy to sustain the sermon at the very end. And therefore regardless of how clever, or important, or theologically sound, or true, or good the ending was, it doesn't sound like it because you are tired. A lot of our difficulties in preaching can be traced back to the fact that we were tired.

Now, thirteen ways to end the sermon.

1. *End the sermon as it began.* Some very good sermons end as they began. For instance, you may have a passage of scripture that is your text. And you read it and then you deal with it, you question it, you punch on it, you pull something out of it, you wonder about it, you tease thoughts out of it, and then you come to the end and you read that text again. It's a different text now.

   One might split a story and have part of it, have a good bit of material about the matter in the middle and then come back to the rest of the story. Mark does that a good deal. Let me give an example from Mark 5. The ruler of the synagogue says, "Please come; my daughter is about dead." Next paragraph: And on the way there was a woman in the crowd who had an issue of blood: "If I could only touch the hem of his garment." There's a beautiful story, a powerful healing story on the way to the house of the ruler. Next paragraph: And when they came into the house, see how it's split apart. That's a remarkable thing, I'm not talking about doing it when you preach on that text; it is just an interesting and helpful way to frame a sermon. Let the end be as the beginning.

2. *End with a simple exhortation.* A good exhortation grows out of the fruit of the content of the sermon. The best example of this is the Letter to the Romans. For eleven chapters, Paul argues—tightly and strongly with all kinds of difficulty—justification by grace through faith. Then he gets to chapter 12 and says, "I appeal to you therefore, brothers and sisters, by the mercies of God, to present . . ." and here he goes, and the rest of Romans is exhortation.

   I once preached on Acts 2:37: what must I do to be saved? One of the troubles with my sermon was that in Acts, Peter had preached a sermon that stirred them to the point of asking, "What must I do to be saved?" And then he gave the answer. In my sermon, I gave the answer without stirring anybody to *ask* the question. I was giving what was not promised, and it was deadly dull and heavy in my mouth. It hit the floor with a thud just beyond the pulpit–it never made it to the first pew.

The preacher does not have to be the one who gives the exhortation. I began my ministry in a little church in Post Oak Springs, Roane County, Tennessee. I was not the preacher except in the absence of the preacher. I was the exhorter. I sat on the front row and listened to the sermon carefully. When he finished his sermon, he sat down. And I stood up and said, "In light of what we have heard today," and I gave the exhortation. This was a very common practice one hundred years ago. A lot of churches tested aspiring preachers by first giving them the role of exhorter. I had to listen *very* carefully to the sermon. Otherwise, there will be a sharp disconnect. But I mean seriously, you don't always have to be the one who gives the exhortation. In any event, let the exhortation have its own integrity and let the sermon have its own integrity.

3. *End with repetition and summary.* I very seldom do this but when I was a pastor, I did it with more frequency. I was a pastor during the civil rights struggles in Nashville, and we had terrible times. I came to the conclusion after about a year of that activity that the most redemptive thing that could be done was to discern the truth from the rumors. There was misinformation on top of rumor, upon suspicion, upon threat. What the most redemptive thing the pulpit can do in a community is to get at the truth. What are the facts in this situation?

There was one family in that church that did not take communion because the father in the family said, "We haven't had a week without sin, we're not worthy to take eucharist, we're not worthy, we're not worthy." What did they need? They didn't need a fist shaken at them or to get fussed at. But what is the text in 1 Corinthians 11–what does it actually say about worthy and worthily and all that?

What is the truth of the matter? And sometimes you want to preach a sermon in which your primary purpose is education. Here's the truth of the matter; this is what actually happened; you can do with it what you will, but this is what was said; this is what was done; this is who was there; this was the point of the meeting; this is where it was held; this is the truth. What you do with that is up to you. But it calls for teaching, naming the points of your argument, summarizing them, and repeating them at the end. It sounds very dull and very drab but sometimes that will be the most important thing, to just tell the truth. And your goal there is for them to hear it and to remember it.

4. *End with a choral response.* The moment after you finish your sermon the choir sings. Some ministers don't think very often about how the fabric of the worship service can be all of one piece: the sermon, the

music, the prayers, and so on. It takes a tiny amount of planning and communication for the preacher and music leader to coordinate the end of the sermon and the beginning of the choral response. It can be a powerful moment when the choir moves directly into some piece appropriately chosen to end the sermon, either in its content or in its ambience.

One time at Cherry Log, I worked with Richard, our choirmaster, to plan for the choir to sing two stanzas of a hymn just before I preached. And then when I preached, I sat down, and the choir sang the last stanza of that hymn: "Jesu, Jesu." But it was important that the choir stay seated, that there be no introduction on the piano, without the choirmaster being up front directing. It was as if the singing just came from somewhere.

I was once asked to officiate at a funeral for a fellow who had moved to this area, retired from playing in a New Orleans jazz band. He played the banjo all of his life. He had gotten old, fingers stiff, but he still loved the banjo and he had the members of his band around in Atlanta and Birmingham here and there when he died. I asked his widow if she could get in touch with the other members of his old band. Could they come and play? And I asked them to be at the funeral home, seated up near the casket, the casket was in front of the podium. And I said, "This is the last thing I will say in the eulogy, and the moment I say that I want you to play jazz." "Are you sure?" "Yes I'm sure." Widow said, "Great." The funeral director said, "What?" But I used the book of Revelation and I ended with "ten thousand harps–and one banjo." And they started playing "When the Saints Go Marching in." They just tore it up; people were standing and applauding. That was the only time I've heard applause at a funeral.

5. *End with an appropriate prayer.* End not with an ad lib prayer, not with a tossed-off prayer, but with a carefully prepared prayer. It will be pastoral; it will be thoughtful, maybe prophetic; and it will be appropriate to the sermon. The prayer will not add to the sermon; it is not just a way of shifting gears and still preaching. It will not repeat the sermon; it will not have new material. And certainly, it will not contain announcements. I mean a pastoral prayer that is short, well prepared, and carefully prepared. And when it is done, everybody will feel that was the only really appropriate way to end that sermon.

6. *End with an invitation to some decision or expression of faith or acknowledgment of some change in one's life.* In different traditions the accent is different. But some sort of opportunity for people to give visible evidence of response is made available. And it can be done in my opinion, most helpfully after a brief interlude after the sermon. But it can be, if carefully woven, a part of the sermon.

It's been my experience as a listener in churches that sometimes a minister prepares the sermon and may do this extremely well but does not prepare or participate in the preparation of the rest of the service. And so the fabric has a lot of holes in it. Sit down with the worship committee, the worship leader, the music master, or whoever and go through it carefully. There can be in the choosing of the end of the sermon, the choosing of the hymn, and the careful choosing of the words between, it can be all of one piece.

7. *End with a story.* Now you can be easily seduced here, because you hear a really good story at some convention from some speaker from Southern California and it wants to jump into your next sermon. It will not wear the harness or pull the plow—it just wants to run wild and free in your sermon. And you are working on the sermon for next Sunday, and that thing is standing up there on your desk saying, "Preach me; I'm a good one."

Isocrates said the first law of communication is appropriateness. Sermons *do* things as well as say things. Does *this* story do it? Does *this* story say it? What does it do? What does it say? Make sure the first law of communication is observed. The story should be appropriate in the sense that it gathers up the sense of, or the content of, or the experience, or mood of what the sermon did and said.

8. *End a sermon with silence.* In some of our services there's not any room for silence. We are just racing through, we are going to get out before the other churches do: "We will be out of here in a few minutes. Fasten your seatbelts we are starting church." Just some silence, some time for reflecting, it can precede the pastoral prayer, it can precede the sermon, it can follow the sermon. Just sit down and wait a little bit before anything else happens. Silence, not negative silence, not anxious silence, not awkward silence. "Did somebody forget something? We are usually racing along, so maybe somebody forgot to be here today?" No, no, no, no. You don't have to put a note in there that says, "Silence. I want to talk to you about silence, which we are observing when I get through talking, we are having silence." If you just sit down; you've been preaching and you are the only one up there, you sit down and sit still, it will take awhile for some people because they don't know what to do with it. They are accustomed to "multitasking"–they will be tempted to pop open their cell phones. It will take a while, but there are a lot of people who will welcome that silence. Silence gives them time to assimilate it, to accept it, to make it part of themselves. Just silence–unrushed silence.

The classic, dramatic, over-the-top example of messing up at the end of a sermon is when you go to gatherings and just go pour your heart out on this sermon, giving every ounce of energy, and prayer, and thought you have left and finishing in a sweat. And then the one

in charge gets up and says, "Thank you Fred. That was a good message. I've been handed a note that there is a blue Plymouth in the
parking lot, with North Carolina tag, and it has its lights on." It just
erases it. What happens after you get through talking is extremely
important. Just everybody be quiet.

9. *End with a question.* Asking a question is easy—asking the *correct* question is difficult. (Some people find it easy because they don't have to
answer their own question.) It needs to be appropriate to the message.
What question comes up through all of this, what is really the question
at the heart of the matter? You may repeat it, but please, ask no more
than one question. One question, you can say it different ways at different times, and end with that question, but it is just one question.
When I hear a whole bunch of questions in sermon, I suspect a lack
of preparation. "Don't you think we ought to be giving more to our
church?" "Don't you think we ought to be more faithful?" "Don't you
think we need to be having more prayer and Bible study?" In other
words, the preacher didn't know what single question to ask.

What one question do I want the listener to take seriously? It needs
to grow specifically out of the message. For example, I was preaching a sermon titled "Was It Just a Coincidence?" And from biblical
material I used the case of Alexander's and Rufus's father, according
to Mark 15:21–22, with Simon of Cyrene, who just happened to be in
Jerusalem that day, and happened to be standing near the street, and
happened to have been present when a Galilean being crucified fell
beneath the cross. And he just happened to be the one the soldiers
pressed into service. Was that a coincidence?

And I took a number of cases that could be explained reasonably
enough as coincidence. If there is not the possibility of something
being opposite of what you are saying, then what you are saying is not
valid. There has to be a "no" available for the "yes" to be valid. If you
can't explain something some other way, then God had nothing to do
with it. God is not coercing faith.

The way the sermon ended, I was in the home of a couple, a
middle-aged couple, and just visiting when I asked, "Where did you
meet?" And she said, "Well, we met in a hospital emergency room.
I got Friday nights off, I worked the first part of the week, but I had
Friday night off. But just before I was getting ready to go out for some
social event, the hospital called and said, 'The Friday-night emergency room nurse is ill. Can you come in?' And I objected, and I was
angry, and I went in to work her shift. During the night of that Friday-
night shift, Earl was brought in with a ruptured appendix, and I had
to attend to him. He was a very poor patient, but I tended to him."

Earl, trying to keep distance from his feelings, said, "Yeah if I hadn't been crippled up with that appendix she wouldn't have got me."

"We've been married forty-two years," she said.

"And it was on Friday night and it was not your shift and Earl was brought in with an appendix ruptured and you took care of him, now you have been married forty-two years?" I asked.

"Yes, that's right," she said.

I turned to Earl, and asked, "Earl was that a coincidence?"

Well Earl is not there. I'm not asking Earl. I'm asking people to think about the way they think about things that happen. Sometimes people want to say God's involved, but they think "maybe I'm surrounded by Philistines" and they'll laugh. Why not say it and take the gaff. No it's not a coincidence. So I just said, "Earl was that a coincidence?" and I sat down.

I've written on the early years of my call to preach, *Reflections on My Call to Preach: Connecting the Dots.*[2] There is just a lot of that in there I didn't even think about until I started looking back on it, reflecting on the people who were in my life at a certain time in life. If you put it all together it may constitute a call, but I still can't say with certainty if I've been called. I may go to my grave not knowing, but it doesn't have anything to do with what I do. There are a lot of uncalled preachers who do accidentally more than the rest of us do on purpose.

10. *End the sermon with a fractured syllogism.* You know what a syllogism is: major premise, minor premise, conclusion. All sinners are punished, Jim is a sinner, Jim is punished. Suppose you have a fractured syllogism. Your sermon is structured as a fractured syllogism. All sinners are punished, Jim is a sinner, Jim is forgiven. It has a little O'Henry quality to it but it's the gospel truth. All God's faithful are blessed, Mary is faithful, Mary is suffering. That's the way life is; that's why they called you to come and talk to them.

11. *End with a refrain.* This comes from singing hymns with refrains. Refrains are to help the congregation to participate. The song leader would be up lining out the stanza. And then there would be the refrain, such as, "This is my story, this is my song, praising my Savior all day long." By the time you go through it three or four times, everybody knows it. That's where everybody joins in: it's a refrain. It deepens it, makes you remember it, you will never get away from it, it is participation by the listener.

A refrain can be most powerful. Recall Shakespeare's play *Julius Caesar.* Caesar has been assassinated. One of the assassins is Marcus Brutus, a close friend of Caesar. Mark Antony gives the funeral oration, and he has a refrain. "Caesar did this, and this, and this for the Roman people. But Brutus says he was ambitious, and Brutus is an honorable man. Caesar did so and so, bought bread for the poor and parks for the children, and this, and this. But Brutus says he was ambitious, and Brutus is an honorable man." By the time he does that about five times, the crowd is just angry, just mad as boiled owls. They want to grab Brutus and kill him. Brutus escapes from Rome and is captured and killed near Philippi.

The use of the refrain is very common in the African American tradition of preaching to which I've been exposed. There was a pastor from California who spent a few days at the Craddock Center one summer, talking, preaching, and reflecting on work she was doing. Her father had been a Pentecostal preacher and a master of the refrain. For a long time she was embarrassed by the fact that her father was a Pentecostal revival tent preacher. She said, "He was master of the refrain."

I said, "Give me an example."

She said, "He had about twenty sermons. And they were all good sermons. But he preached on Samson: arrogant, strutting, demanding the women, making fun of people, breaking heads together, doing all kinds of stuff, robust, handsome, mean as a snake, happy go lucky, irresponsible, 'Daddy I want that woman for my wife.' 'But son, she is a Philistine.' 'Daddy. . . .' 'OK.' He was one of those guys—arrogant, striding through the world—who fell victim to a woman: a woman like many others that he himself had victimized. And his hair was cut off and he lost his strength. He was blinded, chained, and put to work at the grinding wheel making grain for the Philistines and people going by would laugh at the mighty Samson. Laugh at the fellow, 'Where's your strength now?' I won't go through the whole story of Samson. You know the story of Samson. But the refrain he used was a verse in Judges (16:22): 'But Samson's hair began to grow again.'" Thus in the story of Samson is the story of grace. His hair came back. (I envy him for that.)

But she recalled several of the sermons that had that quality, and in all of them, the refrain was a line from scripture. And that was woven into the sermon and ended with that refrain. And then came the call to receive the grace of God. That must have been a powerful thing. But the fact that he didn't have much formal education and preached under a brush arbor was an embarrassment to her. And now she is probably in her early sixties and wants to reclaim her father. She remembers twenty sermons. I've encouraged her to remember them carefully and write them. It was a beautiful example of a refrain. I try sometimes to have refrains, sometimes with a measure of success, sometimes not.

Or, take Tony Campolo. He had a speech titled, "It's Friday, but Sunday's Coming." "It's Friday, but Sunday's Coming," with an increasing participation in the audience on what that means, what that means, what that means, Easter. That is an obviously powerful use of a refrain.

12. *End with a broken sentence.* You can finish it with body language: the shrug of a shoulder, the thump of a table, and so on. You can say part of the sentence, "Ask and you will receive, seek and you will find, knock. . . ." You could do that at the end of a sermon and their lips would be moving, "And it shall be opened to you." And they are saying it, you are not saying it, they are saying it. But you've got to build to that point. I've been told that violinists can be sawing away and doing their thing, and just capturing every heart and mind and ear in the concert hall. And swooping with that bow and coming back with that bow, and they reach a point where they can go like that and not even touch the violin, and you swear you heard it. It's possible to preach that way, and they will come out and appreciate something, you didn't say it, they said it. They have to know you and know that you sometimes will expect that of them. Strangers can't do it too well. I have on occasion stopped at the end and not really planning to but realizing my emotions have reached the surface by saying, "I can't say the words. You know what they are." And I think they did. I hadn't planned to do it that way.

13. *Deliver just the first one-half of the sermon, and then let the people create the second half.* Now, that may be asking too much, but it was, in some times and places where I have lived, done with some effectiveness.

I had a seminary student some years ago whose name was Jack. Everyone called him "Crazy Jack." I didn't start it but it was just natural to call him that. He wore torn blue jeans with a red bandana tied around his knee.

I asked him once, "Jack what's with the bandana?"

He said, "Yeah, man."

It was customary for students to preach a "senior sermon" at a chapel service. When Crazy Jack became a senior, he was duly asked to preach a senior sermon. He read from Matthew 16: "You are Peter, and on this rock I will build my church, and the gates of Hades will not prevail against it" (Mt. 16:18). He said,

I think some of you met my brother when he visited me here. If you think I'm crazy, you should meet my brother. He came in to town once on a freight train from Elgin, Illinois. He loves hopping freight trains. He just has this thing about trains; he loves trains. He can tell you when the trains were started, how wide the gauge, how long the tracks, and what kind of fuel they use. He can tell you all about the development of the train, the building of the transcontinental railroad, and the driving of the last spike. He can tell you how the growth of the train was the growth of the country and how much it made from millions and millions of people. And how many millions of passengers rode the trains. The train was "it." My brother loves to tell that wonderful story of trains. But then he turns sad because trains are kind of out of favor now: weeds growing up in the tracks, tracks rusting, few passengers, seldom a freight train. He was almost in tears when he hopped a train and left town. He just has this thing about trains. Now me, I have this thing about the church.

And Crazy Jack sat down.

I remember the audience not being favorably impressed with Crazy Jack's senior sermon. Most of the faculty members just shook their heads as they left the chapel. But what Crazy Jack told about the story of the train from its beginning, to its grandeur and great success, and then decline. Now he expected the audience to take the word "church" and do the same thing.

Is this type of ending too much to ask? I don't think so. If an audience knows the speaker, trusts the speaker, the commitment and love of the speaker, they will do a lot of the work, if you give them the chance. The permission to finish the sermon is also a demand to finish the sermon. There will be a few who will later tell you, "You need to help me a little with that, I guess I wasn't listening too carefully." But it will be powerful.

One other example from my own experience; you may have heard it before. I was in western Canada to deliver lectures, and it was in October. I wrote the host, the head of religion department at the University of Winnipeg, "I haven't been in that part of the world in October, so how should I dress?"

"Well, bring a jacket and maybe pack a top coat; it can get chilly in October."

I gave the opening night lecture. During the night it snowed, and snowed. It snowed about a foot and a half. It snowed against the door so that I couldn't get out the door. The university cancelled the classes; the lecture was cancelled. My host called me and said, "Everything is cancelled. Even if you can get to the airport, I don't think there is any reason to because the planes are not flying." I mean, he cut me loose there in Winnipeg. But he said, "If you need something to eat, where you are staying they don't have any food. But you can go down the street. When you go out the door . . ."

I said, "I can't get the door open."

"Well somebody will help you. Turn right and go down to the next corner and turn right again and in the middle of the block is a little bus station restaurant. It's probably open."

I put on all the clothes that I had brought, totally inadequate. Finally, I got the door open, went outside walked through that deep snow down the street to the corner, turned right, again and there was that little depot restaurant and it was open. And everybody in western Canada was there. Finally some people at a booth said, "You can sit here." So I scooted in there with the strangers.

A big man with a greasy apron came over and said, "What for you?" And I said, "Can I see a menu?" He said, "We are serving soup." And I said, "Well I don't usually eat soup for breakfast." He said, "Do you want any soup?" And I said, "Soup is what I would like." He brought soup and put it in front of me, it was hot, but it looked the color of a mouse. I tasted a little bit of it and started reeling against the heavens and against Winnipeg and everything. I didn't know what I was going to do. People around me were eating that soup. The door blew open, and this woman came in with no head covering. She had on a ragged old coat, but there was snow in her hair. She was obviously a street person. She came in and somebody said, "You can sit here, lady." They scooted over and she got in there.

The big man in the big greasy apron came over and said, "What do you want?"

"A glass of water."

He said, "You have to be a paying customer."

She said, "I just want a glass of water."

"We are crowded in here lady; either buy something or get out."

"Well, can't I stay long enough to get warm?"

"You have to buy something or get out!"

So she stood up. And then strangely enough everybody else in the room also stood up and started heading for the door.

The man in the big greasy apron relented and said, "Wait, wait, wait. Everyone sit down. I'll give her some soup."

So everybody sat back down and started eating their soup. I started eating my soup. The woman started eating her soup.

"Who was that?" I asked the people who let me sit at their booth.

They said, "We don't have any idea, but if she ain't welcome, we ain't welcome."

So I ate the soup—and now it was pretty good soup. When I finished the soup it seemed to me that I'd had this before. It tasted familiar. Then it occurred to me, it tasted like bread and wine.

If I had continued talking, I'd have been stoned. It was time to quit, no matter how tempted I was to explain that I was referring to the eucharist.

Just leave it there.

17

The Habit of the Sermon

Nettie and I live in Cherry Log, Georgia. If you head out of town on Highway 515, you will go on past Blue Ridge, which is about six miles away. About five miles past Blue Ridge, still on 515, you intersect Highway 60. There is a red light there. Turn left there on Highway 60 and go through Mineral Bluff. Mineral Bluff is a small town; it has one right turn. That takes you toward Murphy and Andrews, North Carolina. Before you get to the North Carolina state line, turn off on a road to the right, there are some harvesting fields there, but then there is the mountain. Eric Rudolph hid out in that area. Stay on that road, but be aware that none of it is paved. Part of it is gravel and part of it is dirt. If you stay on it until the road ends, you will come to a cabin where the oldest person in the world lives. I didn't believe it either at first when I was told about him. But since I enjoy talking with old people and learning from their wisdom, I went to see him.

Like I said, he is the oldest person in the world. Out of courtesy, I didn't ask his age, but I did ask him some questions about creation. I was disappointed at what he said. I thought I would get glowing reports of the morning stars singing together and how wonderful it must have been.

"Oh no," he said. "It was an absolute mess."

I asked him to explain.

"Well, everything was happening for the first time and nothing knew what to do," he said. "We had birds walking everywhere they went. Rabbits tried to climb trees. I saw a robin try to lay her eggs and then try to build her nest. It was unbelievably frustrating. It tried to snow in July. There were no seasons. The real problem, you see, was that no habits had yet been formed. It was total chaos."

Order begets order—and order begets freedom.

A lot of stuff that passes for "freedom" is really just panic and fear. At the bird feeder at the back of our house, beautiful cardinals come to eat the food we put out there. The birds take a peck, look around, take a peck, look around, take a peck, and look around. They look for the cat, take a peck, look around for other birds competing for the food, take a peck, and look around for the cat again. Some people say, "Be free as a bird." But those birds would trade that "freedom" in a heartbeat for real freedom.

The reading of a novel is a delight for a lot of reasons. One reason is that it is a controlled experience. There is a focus on a few characters. There is a focus on one stream of life, and all the rest of everything is forgotten for a moment, and I get to concentrate on a delightful movement from chaos to resolution. It is controlled. I benefit from that control.

I am speaking in behalf of habit. Habit is our friend. Habit is necessary for life. And a very important piece to delivery of sermons is the formation of habit.

Unfortunately, some poor choices repeated often enough can turn into bad habits. These bad habits have tarnished the meaning and power of "habit." Since habit has suffered a bad reputation, it needs "character witnesses." I am representing myself as a character witness for habit.

I have no profound definition of habit. A habit is a well-established behavior that seems to be more or less automatic. That is when the freedom comes. I do not enjoy riding in a car with someone who is learning how to drive. "Now I will press the brake. Now I will turn the wheel. Now I will flip the turn signal." I am scared of getting into a wreck because the driver is consciously thinking about how to drive.

I don't want to be around people when they are in the "thoughtful" stage. I've never really done well at something until I've practiced so often that it was relegated to my spinal column and didn't require my head at all. I didn't have to "think" about it. That can sometimes seem to be a bit of a frightening experience. I have driven through on a highway where there is a string of towns and each one has a red light. After I have gone for a while I ask myself, "Did I stop for that last light? I don't remember stopping for those lights. Did I run those lights?" No, I did all right because I have gotten good enough at it that I have left my mind free to other things. I know there are some curbs on that but the state of "thoughtlessness" is when a person is free.

Habit is well established to the point of seeming to be automatic. How does habit become established? Two things establish it: repetition and satisfaction. Repetition alone won't do it. Going to church every Sunday won't form a habit unless there is some satisfaction. The two together create habit and habit is a wonderful thing.

For the last year and one-half of my teaching career at Candler, I suffered from Guillain-Barré syndrome, which is a paralysis. I was totally paralyzed from the waist down and partially paralyzed from the waist up. I have a residue of that disease that is spasmodic and uncertain in its coming and going, and I have a permanent residue of weariness in the legs. I don't preach both services anymore. I cannot stand that long. I live with that. But there is a come-and-go capacity in my hands. I was once able to sign my name without thinking about it; it was automatic. I still can sometimes sign my name automatically. But sometimes I have to think about it and then tell my hand to write the letters, "F-R-E-D."

It is disconcerting to have to think about what I shouldn't need to think about when the habit breaks down. Sometimes it is with the feet. I will be walking along when I will try to make two steps in a row with the left foot, which is not the correct way to walk. Some of you have noticed that. I was once on a little three-step footstool to cut a limb off a tree. When I started down, I stepped down on my left foot. Then, instead of going to my right foot, I stepped again with my left foot and fell to the ground. It was one of those moments when I had to say, "Now the right foot. Now the left foot." Ordinarily, it would have taken no thought. It is a breakdown of habit. It is such a waste of time. It's also a bit embarrassing when people ask me to autograph one of my books for them, and I am signing it like I don't remember my name. What is bothersome is that I have to give time and attention to what ought to be *automatic.*

Repetition and satisfaction form the habit. There are countless benefits to possessing habit. When my mind is free, so much of life is relegated to the spinal cord and I don't have to give it a thought. My mind is free to imagine, to think, to solve problems, to deal with all kinds of things that otherwise would tie up my thoughts and time.

I observed a lot of seminary students and ministers waste a whole lot of time just thinking about what they shouldn't think about. I know some pastors who are twenty or thirty years into their ministry and who are still every week thinking about when and where they are going to study for their sermon. They pick up some books, a pen and paper, and go into the dining room. After a little while, they migrate to the den, then maybe to the porch, then to their bedroom, all the while asking themselves, "Where can I find a good place to study?" They are making their head do work that has *nothing* to do with what they want to be doing. What they need to be doing is preparing sermons, but instead their minds are thinking about a place and a time to study. I would imagine many of us waste *years* of our lives with things we shouldn't even think about because they should be automatic.

Practicing habit sharply reduces the time required to do something. A good habit increases productivity. W. Somerset Maugham, the great British novelist, went to his typewriter every morning after breakfast. He wasn't wandering through the house wondering when the muse was going to visit him and inspire him to write. He went to that same chair, at that same desk, at that same old typewriter, and sat there. The motion of his body told the rest of his being, "You are at the typewriter, and you are a writer. Now write."

I had the same roommate during all four years of college. He spent so much of his time "lining up" when he tried to study. He would line up his pencils, and then line up his paper, and then line up his books. And then he would say, "I think I will go over to the library." I would see him an hour or two later with his stuff still looking around for a good place to study. He was a sharp, brilliant person. I am sure that he robbed himself of ten years of productivity because he never formed habit. To this day, he doesn't have a habit because he likes to be "free." In truth, he is held captive by his choice to refuse habit.

One of my habits is to write one page every day, six days a week. In the course of a year I write the equivalent of a book. I don't ever sit down and say, "I am going to write a book." Much of what I write never sees the light of day; it is not worth it. It doesn't fit in with anything. Still, I write one page a day.

Bishop William Cannon used to stop me in the hallway at Candler and ask, "You still writing your one page every day?"

"Yes, one page every day."

"Well, you must write a lot that way."

"Yeah, I write a lot that way. Just one page a day."

I write my one page in the evening. I always write in the evening, not the exact same time every evening because evening activities will throw my schedule off a bit. But before I go to bed, I have written one page.

One page of what? Well, sometimes it is pure malarkey. Sometimes I write about a conversation I had. Sometimes I will write one page about a biblical text that I am trying to understand. For example, I wrote one page about David running from Saul with his little band of soldiers. One day he looked across toward Bethlehem, which was his hometown and he thought about that well where he used to drink as a boy. He said, "Oh, if I had a drink of water from that well." His lieutenants jumped over each other to get a cup of water from that well for him. They went through enemy lines, got the cup of water, came back through enemy lines and handed it to him. And he poured it on the ground saying, "I cannot drink the blood of my friends." I was moved by that story. I wanted to claim it, own it, assimilate it, and I wrote it in a way that I could tell it.

Only one page; I never write two pages. It does *not* matter whether it has something to do with next Sunday's sermon. That's not the point. Just write one page.

There is nothing more uninspiring as a blank page. Write about how you went to the nursing home, you spoke to a woman going in and out of amnesia or dementia, or something like that. Don't romanticize it; just write it up. What did she say, what did you say, what did she say, and what did you say? Then put the page away. I just put it in a file of stuff. I am not organizing it. I am not doing anything with it. It may or may not appear in something written or spoken. That is not the point. I write one page every day. Sometimes out of those pages a book has come.

Disciplined habit is so extraordinarily fruitful. Sometimes a good habit will carry me along when my heart is not in my work. I have had people tell me that they go to church not particularly interested in being there. But it is Sunday morning and they go to church. There are silly people who ask, "What good is going to church out of habit?" Because that is the number one reason to go. And those who go out of habit often find they have unexpected extraordinary experiences.

Habits will carry me through the times when my heart is not in it. If you don't think those times will occur—well, you know better. This is an advantage of people who belong to liturgical churches. The regular order of worship does not depend on how many are there, or how they are feeling, or if there is a quorum, or anything else. This is the worship for the day. There are people who show up as dead as 4:00, but they go through the discipline of worship because it carries them.

I think of the women who attended to the body of Jesus. Luke says between the death of Jesus and their going to dress his body fell the Sabbath. They observed the Sabbath. After the Sabbath, they came to the tomb with spices. Now why did they wait? Because it was the Sabbath. Because the order of their lives had to stay fixed, especially when they had lost the one person most important to them. They did not go running around in chaos. They kept the routine of life. Friday evening at sundown, everything shut down, they began Sabbath prayers, Sabbath songs, the Sabbath foods, and the Sabbath gatherings. And that carried them to Easter morning. I think it was their survival. I think it was their preparation for the resurrection.

I once went to preach for a gathering of churches in Newton, North Carolina. I was housed in Abernathy Retirement Center. Newton had motels. There was a Holiday Inn right near to one of the churches, but they put me up in the retirement center. I was insulted, but kept quiet. When I went to the retirement center, I was introduced to the director, a very pleasant woman. She said, "Now, when you come for breakfast, please wait until the others are seated because they sit in the same place every time." Don't get in one of their places. They are trying to stay alive and stay sane. *Don't take those habits away.* This is why you do some people a real favor if your sermon has a flow to it that is highly predictable.

Highly predictable. Now, I may contradict myself in a moment. For now, please let it stand like it is. Church is one of the last places where people can go and not feel like they will be ambushed. Unfortunately, it is quite possible to go to church and feel ambushed.

I preached at a church in Louisville, Kentucky. The minister said, "You go in with the choir. I will be in shortly." I went in with the choir. I thought he was going to stay at the back and have a prayer or something.

He disappeared. After a few minutes, he raised a window from the outside. He then crawled through the window at the side of the sanctuary, wearing a robe, walked across in front of the table, and sat beside me. It was disconcerting. Afterward, I asked, "What's this coming in the window business?" He said, "These people come and sit in the same place every Sunday. I just wanted to shake them up." I know what he was *trying* to do, but he had no appreciation of the composing nature of daily habit.

New ministers frequently want to go in and change things up and put their stamp on things. Soon enough they find that they have opposition "always crossing my path and blocking what I am trying to do." You haven't respected their habits. Habits sustain a person through very difficult times.

Now, sometimes a habit is a problem. Someone says, "But I like to preach prophetic sermons. If it is highly predictable, same pattern, same flow, same style, then when can I be prophetic?" It is in that same flow and same style that you can be prophetic because if you come out wearing a Hawaiian shirt, and dancing a little jig, and reading something backward, and doing other kinds of cute stuff and you want to preach a prophetic sermon, they have burned up all of their "listening calories" trying to figure out what in the world you are doing. Do what you usually do and they will listen to that then all of a sudden, they've received a word of prophecy.

I am sometimes asked whether it is best to preach from the pulpit or not. In general, I am in favor of the habit of preaching from the pulpit, and I would need a very good reason for moving away from it, such as the church is remodeling their facilities. I'll go to conferences and there's some hot shot talking about how "I just take a handheld microphone or a lapel microphone and go back and forth and the people really like it." That is not a good enough reason. Ask yourself, "What really am I achieving by moving around?" I don't want to "burn" the extra calories as listeners watch me and observe me. It takes enough "calories" to see me in my familiar place.

Now, I know there are occasions when coming down to the front and just talking with the folk are quite appropriate. But to just be moving around for no apparent reason is wasteful burning of their listening energy. Remember that when you set foot into that pulpit, you are stepping into a place where a lot of important things have happened: memorable sermons were preached in which someone heard Christ and came down to the front to profess their faith and receive Christ. To discard that is to discard something important.

Jesus went to the synagogue as was his custom, his habit. And on the Sabbath, when he was in the synagogue at Nazareth, the attendant got the scroll, opened it to Isaiah, and handed it to Jesus. He read from the scroll and gave it back to the attendant (Lk. 4:16–30). "Wasn't that beautiful, what we have every Sunday? He is such a nice young man. His mother, brothers, and sisters are here. Didn't he read well?" Then Jesus said, "This scripture has been fulfilled today in your hearing." He got to talking with them and pretty soon they were as angry as boiled owls and they wanted to throw him over a cliff.

Within the habit is the freedom to be prophetic. If you use all your freedom showing how free you are there is no juice left for the prophetic sermon. Nobody is listening anymore. It is sophomoric. Even if the content is true, your actions are sophomoric.

Preaching with predictability has a positive pastoral care effect. It also can be the vehicle for preaching prophetically, so that when you do the prophetic thing, it will be genuinely prophetic and will not be couched in a lot of surprises and stunts.

I recommend a habit of reading good material. Those who have been my students know I urge you to read that which has *nothing* to do with the sermon next Sunday's or any Sunday. Just read good literature. I am going back and reading again right now Chaim Potok's *The Chosen*[1] and *The Promise*.[2] They are delightful. Potok is a very good writer, neat and clean and takes me into the world of rabbis and rabbinic schools. Reading Potok has nothing to do with any of my work, except the work that I need to do on me.

When I retired, I increased the habit of reading to thirty minutes in the evening. It used to be twenty. I don't read longer than thirty minutes, especially if the material is really interesting. When it is really interesting, I will be tempted to read longer. That is a mistake. Put your marker where it is really interesting. You will be eager to return to it the next evening.

The same is true for study. When you have a breaking moment of clarity in your study, take a break. Don't wait to break until you are weary and reach the point of diminishing returns. You will not want to come back to it because it was such a dismal pit you were in. If you break at the peak, you will want to get back to that study.

Some books are a duty, some a delight. Some are suggested. Some are urged. *The Life of Elder John Smith* by John A. Williams[3] was delayed for years. I don't know why. Maybe the small print. Finally I read it. "Raccoon" John Smith (as he came to be known) was a southern Appalachian Mountain preacher. He had very little education but had an extraordinary mind. He memorized much of the Bible. I am fascinated by him living back there in those mountains, trying to raise crops, tilling a garden, children dying in infancy. No matter what, he kept at it. He was German. His father was George Schmidt. They lived in an area where people didn't like Germans. George said, "From now on, your name is Smith." They were Germans, Pietists, became Baptists; thrown out by the Baptists, became Presbyterian; not allowed to preach, became this, became that. It is an old book, out of print. The covers are coming off my copy. I don't know why I hadn't read that before. I was told to read it by a woman in the mountains. I read it. Most of the books I read are recommended by other people or given to me. I like it when people give me books.

When we were in the Bahamas on a preaching mission, churches had lost their libraries, ministers had lost their libraries, but when I left they gave me a gift. They gave me a copy of the British Methodist hymnal. It is the copy that doesn't have the music, just the words. I read some of that every evening. It is poetry: the words, no tunes. I make up tunes and hum them. It is a delightful thing. Thirty minutes is tops in the evening.

I recommend a habit of study. I always say, "Find a time, find a place, and do it." Here is my habit, for what it is worth. Now that I have been retired for several years, this is my routine: I am through with my breakfast and preparing myself for the day at 7:30. I study from 7:30 until 9:00. An hour and one-half each morning has such cumulative effect. You know how much time of study that is in the course of a year? It really adds up. Sometimes we make the mistake of thinking that these little pieces aren't really any good. "When I really get a good stretch of time, I deserve a sabbatical, when I get three months, six months, I am really going to produce." Nah. Just a little bit. My father said to me once, "Son, if someone offers you a job of honest labor and will pay you for a day's work with a grain of corn with a promise that they will double your pay every day and you can work for them for three months, take the job. At the end of three months, you will be rich." A grain of corn, then two grains, then four grains, then eight grains, then sixteen grains. I am not getting anywhere, then all of a sudden I am rich with grains.

It is such a blessing to have habits of reading, study, and the discipline of the same place and at the same time. I never take a newspaper or magazine to study. When I hit that somewhat uncomfortable chair, my body says "study." I don't wait thirty seconds into it. No warm-up time, no exit time. That is it. At 9:00 a.m., I stop. Next day it is the same. Next day it is the same. It is that way for six days. That is my habit.

"Don't you have interruptions?" you might ask. Of course I have interruptions. But if I don't have a habit, I don't have interruptions. You are just hoping the phone will ring. Maybe you are hoping to have a funeral. It is just like following a pattern of preaching whether it is the lectionary or a schedule of preaching text that you have devised for yourself. Somebody says, "Doesn't something come up to cause you to need to vary from that schedule?" Of course. But it is the *varying* from the habit. If you don't have a habit and a schedule, there is nothing to vary from. If there is an interruption it has to be important enough, it has to be an emergency of such importance that it can scoot away the page that I wanted to write. But if I don't have anything on the page it is just like a vacuum and sucks it in.

I am saying what you already know. Still, I just keep running into so many ministers who struggle to make good use of their time, but seem allergic to habit. Habit is our friend. Those of you approaching graduation, those of you fresh in the parish, what do you do on Tuesday? You used to go to class on Tuesday, now what do you do? "Well, I hadn't really thought about it." Get some habits. You say, "But I am an evening person." OK, study from 10:30 to midnight, six evenings per week. If you establish the pattern and follow the discipline, it will set you free.

My family always knew it. My children, when they were young, knew it. When I got up out of the chair from studying I was free to play with the kids or go walking, help them to learn, ride a bike, or whatever. I was not studying; I was with the kids. When I was with the kids, I was not studying. When I was studying, I was not with the kids. How many of us defeat ourselves? When we can't play a game of tennis because we should be studying and we think, "I want to play a game of tennis." Neither one is done and neither one is enjoyed because of the absence of habit.

I think I have said "habit" at least twenty-seven times so far. I am not going to say it anymore; otherwise, I might get into the habit of saying it. When you experience repetition plus satisfaction, people will marvel at how much you accomplish.

"When did you do that? When did you get that done?"

"Well, from 7:30 to 9:00 every morning."

"Well, I read from 10:30 until 11:00 in the evening."

You know all of this. You probably want to talk about something else, because this sounds a lot like discipline. I guess that is what it is. That is the habit of the sermon. That is what sets you free to be playful. Some of you have noticed that I enjoy the playfulness of the sermon; I try to stay light on my feet. What gives me that lightness is that I have a disciplined pattern of study and incidentally, I know what I am talking about.

And that sets you free.

18

Once More with Feeling

I want to talk to you about emotion in preaching. It is a subject much neglected because it's complex to deal with. It involves ethics: "Am I manipulating people? Am I engineering their emotions? Is that Christian or un-Christian? Does the result justify the means for doing it?" Historically emotions were regarded as cheap, a characteristic of the unwashed masses. In this way of thinking, emotion certainly had no place among the educated and sophisticated elites.

Some have no access at all to their emotions; others have their emotions ready and available at the drop of a hat. Some are afraid of their emotions; some enjoy them freely.

What is emotion in preaching? Is emotion a matter of the relationship of the preacher to the subject matter? "How do I feel about it?" Is that even a factor to be considered? Dietrich Bonhoeffer started his academic career by teaching preaching. A young and confident Bonhoeffer argued that preachers should not be emotionally involved in their preparation or delivery of sermons; that there should be distance between the preacher and the sermon.

Dietrich Bonheoffer was obviously a quite different person after many years of resisting the Nazis and then being imprisoned by them. But he is not alone in his early idea that there is little to no relationship of the subject matter to the speaker.

I've met only one teacher of oratory in my life. Earl Oberg was a professor of oratory. He had retired when I met him. I went to see him present *A Christmas Carol* by Charles Dickens. He would walk out on stage without music, or decoration, or props and stand there. He was a short man with a face like Spencer Tracy. Yet when the welcoming applause ended and the house was hushed, he began, "Marley was dead: to begin with."[1] For the next two-and-a-half hours, he took the audience on an unforgettable journey through Dickens's classic. He traveled the world performing *A Christmas Carol.*

Oberg came out of retirement to give a lecture on oratory. I went to hear him. He talked about emotion. He said something to the effect of, "You should be able to project the emotion that is appropriate to the *material,* regardless of how you happen to feel about it. You might have a temperature of 102 degrees and be sicker than a dog. That is not the point. You convey the emotion that is appropriate to the material. You convey it in such a way that it is almost magic."

He demonstrated several different ways of projecting emotion that were absolutely fascinating. He said, for instance, "Some of you have seen me walking across the campus with my dog, Lonesome. I found the dog as a pup along the street. For thirteen years now, Lonesome walks with me everywhere. I walk early every morning across the campus. Every morning you will see us walking there." He paused and then said, "Well this morning . . . ," as his eyes welled up with tears and his chin began to quiver. We were all sitting there thinking, "Lonesome died." Then he said, "Gotcha!"

As preachers, we don't want to say, "Gotcha!" But Oberg's contention was that emotion registers the relationship appropriate to the subject matter, not the relationship of the speaker to the subject matter. As far as he was concerned, a very effective sermon could be printed and published and preached by someone who did not have any belief in God.

Some people believe emotion is the engagement between the speaker and the listeners–and the subject matter is irrelevant. There is such a relationship built up over the years between a preacher and a congregation that whatever we do tends to be well received. In this way of thinking, the preacher could read the phonebook in the pulpit and the listeners would love it, because they love the preacher. Whatever we do is "marvelous" because of the mutuality of loving relationship.

I received in the mail something like a "pastor's newsletter" although the person who puts it out has been retired since Moses. He told about a matter involving a classmate who had graduated from a small university in 1950s. He said,

> A friend of mine, long retired, decided to go back and visit the campus. While he was there the basketball team was scheduled to play a rival college, so he decided to go watch the game. During the basketball game the team was a little bit behind and the students began to cheer on the home team by yelling, "Forty-two! Forty-two! Forty-two! Forty-two!" The graduate of long ago talked to some of the students after the game. "Why were you yelling Forty-two! Forty-two! Forty-two?" he asked them. None of them

knew. They said, "They were doing it when we came here. We just keep doing it." The visitor, the alumnus from years ago, said, "I will tell you how it started. We had a student when I was here named Myers. He was just a farm boy. He played basketball and played well. But he was frequently on the bench. When the team got behind, the students would yell for him. He wore forty-two. The students would yell for him to come out. The coach would finally relent and let him play and that frequently turned the tide from defeat to victory. So every game if they were a little behind the students would yell, 'Forty-two! Forty-two! Forty-two!' and out would come this fellow named Myers and save the day." Fifty years later, the current students are yelling, "Forty-two! Forty-two! Forty-two!" and do not know why.

Preachers can forget why we do what we do. We have to think through whether or not we are suffering from compassion fatigue. And we should know the difference between compassion fatigue and whether we have grown cold toward God, or the ministry, or the pulpit. I need to know whether I have intense emotions or mild emotions. I need to know whether my environment or training has drained from me any show of emotion or whether it is available to me and useful and healthy. I should know how I feel about preaching on a certain Sunday morning when I don't want to at all.

A friend of mine had the good fortune of being a pastor of a church that did not like him. A special board meeting was called at 8:00 a.m. on a Palm Sunday. The cut palm branches were out, the kids were lining up to process into the sanctuary and to shout, "Hosanna!" In the special board meeting, the chair told the pastor, "Upon the request of the pastor-parish relations committee, we have to ask for your resignation." Hosanna. He had to preach two services that morning. He did. He told me he felt like a hypocrite preaching the sermon he had prepared. "I should have just told them how I felt," he told me.

It is not about how you feel—but it is how you feel. This is how I feel. I need to work through that. You need to work through that. I know ministers who every Sunday morning step out of domestic wreckage and preach the gospel of Jesus. Others step out of congregational chaos and conflict and preach the gospel of Jesus. How in the world is that possible? Well, it happens all the time.

As a Baptist minister down in Florida said, "Some Sundays I climb into the pulpit wearing iron shoes." When I feel that way, should I just say I don't feel like preaching today? I have prayed the same prayer every morning for the last thirty-five years, "Gracious God, I am grateful for work more important than how I happen to feel about it on any given day." That does not mean that I do not give thought to my emotion. I know emotions are very complex and capable of manipulation. Some of us can manufacture emotion.

I realize that we are not all in the same place with reference to levels or intensity of emotion. Nor are we all at the same place in the forms of its expression. Some people find preaching such a delight. I use the word delight in the Augustinian sense: that you do the other work of ministry just looking forward to Sunday. That marvelous moment when you have a conversation going with that congregation and Sunday is the highlight of your week.

For other people, the pulpit is a chore to be endured. They enjoy the counseling, or the administration, or the teaching, but not the pulpit.

There are ministers who would like to have a ministry without a pulpit. There are others who came charging into the ministry almost messianically. But that charge has faded away, is dying away, and is frighteningly absent. The days of wine and roses laugh and run away. Some of you dread such a day if it ever comes. Continuing to try to preach Easter as though you had a wild flower morning and a butterfly afternoon, when in truth you had neither.

Your emotions are extremely important. Some desire to have more passion for the pulpit. I hear a frequent lament of an absence of passion in the pulpit and I don't know why. No stirring of the heart and mind on the part of the minister. And your listener senses the absence of emotional engagement as you don't believe your own sermon, or you don't think it is important. That is the way it is telegraphed to the listener.

By underscoring emotion, I do not intend to minimize in any way the role of the intellect or volition or will. Most of us have been schooled in Paul Tillich's three distortions of the faith: emotionalism, intellectualism, and volitionalism. Some preach it as if it were constant activity, some as if it were a matter of thought, some as though it were a matter of feeling. All of these alone can be distortions and I do not want to get into that, although I am aware of it.

I recall reading about Oliver Wendell Holmes Jr., a justice of the United States Supreme Court, and the running argument he had with his father. His father was a medical doctor and a poet. Father and son argued often about "feeling." Oliver Wendell Holmes Sr. said to his son, "You don't feel anything about anything. You just study, reason, and draw your diagrams of reasoning and you come to a conclusion, but you don't *feel* anything."

"Father, isn't knowing just as good as feeling?"

"No, son, it isn't."

The poetic father and the logical son argued about this for years. They were both right, of course.

How one feels about a task is not the register of its effectiveness. We know that sometimes the most effective things we do in ministry will be done without enthusiasm. Sometimes we know the moment we finish preaching a sermon that it was a clunker. We feel like going around the rest of the week apologizing to everybody. And then someone calls and says, "I want you to know you touched me Sunday in a way you never had before. Thank you so much for that sermon."

We do not know how to evaluate ourselves effectively, so it is a waste of time to get into introverted and convoluted evaluations. Stop printing those little sheets to get everyone to evaluate your sermon so you can get a doctor of ministry degree from someplace. Just leave it alone.

In what follows I am going to assume a simple definition of emotion. Emotion is the body's response to value. As you may remember from Psychology 101, an emotion has five components:

1. *Perception of an emotive situation.* For example, a snake lying in the path where you are walking; a crying child standing in the middle of the street alone; an elderly couple walking down the sidewalk, holding hands; an expectant group of people with their faces turned upward toward your pulpit on Sunday morning; a green tent spread over a fresh grave. So the first step is to perceive an emotive situation.
2. *Involuntary internal changes.* Changes in the chemistry of your body, the blood begins to race, the heart beats faster, adrenaline is released, more sugar into the blood stream, electrical resistance of your skin. The body changes involuntarily, you don't tell your body to do it. It just does it immediately.
3. *Immediate overt behavior.* You freeze, you rush to the child, you scream, you smile, you weep.
4. *Feeling.* I want you to notice how far down the line feeling is in the five components of an emotion. If you try to change your feelings without changing what you consider an emotive situation, it is just artificial.
5. *Adjustment.* The body gets back in place; all the chemistry settles down, you are as you were.

If you have a prolonged period of lacking emotional engagement or investment in the pulpit, you have reason to be concerned. If you have cultivated a kind of indifference, you know how to make the heart a desert and then call it peace, to guard against pain or disappointment or vulnerability then your problem lies beyond homiletics itself.

I am going to make a few remarks about emotion, but I will not assume that any of you have reached the point of *acedia*–that is the Greek word for "I don't care." Acedia is that condition capable of taking over anybody's life, especially the lives of people who are capable. It can be when you are still young, it can be while you are at the peak of your power, it can be when everything is going your way and you are the envy of everybody else in the ministry. It is possible to lapse into, to fall into, and to be entrapped in acedia. "I really don't care." I think the best treatment about it is by

Kathleen Norris, *Acedia and Me.*[2] It is autobiographical, it is very probing, and in some places painful.

Starting in the fourth century with a monk named Evagrius, acedia was called the "demon of noontide," from Psalm 91:5–6, "the arrow that flies by day . . . the destruction that wastes at noonday." The Greek translation of destruction is "demon," the demon that comes at noon. Noon is the time when the sun is overhead and there is no shadow. I have the world by the tail. So why am I not interested in what I am doing? Some may know what I am talking about; others may fear it like the plague because it is a plague. And for the majority who are not in acedia, I hope you will use this material to process your feelings, and in doing so, use "preventive medicine" against that dreaded phenomenon.

Let me mention a few symptoms as persons may approach such a condition. Lack of energy: remember, emotion is basically a bodily function, so a lack of energy may signal a problem. Or a lack of interest even while I am telling everybody how important my work is: "I know it is important and life changing. I believe people are called to do the ministry. I think it is important, major work, but I am not interested in it." Whenever preaching is done for the purpose of getting solace for oneself rather than strength for the congregation, that is a bad signal. "I am asking for your support, your tears, your solace, your sympathy." Some have cultivated cynicism to cover acedia. It is real cool to be cynical about all of it, to joke about all of it. One sign of its approach is looking for something cute and clever to break the boredom of it. It is like the old song of the woman who was taken by her father to the circus. She saw the acrobats and clowns and performers on the high wire and the trapeze. She turned to her father and said, "Is that all there is to a circus?" Do I spend a good bit of my time thinking of something clever to "get" them? Why do I need to do that?

Another symptom is hyperscheduling; scheduling yourself 24-7. "I am so busy, busy, busy; I wish I had time," when actually what I am trying to conceal is my lack of interest and my boredom with what I am doing.

Another symptom is overexposure of one's self to the stimulants that are in the culture. A lot of things are stimulating. Television is working harder and harder to keep your interest by being more and more stimulating. The language and the displays of the human body, all kinds of configurations of relationships, are used to stimulate you, to keep your eye on the screen. Well then, what is next, and next, and next? Circuses and bread, circuses and bread, circuses and bread.

One signal is when you compete with oneself. That is deadly. People come out the door and say, "That was your best sermon." You should be happy with that comment, but fears sets in: "Now, what am I going to do next week? I should have held back a little bit." There is a well-known minister—you would know him if I mentioned his name—who calls me at least every other week and asks in obvious desperation, "What are you reading? What are you talking about? What's happening?"

"What's the matter?"

"Fred, I really did well last Sunday. Everybody said that sermon was one of my very best." Every time he calls me, he says something like, "That was my very best."

He says in despair, "Now what am I going to do? I can't have one worse than that, I have to have one better." He is competing with himself even though he knows that he will lose the competition. It is deadly.

Another symptom is to become overobsessed with information. I remember hearing a lecture by Robert Frost in which he talked about his poems, including "Stopping by Woods on a Snowy Evening," which is famous for the phrase, "But I have promises to keep and miles to go before I sleep."[3] He gave the lecture to a university crowd and there was a little period of question and answer. The first hand went up. "Yes young man, what it is?"

"You spoke of promises to keep. What were the promises?"

Frost said, "If I wanted you to know, I would have told you."

I recall the year I was a fellow at Yale. I met Eberhard Bethge, who was the good friend and biographer of Bonhoeffer. He was there with Frau Bethge. His purpose was to talk about Bonhoeffer, and mainly he was going to read several as yet unpublished letters that he received from Bonhoeffer.

So he got up to read; she was seated near him. He got up to read in English because most of us couldn't handle it otherwise. The first letter he started to read began with Paul's expression in Philippians 1:3: "I thank my God for all my recollection of you."

"Mr. Bethge?"

"Yes, what is it?"

"Now are these letters coming from the period in which Bonhoeffer was more involved in romanticism or in rationalism? Or had he moved already to existentialism?" Frau Bethga tugged at Eberhard's coattail and said, "I don't think this is the time." And they got up and left.

What are the causes for the exhaustion of emotion, for compassion fatigue, for the acedia? I think one of the causes, first of all, is failure to give adequate attention to the condition of one's body. Inattention to one's physical condition lies at the base of much emotional lack. You know the ancient students of the human body talked about the different emotions being related to the different fluids in the body, like bile. Those fluids were called "humors." We still use the word—good humor, bad humor. That's a fluid that goes through the body and affects the personality. Now, those ancients, with their primitive psychology and physiology, had some truth to it, it lies in your body.

When I taught at Candler, I tried a gimmick to create a "teachable moment." It didn't work. I found someone who owned an old violin that no longer worked. The strings and other parts were shot. I asked to borrow the old violin. I wasn't going to play it. I waited for a rainy day. When it came, I put the old violin out in the commons area where students went from class to class and sat around and bemoaned that they had afternoon classes and such. I took the violin out of its case and just put it in plain view in the commons area in the rain while no one was around. I then went to my classroom and greeted students as they arrived. Students entered the room commenting how rainy it was, how they were so busy, and so on.

I waited for someone to ask, "Who was the idiot who left a violin out in the rain?" That was to be my teachable moment. I would respond, "Well, it is no different than mistreating one's body by eating moon pies, chasing them down with colas, getting no exercise, and then wondering why one is obese."

It didn't work. *Nobody* said *anything* about the violin in the rain, and I didn't bring it up.

I think part of the cause of this emotional lack is a failure to appreciate routine; the failure to appreciate the contribution of the regular, normal, repetition of life. Repetition is healthy. We couldn't have our great music without repetition. Repetition has a cumulative effect. Children know this. When you read them a story at bedtime, what do they ask?

"Read it again."

"I just read it."

"Please?"

"OK, see the bunny hop in the woods, hop, hop."

"You skipped a hop."

"OK, hop, hop, hop."

"Do it one more time, please?"

Over, and over, and over. There is something soothing and right about repetition. As much of your life that you can gear into healthy routine, the happier and more productive you will be.

Part of the difficulty, I think, is an under-appreciation for emotion. I don't know who is responsible for this. For preachers, it is often the academy. A lot has changed in theological education since I was in seminary, but there are places that heap exhortation on students in ways similar to the ways of my professors. They used to say things such as "Feeling boils water, but thinking makes soup." They were a hard bunch. To be fair, I think it was their way to get us to study for our own good. It didn't work very well.

I recall in undergraduate school that it was generally understood that emotion was a factor in the lives of people who were not educated or sophisticated. The ordinary unwashed masses get all riled up; they get emotional, angry, and form mobs. They run by their feelings. But for the chosen few who made it through the academy, we acquired the discipline of "self-control" and "reasonableness" and thus don't feel anything. That is just not true.

Part of the difficulty may be that we expect too much out from emotion. Ministers can get sucked into a totally unrealistic expectation of chronic happiness and good cheer: "I have to feel 'up' all the time. Everyone expects me to feel 'up' all the time. Every morning is like Easter morning." Well, that may be true for a few of us. Some of us are not morning people at all and it is too bad that we have to preach in the morning: "I could give them a 'whizbanger' at about 4:00 in the afternoon. But they want me to talk in the morning, so I have to appear to be really on top of my game and really full of zip and vinegar when I am not." You don't have to act like and feel like you are on a high all the time. When the company comes somebody has to run the vacuum. It is not exciting, but it is important.

I think many of us underestimate the amount of energy that is drained from us, from just the normal comfortable socializing that is a part of ministry. For instance, somebody will say, "Some of us are getting together to have a light supper at 5:30. Since you don't have to speak until 7:00, we want you to join us for supper, too. These are all friendly folks." I don't care who they are. When there are so many bodies, with so many minds, and so many tongues, and with so many activities in a room, there is an expectation on you. Even if you don't say a word, it drains energy. I will refer to this shortly and I hope you will keep in mind some sense of the measure of your tank. How much can you hold? How much emotional energy can you sustain? If you drain it out by 7:00, then you will go into the 7:00 service already tired, but you might not be aware you are tired. Socializing takes a lot out of us. How much it takes out of you depends on how you are constructed. Some of us have a fairly large tank for emotional energy. Some of us don't have much of one at all.

I learned long ago, although it was a price my family paid, in part, to not go to ball games on Saturday. It was a big price to pay because Saturday was the day they played football. If I go to a ball game, I am an intense participant. I don't get up and yell, or dance around and throw my popcorn, or anything like that. But I am very intensely engaged in the game. The "elastic" is stretched for three hours on Saturday and I want to stretch it again on Sunday morning, but it has lost some of its elasticity. I don't have a large enough tank of emotional energy to make me an active participant in a ballgame on Saturday, especially Saturday evening, and then preach on Sunday. The same is true for bright, happy parties or other engaging or demanding events. For me, Saturday is the day of preparation for Sunday. There are two major areas of preparation for the preaching moment. The first area is to prepare the sermon—we do that prior to Saturday. On Saturday, we have to prepare ourselves.

I am not recommending that as a "menu" for you; you know how much you can do. Some of you may still be riled up about the game on Sunday morning and it energizes your sermon. But I doubt it.

I urge you to give attention to your body through a Sabbath rest program. A Sabbath program for your own situation. I know some of you have had those Lily grants that allow you to go away for three to six months, to be entirely separated from all your chores and supposedly have a very refreshing experience. I hope those who have taken advantage of these have found them worth the rest. But I am thinking more of your regular, daily, weekly schedule. A Sabbath rest is a scheduled time for a change of behavior. Not large chucks of time (who has them?), but a way of scheduling your life daily and weekly so there is Sabbath rest built into the routine of what you do. I emphasize the word *schedule*. That means discipline. As I have said many times before, there is no freedom, no pleasure, apart from discipline. A scheduled time sets you free, so that when you play, you play, and when you work, you work. Many people get so messed up about this that they cannot enjoy a game of tennis or golf or a walk in the woods because they are worrying, "I should be studying or preparing my sermon." But then when they go to the study to prepare the sermon, they think, "I need a break. I need to be walking in the woods; I need to play tennis or golf." The result is that neither play nor work are enjoyed–they are just garbled together, resulting in a general state of weariness and a lack of pleasure. It is possible to enjoy play when you play and to enjoy work when you work, but you need to know the difference and to have time scheduled for each.

Now a change of scenery during a sabbatical is helpful to some and to some it is not. A change of scenery has never been that helpful to me. I recall hearing (I think on a tape) a sermon by David McCrackin, in New York City. He had a sermon on the geographical cure. His text was, "Oh, that I had the wings of a dove, I would fly away and be at rest." Then he told a story about a bus driver on the city streets of New York running his bus every day; going to the bus barn, leaving his car, picking up the bus, in the evening taking the bus to the bus barn, getting in his car, and going home. Everyday, everyday, everyday, everyday. One morning he went to the bus barn, parked his car, prepared the bus for the daily route through the city, but this time he just drove the bus to Miami, Florida. We all know something about the bus driver's feelings, but his action is not really a cure for anything, is it?

A change of scenery might help. There are a lot of places I enjoy very much; it is just that I don't want to get all tired out getting there. One of my favorite places is Ireland, especially the rural areas. I have not spent a lot of time there, but some. I recall a time when our family was in rural southern Ireland. We had a detailed map. We were looking for a historical church building, not operating anymore, that was about one thousand years old. We couldn't find it, but it had to be close. I put my finger on the spot on the map where the church was marked and walked over to a little pub. There standing outside the door was a pleasant redheaded fellow, probably in his sixties. I showed him the map and said, "I want to get to this place where there is a very old church." He looked at the map, then he looked at me and said, "Have you the petrol to go the beauty way?" I said, "I think so." He said, "Well, you are on it." We were and we went. Encounters like that are pleasant to me. But it is a long plane ride to Ireland.

I also suggest that you prepare your own schedule. I know that all scheduling is not up to you and other people do things that call for your attention that you didn't schedule. As far as it is in your control, I suggest putting back-to-back events that make different demands on you. This is true when you are in school. If you can schedule classes back-to-back that are very different so they don't bleed into each other or require the same kind of attention, then it is relaxing to you; it is a kind of built-in sabbatical. Put back-to-back activities that have different mental, physical, or emotional demands and you will find them less tiring and a way to refresh yourself in the middle of your work.

May I suggest, also, that you welcome whatever truth there is in the James-Lange theory of emotion.[4] It is the opposite of the way many of us think. Instead of feeling and then doing, like "I feel afraid so I will run," they say you can run and that will make you afraid. It is not feeling and then doing, it is often a case of doing and then feeling. There is a lot of truth to that, I think. I could get out here in the parking lot, start running and looking over my shoulder and make myself afraid. It works that way.

I have suggested it to my students, "If you don't feel like reading the textbook, that's the best time to read it. You do it and that makes you feel like it. You'll find yourself saying, 'Hey, this is not a bad book after all, this is very interesting.'" You know how you got to it? By just doing it. How does a motor start? By turning over. How does a walk or a run start? By taking the first step.

This was one of the big areas in the civil rights times when we were fighting over integration matters and so many people, in the churches too, were saying, "When our hearts are right, we won't have any problems. When everybody has love in their hearts, we won't have any more of these segregated meetings, we will not have any more of this painful civil strife. But we have to feel it in our hearts first; otherwise, we are just being hypocrites if we do it without feeling it."

The trouble with that is it is not true. In one of my Sunday school classes, a man said, "The government can pass laws about integration if it wants to, but it is not going to really happen until we feel it." So it is that the churches have been backed up in the social activity all the way to Chicago even though the light is green while we tinker with our carburetors trying to get our feelings straight so that when we feel right then we will do right. Why not just do and then feel right about it?

My mother taught me that nothing is right unless you feel it first in your heart. I loved my mother, but on this point she was in error. In many areas of my life, I have had to do the work first, and then I felt right about it. The feeling followed the action. Unfortunately, many ministers have talked themselves into a whole ministry of inactivity by waiting to do work until their hearts were right.

I want to continue by suggesting to you that you read and write poetry. I don't do this very well. I have not written much poetry. I am now reading a lot more poetry than I did. I don't know why I didn't read more poetry when I was younger. It is stimulating, it is biting, and it is life changing. I was once on a program with Maya Angelou. It was years ago in San Diego. She and I were in the program. She was first on the program. My goodness what a demonstration of power she was! She sang, she read her poetry, she even danced right there on the stage. Then it was my turn. What a lump of clay I was after that. She was a tough act to follow. I talked with her afterward. I asked her, "Why is it when you have a task so difficult as to improve the condition of the black woman in America you choose as your weapon poetry? Is not that a little fragile to do such a big job?" She looked at me and said, "Poetry is winged for the heart. Some of you white preacher types just go bruising the tree but you never chop one down. I chose poetry–it goes to the heart." So it does.

Have you thought much about the fact that the prophetic oracles in the Old Testament, the inspired speeches of the prophets, are poetry? Some of the translations of the Bible make it quite clear by the way they arrange the text. It is written in the text like a poem. It is a poem. Beautiful. Some of them were probably set to music. I don't know why we think our business is so extremely important that we cannot use something fragile like poetry.

We think we need strong, powerful prose. Not really true. Here I am suggesting that you do something that I have not done well nor often enough and that is to read and sometimes write poetry. The reasons are several. One is it is good for the healthy emotional life. Another reason is the language of poetry gets you back to the primary function of poetry and takes you back to the visceral nature of poetry. Read Psalm 22:16–17, 21: "For dogs are all around me; a company of evildoers encircles me. My hands and feet have shriveled, I can count all my bones . . . Save me from the mouth of the lion." It is so extraordinarily strong. Not full of those abstract words like "righteousness" and "stewardship," just primary seeing, tasting, smelling, feeling, and saying.

One source of great poetry is the hymnal. When our church, the Disciples of Christ, put out *The Chalice Hymnal,* I wrote to the editorial committee and requested they also print some copies that are words only, so it is a book of poetry because that is what hymns are, poems set to music. Leave the music out, then it will be a smaller book and handy to use for devotions, to take in a suitcase on a trip, to put in one's satchel. They said it was too expensive and did not do it. I hope some day it will be done.

Read the hymnal. Some of those stanzas are powerful. The African American tradition includes a lot of poetry and hymns within the sermon itself. The Wesleys who wrote so many songs included it also in preaching. Sometimes it is helpful if you just communicate with someone else with a poem. It may not be a prizewinner, but it says what you think, as well as what you *feel*, and what you are doing. It is a marvelous thing.

I received some years ago the gift of a poem. Unexpected, surprising really. I was in Eastern Kentucky, at the Appalachian Lay Pastors School. I was there to have sessions with lay pastors on preaching and there was a middle-aged woman who came before the first day and asked if she could be in the class. I said, "Have you registered?" She said, "No. I am not registered for any of the classes. But I would like to come to this one." I asked, "Why?" She said, "I just like to hear the stories about Jesus." Well, anybody who wants to hear the stories about Jesus should be admitted. So I admitted her to the class. She sat in the back. She never said anything, but she was there every time and her face registered interest. She thanked me at the close of the school. About two weeks later, I received an envelope in the mail with a Kentucky postmark. It contained this poem from this woman:

There is the hint of quiet rain coming soon,
Not much
enough to soothe the greening needs
of outstretched leafy arms and hidden moss
shy and quietly waiting for the damp

There is the hint of quiet moments coming soon
Not much
enough to soothe the thirsting needs
of outstretched anxious hearts and hidden selves
private and silently waiting for the peace.

She gave me that. It is a poem by an unlikely person. You also may believe you're an unlikely poet, but you can write a poem. Give one to a child at school, give one to a neighbor. Read one from the pulpit as a gift to your church. It is a marvelous way to keep alive your own emotions and your own emotional investment in what you are doing in the pulpit.

I further suggest the sermon you preach be your own sermon. I know that is an old song and you have heard it from all your teachers and mentors and you have read in all your books, "preach your own sermons." I am not adding anything to that, but I am certainly not subtracting anything. It is not a matter of plagiarism, it is not a matter of saying, "I gave credit to the person by whom it was written. I gave credit because it was copyrighted. I didn't steal it." I am not talking about plagiarism. I am talking about *passion.* How can you eat off someone else's plate and be passionate about the meal? Let it be your own. True and genuine emotion arises out of the material itself. It is not a case of preparing a sermon and then adding emotion to liven it up. You don't add it. What you want to do is prepare the sermon and if it is totally your own, you will feel strongly about it. I don't mean to be defensive or protective, but out of that material will come the appropriate passion in volume and in nature of expression. The appropriate passion comes out of a sermon that is one's own.

As far as is possible, I suggest you reexperience your sermon at two points: one in the latter stages of preparation. You have prepared the sermon. It is all there—manuscript, or notes, or whatever you use. Now reexperience it. Feel the feelings you had as you put it together. Sit somewhere in a room, lean back, stare at the ceiling and say that sermon, feel your way through the sermon—have what is called a feeling intelligence. Feel the passion of it, the interest of it, and the importance of it. The other time to do it is when you are in the pulpit. Let your preaching be your reexperiencing of your material: you feel it, you hear it, you taste it, you touch it, you know it, and you say it. It is very exhausting. Coming down out of the pulpit you want some time alone to kick a rock down a road, rethink, debrief yourself because you have just been totally engaged and invested in what you are doing.

Now I know this is different from what Dietrich Bonhoeffer said in his early days of teaching preaching. He argued that preachers should not be personally engaged in what they are doing. I can't buy that. I am sure he would not have believed in that later in his life either. Some people will attend your sermons, not because they believe what you say, but because *you* believe what you say. The power of that passion keeps their attention and gives life to your sermon. Reexperience in preparation; reexperience in the delivery.

May I say that healthy emotions are accessible to you only when you are free? If you are tied in a knot for some reason, embarrassed to be up in front of the people, not really prepared yet, haven't adequately worked it out, then you are afraid someone is going to come in who knows something about the subject. When they walk in the pores of the skin close up, the voice tightens and changes and you wish you were somewhere else. There is no free flow of emotion if you are in a knot for whatever reason. You have to be free.

True, genuine, healthy emotion flows through the veins of a person who is free. And the way you are free in the pulpit is to *know* what you are talking about and to *believe* it is important. That is what sets you free.

In the process of the sermon, I urge you to keep explanations to a minimum. Not a lot of explaining things. People can figure it out. You don't have to explain everything. It is like a person telling a joke and then explaining the joke. I would rather not get the joke than to have you explain it to me. Sermons that are full of explanations are dull and they are boring, and much of it is unnecessary. We deal in images, we deal in metaphors, we deal in hyperbole, and all kinds of styles and ways of speaking but explanations *only* if necessary.

I recall reading, I don't remember where, about the Five Civilized Tribes on the Trail of Tears into Oklahoma. There was written up a reporter's conversation with one of the women. She was of the Creek tribe. She made the trip to Oklahoma. The reporter asked her if she had any children. She said, "Yes, I had six children, but they are all dead except Adam, Rachel, Joseph, Wes, and Annie." Isn't that something? You want somebody to explain, but you don't want somebody to explain it. Why would she say, "They are all dead; all six are dead, except . . ." and she names five that are not dead. What is she feeling? Don't tell me. Don't try to give me a theory. Don't dig out your theology and psychology. Leave it alone. Just let it rest there in the heart and mind of the listener. I can't explain it, but I am profoundly moved by what she must have been feeling over the death of one of her children.

May I suggest, also, in the arrangement of your sermon, that the movement of your sermon be primary, not the structure. Nobody is going to take a picture of the structure of your sermon. It is going to be heard; it is going to be vibration over the ear. It does not matter what it looks like on paper. It is what it sounds like and the sounding like is based on its movement. Does one part anticipate the next part and are the listeners gratified by the sequence? That is good movement. That has built into it anticipation. The greatest single source of pleasure that anybody has is anticipation. The joy of Christmas is anticipation. The anticipation of the end of school or other significant events in one's life–there lies the pleasure. It is important that anticipation be built into the sermon for the sake of the listener; they love to anticipate where the preacher is going and they like to run ahead and be sitting on the porch waiting on you when you get to the end of your sermon. You may end up on another porch and they say, "Oops, we missed it." They like to do it anyway. Listeners are active in their minds. They like to anticipate the direction and conclusion of your sermon. You are not playing a game; this is not an O. Henry short story.

Anticipation is the chief source of pleasure when listening to a sermon. It is also important to keep in mind that anticipation is a healthy emotion for you. It keeps you alive to your sermon. You anticipate arriving at the end of it. You appreciate the listeners' keen interest in what you are doing. Do not be in a hurry. I suggest maybe you could practice a little bit getting some restraint. Do not release it all at once. I recall a reporter talking with Carl Sandburg: "Mr. Sandburg, you are a man of words, you write poetry, history, biography; you use words; you are a master in the use of words. What to you is the ugliest word in the English language?" Old man Sandburg, that lock of white hair falling down his forehead, looked at the ceiling, then looked out the window, then said, "The ugliest word, the ugliest word, the ugliest, ugliest, ugliest word in the English language, the ugliest word, the ugliest word in the English language, well, the ugliest word is exclusive."

Sandburg held the reporter's attention. He exercised such restraint that the reporter was already guessing what he going to say. Carl Sandburg knew what he was going to say, he just kept at bay his listener with restraint.

If I had been interviewed by the reporter about what I thought was the ugliest word in the English language, I probably would have said something like, "Well, I don't know. Different people have different opinions, but my view is the ugliest word is ___." How uninteresting.

The key to anticipation is restraint. You can practice restraint by telling stories or reading stories to children because they love to guess. They love mystery and to think they know what is coming next, but they don't know. "It's a king." "No, it is not a king. It is an egg. Didn't I tell you?" They will stay with you if there is restraint.

One good way to practice restraint is to tell jokes. I do not mean in the pulpit. That is not a good thing to do. Too many things can go wrong. You could forget the punch line or worse you give the punch line too soon, then it is all shot to pieces and falls to the ground. Practice telling jokes in casual conversation, because a joke has a punch line at a certain point and you don't jump ahead of it or get in a hurry. You build up to it; you make everybody wait for it. Then it comes.

The same is true of a good story. Tell stories to each other. Don't wait until you are in the pulpit and you think you are going to tell a story. You are not going to do it well. Don't wait until you are in the pulpit to tell stories thinking you are going to be like some great narrative preachers. Practice around the coffee table. Practice in the kitchen. Practice with your kids. Practice with your friends. Then when you are preparing a sermon, you will know how important restraint is. This is why I have urged my students through the years, when preparing a sermon, to write the closing sentence first and then let everything else build toward that. It is good discipline and it will fill you and your listener with anticipation.

That is what I want to say to you, except a parting word. I have appreciated very much the workshops, lectures, preaching, and classrooms. I learn from everybody I meet who is a preacher. I appreciate you and thank you for being here today and through the years.

I hope to meet you somewhere near a pulpit down the road.

Notes

Foreword

[1] His remark appears on the first chapter of this book as statement number 9.
[2] His remark appears on the first chapter of this book as statement number 7.

Chapter 1: Between the Ear and the Mouth

Minister's Week, Candler School of Theology, Emory University, Atlanta, January 16, 1991.

Chapter 2: New Testament Theology as a Pastoral Task

Minister's Week, Candler School of Theology, Emory University, Atlanta, January 14, 1987.

Chapter 3: Preaching as Storytelling: For Instance

Furman University, Greenville, South Carolina, July 2, 1980.

Chapter 4: Preaching as Storytelling: Sustaining the Power

Furman University, Greenville, South Carolina, July 3, 1980.

Chapter 5: Preaching as Storytelling: The Form

Furman University, Greenville, South Carolina, July 3, 1980.

Chapter 6: Preaching as Storytelling: Additional Practical Suggestions

Furman University, Greenville, South Carolina, July 4, 1980.

Chapter 7: The Sermon as a Twice-Told Tale: What Is a "Twice-Told Tale"?

The Sprunt Lectures, Union Theological Seminary, Richmond, Virginia, February 4–6, 1991.
[1] Henry Wadsworth Longfellow, *North American Review* 45 (July 1837): 62.

Chapter 8: The Sermon as a Twice-Told Tale: Funds in the Memory Bank

The Sprunt Lectures, Union Theological Seminary, Richmond, Virginia, February 4–6, 1991.

Chapter 9: The Sermon as a Twice-Told Tale: Resonance with Human Experience

The Sprunt Lectures, Union Theological Seminary, Richmond, Virginia, February 4–6, 1991.
[1] Don Browning, *Reviving Christian Humanism: The New Conversation on Spirituality, Theology and Spirituality* (Minneapolis: Fortress Press, 2010).

² Kenneth Burke, *A Grammar of Motives* (Berkeley: University of California Press, 1969).

³ Edgar Lee Masters, *Spoon River Anthology* (Lawrence, KS: Digireads.com, 2005), 12.

⁴ Forest Carter, *The Education of Little Tree* (Albuquerque: University of New Mexico Press, 2001).

Chapter 10: The Sermon as a Twice-Told Tale: The Form of the Sermon

The Sprunt Lectures, Union Theological Seminary, Richmond, Virginia, February 4–6, 1991.

¹ Wayne Booth, *The Company We Keep: An Ethics of Fiction* (Berkeley: University of California Press, 1989).

² Ibid., 12.

³ Donald Barthelme, *Sixty Stories* (New York: Penguin Classics, 2003), 225.

⁴ Booth, *The Company We Keep*.

⁵ Kenneth Burke, *Counter-Statement* (Berkeley: University of California Press, 1968), 31.

⁶ Ibid., 124.

⁷ Joyce Carol Oates, *Contraries: Essays* (New York: Oxford University Press, 1981), 116.

⁸ Henry Louis Gates Jr., *The Slave Narratives* (New York: Penguin Press, 1987).

⁹ Ibid., 2.

¹⁰ Claude Lévi-Strauss, *The Elementary Structures of Kinship* (Boston: Beacon Press, 1969).

Chapter 11: The Sermon as a Twice-Told Tale: New Words to Old Tunes

The Sprunt Lectures, Union Theological Seminary, Richmond, Virginia, February 4–6, 1991.

¹ Naomi Margulis Maurer, *The Pursuit of Spiritual Wisdom: The Thought and Art of Vincent Van Gogh and Paul Gauguin* (Madison, NJ: Fairleigh Dickinson University Press, 1998), 31.

² John Keats, *The Major Works: Including Endymion, the Odes and Selected Letters* (New York: Oxford University Press, 1990), 380.

³ Robert W. Funk, *Parables & Presence: Forms of the New Testament Tradition* (Philadelphia: Fortress Press, 1982).

⁴ Elizabeth Barrett Browning, "Poem XLIII," in *Sonnets for the Portuguese: A Celebration of Love* (New York: St. Martin's Press, 2007), 51.

⁵ Joseph Conrad, Nostromo, *A Tale of the Seaboard* (Lawrence, KS: Digireads.com, 2007), 233.

⁶ Ben Jonson, "Song to Celia," in *The Complete Poems* (New York: Penguin Classics, 1975), 106.

⁷ William Ernest Henley, "Invictus," in *101 Famous Poems*, ed. Roy J. Cook (Columbus, OH: McGraw Hill, 2003), 95.

⁸ John Donne, "Holy Sonnets, XIV," in *Poems of John Donne*, vol. 1, ed. E. K. Chambers (London: Lawrence & Bullen, 1896), 165.

⁹ http://www.lyricsplayground.com/alpha/songs/s/stealawaytojesus.shtml.

¹⁰ http://www.cyberhymnal.org/htm/w/h/e/whenisur.htm.

¹¹ http://www.cyberhymnal.org/htm/l/o/loveofgo.htm.

Chapter 12: Preaching and the Nod of Recognition

Franklin S. Hickman Lectures, Duke Divinity School, Durham, North Carolina, October 29, 1984.

Chapter 13: Preaching and the Shock of Recognition

Franklin S. Hickman Lectures, Duke Divinity School, Durham, North Carolina, October 29, 1984.

[1] Herman Melville, *The Enchanted Isles* (London: Hesperus Press, 2002).

Chapter 14: Preaching and the Same Sermon Every Week

Chevis F. Horne Preaching and Worship Conference. Baptist Theological Seminary, Richmond, Virginia, April 13, 1999.

[1] A paraphrase of Emily Dickinson, "The Bustle in a House," in *The Complete Poems of Emily Dickinson*, ed. Thomas H. Johnson (New York: Back Bay Books, 1976), 489.

Chapter 15: Wanting Out

Virginia Conference Pastor's Convocation based on Hebrews 6:1–12, January 1, 1988.

Chapter 16: Thirteen Ways to End a Sermon

Craddock Center's Preaching Workshop, Cherry Log Christian Church, Cherry Log, Georgia, October 6, 2008.

[1] Edgar Allan Poe, "The Philosophy of Composition," in *The Portable Edgar Allan Poe*, ed. J. Gerald Kennedy (New York: Penguin Classics, 2006), 543.

[2] Fred B. Craddock, *Reflections on My Call to Preach: Connecting the Dots* (St. Louis: Chalice Press, 2009).

Chapter 17: The Habit of the Sermon

A Celebration of Preaching, Candler School of Theology, September 18, 2003.

[1] Chaim Potok, *The Chosen* (New York: Ballantine Books, 1996).

[2] Chaim Potok, *The Promise* (New York: Anchor, 2005).

[3] John A. Williams, *The Life of Elder John Smith* (Cincinnati: Standard, 1904).

Chapter 18: Once More with Feeling

Craddock Center's Preaching Workshop, Cherry Log Christian Church, Cherry Log, Georgia, October 5, 2009.

[1] Charles Dickens, *A Christmas Carol* (New York: Tribeca Books, 2010), 5.

[2] Kathleen Norris, *Acedia & Me: A Marriage, Monks and a Writer's Life* (New York: Riverhead Books, 2008).

[3] Robert Frost, "Stopping by Woods on a Snowy Evening," in *The Poetry of Robert Frost: The Collected Poems, Complete and Unabridged*, ed. Edward Connery Lathem (New York: Henry Holt & Co, 1969), 224.

[4] See Samuel Smith, *Ideas of the Great Psychologists* (New York: Harper & Row, 1983), 157–59.